SCARECROW STUDIES IN YOUNG ADULT LITERATURE

Series Editor: Patty Campbell

Scarecrow Studies in Young Adult Literature is intended to continue the body of critical writing established in Twayne's Young Adult Authors Series and to expand it beyond single-author studies to explorations of genres, multicultural writing, and controversial issues in young adult (YA) reading. Many of the contributing authors of the series are among the leading scholars and critics of adolescent literature, and some are YA novelists themselves.

The series is shaped by its editor, Patty Campbell, who is a renowned authority in the field, with a thirty-year background as critic, lecturer, librarian, and teacher of YA literature. Patty Campbell was the 2001 winner of the ALAN Award, given by the Assembly on Adolescent Literature of the National Council of Teachers of English for distinguished contribution to YA literature. In 1989 she was the winner of the American Library Association's Grolier Award for distinguished service to young adults and reading.

1. *What's So Scary about R. L. Stine?* by Patrick Jones, 1998.
2. *Ann Rinaldi: Historian and Storyteller,* by Jeanne M. McGlinn, 2000.
3. *Norma Fox Mazer: A Writer's World,* by Arthea J. S. Reed, 2000.
4. *Exploding the Myths: The Truth about Teens and Reading,* by Marc Aronson, 2001.
5. *The Agony and the Eggplant: Daniel Pinkwater's Heroic Struggles in the Name of YA Literature,* by Walter Hogan, 2001.
6. *Caroline Cooney: Faith and Fiction,* by Pamela Sissi Carroll, 2001.
7. *Declarations of Independence: Empowered Girls in Young Adult Literature, 1990–2001,* by Joanne Brown and Nancy St. Clair, 2002.
8. *Lost Masterworks of Young Adult Literature,* by Connie S. Zitlow, 2002.
9. *Beyond the Pale: New Essays for a New Era,* by Marc Aronson, 2003.
10. *Orson Scott Card: Writer of the Terrible Choice,* by Edith S. Tyson, 2003.
11. *Jacqueline Woodson: "The Real Thing,"* by Lois Thomas Stover, 2003.
12. *Virginia Euwer Wolff: Capturing the Music of Young Voices,* by Suzanne Elizabeth Reid, 2003.
13. *More Than a Game: Sports Literature for Young Adults,* Chris Crowe, 2004.

The Heart Has Its Reasons

Young Adult Literature with Gay/Lesbian/Queer Content, 1969–2004

Michael Cart
Christine A. Jenkins

Scarecrow Studies in
Young Adult Literature, No. 18

THE SCARECROW PRESS, INC.
Lanham, Maryland • Toronto • Oxford
2006

SCARECROW PRESS, INC.

Published in the United States of America
by Scarecrow Press, Inc.
A wholly owned subsidiary of
The Rowman & Littlefield Publishing Group, Inc.
4501 Forbes Boulevard, Suite 200, Lanham, Maryland 20706
www.scarecrowpress.com

PO Box 317
Oxford
OX2 9RU, UK

British Library Cataloguing in Publication Information Available

Library of Congress Cataloging-in-Publication Data

Cart, Michael.
   The heart has its reasons : young adult literature with gay/lesbian/queer content,
1969-2004 / Michael Cart, Christine A. Jenkins.
     p. cm. — (Scarecrow studies in young adult literature ; no. 18)
   Includes bibliographical references and index.
   ISBN-10: 0-8108-5071-0 (alk. paper)
   ISBN-13: 978-0-8108-5071-2
   1. Young adult fiction, American—History and criticism. 2. Homosexuality and
literature—United States. 3. Teenagers—Books and reading—United States. 4.
Gays in literature. 5. Gay men in literature. 6. Lesbians in literature. I. Jenkins,
Christine, 1949- II. Title. III. Scarecrow studies in young adult literature ; 18.
PS374.H63C37 2006
   813.009'928308664—dc22

2005031320

∞™ The paper used in this publication meets the minimum requirements of
American National Standard for Information Sciences—Permanence of Paper
for Printed Library Materials, ANSI/NISO Z39.48-1992.
Manufactured in the United States of America.

The heart has its reasons that the mind cannot know.

Blaise Pascal—*Lettres Provinciales*

Contents

Timeline of Events
Relevant to GLBTQ Youth

1969   Stonewall Riots in Greenwich Village (New York City) launches modern gay rights movement. First young adult novel with GLBT content—John Donovan's *I'll Get There. It Better Be Worth the Trip*—is published

1973   First formal meeting of "Parents and Friends of Gays" held in New York City (see 1981)

1973   American Psychiatric Association votes unanimously to remove homosexuality from its DSM-II (the official list of psychiatric disorders)

1977   Entertainer and Florida citrus industry spokesperson Anita Bryant's "Save Our Children" campaign is successful in repealing the Miami-Dade County gay anti-discrimination ordinance (see 1998)

1977   Openly gay candidate Harvey Milk elected to San Francisco Board of Supervisors

1978   Briggs Initiative (Proposition 6), which would have kept gays and lesbians (as well as teachers of any sexual orientation judged to be "advocating, imposing, encouraging, or promoting" homosexual activity) from teaching in public schools, overwhelmingly defeated in California

1978   Former San Francisco Board of Supervisors member Dan White murders Mayor George Moscone and openly gay Supervisor Harvey Milk (November 27, 1978)

1979   First National Gay and Lesbian Rights March in Washington D.C. (October 14, 1979); 100,000 attend

1981   PFLAG (Parents and Friends of Lesbians and Gays) launched as a national organization

1982   Wisconsin passes first state legislation outlawing discrimination in employment, housing, and public accommodations on the basis of "sexual orientation"

1982   The acronym "AIDS" (Acquired Immune Deficiency Syndrome) is first used in public by medical researchers, acknowledging that people in various demographic groups are at risk for this disease (Earlier, the disease was sometimes referred to as "GRID" [Gay Related Immune Deficiency].) (July 27, 1982)

1982   *Board of Education, Island Trees (NY) Union Free School District No. 23 v. Steven A. Pico, et al* (June 25, 1982)—U.S. Supreme Court case affirms public school students' First Amendment right to receive information—a book may not be removed from the library simply because school officials dislike the ideas expressed in it

1982   Gay Men's Health Crisis founded in New York City

1982   Nancy Garden's *Annie on My Mind*, the first lesbian love story for young adults, is published

1983   New virus (referred to as "LAV") is identified by doctors at the Pasteur Institute in France as the cause of AIDS

1984   HIV virus is identified by researchers at the National Cancer Institute as the cause of AIDS. (In 1985 it would become clear that LAV and HIV were the same virus.)

1984   Harvey Milk School for gay/lesbian high school students started in New York City

1984   Charles Howard is gay-bashed and drowned by three teenagers who throw him off a bridge in Bangor, Maine (This incident was the inspiration for the 1991 young adult novel *The Drowning of Stephan Jones* by Bette Greene.)

1985   President Ronald Reagan first mentions AIDS in a public speech (Sept. 17, 1985)

1985   Movie star Rock Hudson comes out as gay and as a PWA (Person with AIDS), which "gives human face to AIDS" (Oct. 3, 1985)

1986   *Bowers v. Hardwick* (June 30, 1986)—U.S. Supreme Court rules 5-4 that Georgia's sodomy laws do not violate the U.S. Constitution, stating that the right to privacy does not extend to private consensual same-sex sexual acts

1987   ACT-UP (AIDS Coalition To Unleash Power) founded in New York City

1987   March on Washington for Gay and Lesbian Rights (October 11, 1987); 500,000 attend

1987   NAMES Project unveils AIDS Memorial Quilt

1987   Barney Frank becomes first U.S. Congressman to self-identify as gay

1990   James Dale expelled from Boy Scouts for being gay (see 2000)

1990   Teen hemophiliac and AIDS activist Ryan White dies of AIDS (April 8, 1990)

1990   *BOE of Westside Community Schools v. Mergens* (June 4, 1990)— U.S. Supreme Court rules that the 1984 Equal Access Act (requiring public schools that allow non-curricular student-led clubs to provide equal access to all such clubs) is constitutional (see 1998)

1992   Colorado passes Amendment 2 outlawing gay rights legislation (see 1996)

1993   March on Washington for Lesbian, Gay, and Bisexual Rights and Liberation (April 25, 1993); 1,000,000 attend

1993   "Don't Ask Don't Tell" policy adopted by U.S. military (Department of Defense Document 1332.14)

1995   *Stevana Case, et al, v. Unified School District no. 233, et al* (November 29, 1995)—U.S. Court of Appeals, 10th Circuit rules that the

Olathe (Kansas) school board and school superintendent violated the U.S. Constitution by removing a book (young adult novel *Annie On My Mind,* by Nancy Garden) from the school library because school officials dislike the ideas expressed in it. The judge orders the novel placed back in the school library

1996   *Roemer v. Evans* (May 20, 1996)—U.S. Supreme Court rules 6-3 to strike down Amendment 2 of the Colorado State Constitution (denying homosexual and bisexual people coverage under anti-discrimination laws and ordinances) as violating the equal protection clause of the U.S. Constitution (see 1992)

1996   *Nabozny v. Podlesny* (July 31, 1996)—U.S. Court of Appeals, 7th Circuit, rules that public schools have a constitutional obligation to protect students from anti-gay harassment As a result, former high school student Jamie Nabozny successfully sues Ashland Wisconsin School District for four years of anti-gay harassment and assault by high school classmates and is awarded $900,000

1996   Federal Defense of Marriage Act (DOMA) signed by President Bill Clinton

1997   Ellen DeGeneres, star of *Ellen,* comes out as lesbian in television role and in real life

1998   *East High Gay/Straight Alliance v. Board of Education of Salt Lake City School District* (March 19, 1998)—U.S. District Court for the District of Utah, Central Division, rules that permitting some extracurricular clubs and denying others violates the Federal Equal Access Act. Background: In 1996 the district responded to East High student efforts to form a Gay Straight Alliance by banning all of the school's 46 non-curricular student-led clubs. Despite the ban, however, some clubs were allowed to continue meeting. (See 1990)

1998   Miami-Dade County Commission approves gay rights ordinance (see 1977)

1998   Mathew Shepard, 21-year-old out gay college student, beaten to death by two young men in gay-bashing incident. Shepard's death galvanizes anti-hate crime forces (October 12, 1998)

2000   *Boy Scouts of America v. James Dale* (June 28, 2000)—U.S. Supreme Court rules 5-4 to uphold the BSA's expulsion of James Dale as scout leader for being gay, ruling that the BSA is a private organization and thus can legally discriminate against gay people

2000   Same-sex "civil unions" become legal in Vermont (April 11, 2000)

2003   Harvey Milk High School, which started as a two-room school in the Hetrick-Martin Institute in New York City in 1984, becomes a public school

2003   Court of Appeal in Ontario legalizes same-sex marriage in Canada (June 10, 2003)

2003   *Lawrence & Garner v. State of Texas* (June 26, 2003)—U.S. Supreme Court rules 6-3 that anti-sodomy laws are unconstitutional and unenforceable when applied to consenting adults in private for non-commercial purposes

2004   Massachusetts Supreme Judicial Court rules 4-3 that there is no "constitutionally adequate reason" to deny gay and lesbian couples the right to marry in the state of Massachusetts

2004   San Francisco Mayor orders city officials to issue marriage licenses to same-sex couples (February 12, 2004). A month later, the California Supreme Court orders San Francisco officials to cease issuing marriage licenses to same-sex couples (March 11, 2004)

2004   Massachusetts becomes first state in U.S. to legally permit same-sex marriage (May 17, 2004)

Introduction

$\mathcal{T}$he first young adult novel with gay content, John Donovan's *I'll Get There. It Better Be Worth the Trip*, appeared in 1969. Some reviewers welcomed its publication, while others were skeptical that such a book could ever be appropriate for teen readers. Nevertheless, in the more than thirty-five years since then nearly 200 young adult novels with gay and lesbian content have appeared in the U.S. Although 200 books might appear to be a substantial number, this averages out to five titles per year, which seems hardly sufficient to give faces to unnumbered millions of homosexual youth in the U.S. from 1969 to 2004. We say "unnumbered," since no one knows precisely how many teens were or are homosexual. However, it is possible to make an educated guess.[1]

Certainly, non-heterosexual people have become more visible over the past several decades, and with increased visibility, the labels applied to sexual minorities have proliferated. In this book we use "GLBTQ" as an inclusive short-hand term. Why? Well, in the absence of a single modifier to represent the various orientations of people identified as sexual minorities, this rubric "GLBTQ" (a list of initials that does not exactly come tripping off the tongue but has the advantage of brevity) has come to include those described as "gay, lesbian, bisexual, transgendered, and/or queer/questioning." Some prefer the designation "LGBTQ" to ensure that women are included and visible. We have chosen to use "GLBTQ" in this historical account to reflect the fact that the human rights movement on behalf of GLBTQ people that began with the 1969 Stonewall Riots was originally referred to as the gay rights or gay liberation movement.

Despite uncertainties of statistics and vagaries of descriptors, a look at YA publishing over time clearly indicates that the number of YA novels with gay/lesbian content has slowly increased, growing from an average of one title per year in the 1970s to four per year in the 1980s to seven per year in the 1990s to over twelve titles per year in the early years of the 21st century.

A number of the early novels—and even some of the more recent ones—perpetuate stereotypes in their portrayal of homosexual characters. Some are pictured as unfortunates doomed to either a premature death or a life of despair lived at the darkest margins of society. Others are portrayed as sinister predators lurking in the shadows of sinister settings, or play the role of briefly viewed "fags" or "dykes" who are included only to confirm a more central character's naivete or sophistication. There are also a number of YA novels—most, though not all, of a more recent vintage—that present gay and lesbian characters in a more realistic light. They are portrayed as people of various ages, cultures, incomes, and perspectives, as the friends, family, neighbors, and mentors who are part of the social web of connectedness that teens of all sexual orientations navigate on a daily basis.

Many of these books are well written, well reviewed, and popular with teen readers of all sexual orientations—these are books that teens *want* to read. In certain quarters, however, their very existence remains controversial. A chilling reminder of this fact was seen in early 2005 in the Alabama legislature with the introduction House Bill 30, a bill that would have prevented public and school libraries from owning, purchasing, or making accessible any print or electronic materials that "recognize, foster, or promote a [homosexual] lifestyle." The bill eventually died without debate when the legislature was adjourned. However, in May 2005 the Oklahoma state legislature passed a resolution urging all public libraries to "confine homosexually themed books and other age-inappropriate material to areas exclusively for adult access and distribution." Indeed, some legislators threatened to kill a library-funding bill unless libraries complied with the resolution. Challenges to books with GLBTQ content—particularly those aimed at young readers—are on the rise. These examples demonstrate the role that books can play in political demonstrations of anti-gay sentiment.[2]

Clearly, GLBTQ teens must negotiate a complicated social and political environment that is mirrored (and sometimes distorted) in YA literature. Happily, such struggles can result in gay/lesbian teens finding support from their peers. Since the 1990s, Gay-Straight Alliances (GSAs) have been organized by students in schools across the country. By January 2003, there were an estimated 1,700 such clubs.[3] Many teens, however, who remain uncertain about their sexual orientation or are afraid of public censure still prefer the privacy that reading offers and turn to the "community on the page" that is found in books.

Although young adult novels with gay content have been published for more than thirty-five years, only one book-length analytical study— Alan Cuseo's academic work *Homosexual Characters in YA Novels* (Scarecrow Press, 1992)—and two book-length annotated bibliographies— Marjorie Lobban and Laurel A. Clyde's *Out of the Closet and into the Classroom* (Thorpe/ALIA, 1996) and Frances Ann Day's *Lesbian and Gay Voices* (Greenwood Press, 2000)— have been published about this genre as a body of literature. A handful of journal articles evidencing serious research into the subject have also appeared, some focusing on a small number of titles, others focusing on the responses of teachers, librarians, or school administrators to having one or more of these titles in their classrooms or their libraries. A few studies have even focused on the responses of the teen readers themselves (see Appendix B).

Why this dearth of critical analysis? Well, it is probably not a conspiracy of silence, as we will see in chapter three, though a certain specter of fear has haunted this field since its beginning and has often impeded open discussion. Books with GLBTQ content remain among the most challenged titles in America's public and school libraries, as documented by the American Library Association's Office for Intellectual Freedom, and it appears that the pressure will not be abating any time soon. In 1994 Michael Thomas Ford stated that fear of controversy has often discouraged publishers from issuing gay or lesbian titles.[4] A decade later we continue to be aware that while controversy can build a market for a title, it can also open publishers to criticism, boycotts, and public censure—particularly when a book is aimed at a young audience.

Though the struggle for gay adult rights was symbolically initiated in the Stonewall Riots of 1969 (the same year as the publication of Donovan's novel), it appears that the struggle for the human rights of gay, lesbian, and bisexual teens is still just beginning. Joyce Hunter, a researcher at Columbia University, describes the plight of too many of these troubled teens: "These are kids who are lonely, who haven't got their coping skills developed. And they need support. They need to know that they are not alone."[5] What better way to give that assurance than to share with them good books that offer positive portrayals of homosexual characters and deal compassionately and honestly with homosexual themes and issues? As Lynn Cockett has eloquently written, "A balanced [library] fiction collection should assuage the fears of gay and lesbian YAs, assuring them that they are not alone."[6]

This belief in the importance and value of balanced library collections for gay and lesbian teens is foundational to the collaborative text you are reading. It is our goal both to chart the evolution of the field and to identify titles that are remarkable either for their excellence or for their failures. In the process we also hope to establish some useful criteria for evaluating books with GLBTQ content. Our judgments of the accuracy of character portrayal and the validity of thematic treatment are, inevitably, based on our own life experiences and our understanding of and familiarity with the historical context(s) in which these books have been published and read. We are also drawing upon our collective experience of more than fifty years of reading and writing about young adult literature. If some of our judgments seem harsh and some of our praise lavish, it is due to our continued belief in the power of books to help teen readers understand themselves and others, to contribute to the mental health and well-being of GLBTQ youth, and to save lives—and perhaps even to change the world—by informing minds and nourishing spirits. In order to provide readers—and authors—a critical context in which to evaluate GLBTQ literature, we believe that what is stereotypic, wrongheaded, and outdated must be noted and what is accurate, thoughtful, and artful must be applauded.

That our focus will be primarily on fiction does not discount the importance of nonfiction titles to readers in pursuit of information, affirmation, and community. Biographies, self-help, and advice books aimed at teen readers; informational texts about the social and political history of homosexuality; and first-person accounts of the lives of GLBTQ teens and adults are all useful to the inquiring teen reader.

We have chosen to collaborate, instead of writing independent works, for two reasons: 1) we felt it was important to bring both a male and female perspective to the work and 2) we wanted to include our different professional perspectives as a university professor (Christine) and a literary journalist and editor (Michael). Our previously published work has been targeted at different—though often overlapping—audiences. By collaborating we hope to expand the readership for this work, the subject of which is so powerfully important. Though often of one mind, we do not always agree on issues, interpretation, or the evaluation of individual titles. Just as individual teen readers respond in their own ways to the stories we examine here, so we, too, view the landscape of YA literature on GLBTQ themes somewhat differently.

While striving for a lively style and accessible content, we nevertheless recognize the importance to the credibility of our work of critical apparatus, of framework and structure. The model we have chosen for these twin purposes (described in full in Appendix A) is built upon Rudine Sims Bishop's foundational study *Shadow & Substance: Afro-American Experience in Contemporary Children's Fiction.*[7] Sims Bishop proposes a three-part model to describe representations of African American characters in children's books published in the fifteen years immediately following the enactment of the Civil Rights Act of 1964.

First to appear, she states, were "social conscience books;" books in which race was the problem and desegregation the solution. Next came "melting pot" books, in which racial diversity was present but unacknowledged, and integration was a given. Finally, "culturally conscious" books began to be published, books in which African Americans were portrayed in a culturally accurate manner.

The model we use in this text grows out of Christine Jenkins' research on YA literature with GLBTQ content.[8] Jenkins' framework builds upon Sims Bishop's three-part model for African-American inclusion in children's fiction to create a model specific to GLBTQ content in YA fiction using category descriptors that reflect post-Stonewall GLBTQ history and experience to describe the evolution of YA literature with GLBTQ content from 1969 through 2004. The three categories are:

Homosexual Visibility
Gay Assimilation
Queer Consciousness/Community

Most of the young adult novels with gay/lesbian content from the 1970s and 1980s are stories of "homosexual visibility" in which a character who has not previously been considered gay/lesbian comes out either voluntarily or involuntarily. This revelation may occur at any point in the story with much of its dramatic tension arising from what *might* happen when the invisible is made visible. Consequently, as with "social conscience" stories of racial integration, a previously homogeneous society is interrupted by the appearance of a character who is clearly *not* "one of us." The response to this interruption is the dramatic substance of the story.

"Gay assimilation" assumes the existence—at least in the world of the story—of a "melting pot" of sexual and gender identity. These stories include people who "just happen to be gay" in the same way that someone "just happens" to be left-handed or have red hair.

Stories that contain "queer consciousness" show GLBTQ characters in the context of their communities of GLBTQ people and their families of choice (and in recent years, often their families of origin as well). As with "culturally conscious" stories told from an African American perspective, the audience for "queer consciousness/community" books is not limited to readers from within the culture; rather, these titles are—at least potentially—for readers from all points on the sexual orientation continuum.

Not surprisingly, surveys of public attitudes toward homosexuals indicate that people who say they know a gay/lesbian person personally express more tolerance of and comfort with GLBTQ people than those who say they do not. Could these books perhaps play a positive didactic role in acquainting young readers with realistically portrayed gay/lesbian characters? And could those readers' imaginations be pushed a bit further to see such characters from an empathetic, rather than simply a sympathetic, perspective? Could a young reader not simply feel *for* gay and lesbian people but also *with* them?

Shadow & Substance opens with a quote from the African American writer James Baldwin, "Literature is indispensable to the world. The world changes according to the way people see it, and if you alter, even by a millimeter, the way a person looks at reality, then you can change it."[9] Here it must be noted that Baldwin was a *gay* African American author and that his words apply with equal force to literature with gay/lesbian content. Baldwin's belief in the indispensability of literature and its power to change the world is foundational to our own analysis of young people's literature with gay/lesbian content that follows.

NOTES

1. In the years since the publication of Donovan's book, the U.S. census reported 24.3 million people between the ages of 12 and 17 in 1970; 23.3 million in 1980; 20.1 million in 1990, and 24.2 million in 2000. The 2000 census was the first census to ask about sexual orientation; 4.3 million people (1.5% of the population) identified themselves as gay, lesbian, or bisexual. Given that these figures are entirely self-reported and that openly gay/lesbian/bisexual people may face negative consequences—ranging from social/familial ostracism to job loss to physical harm—it seems likely that their numbers are actually higher than the census count. But even using this low-end estimate of 1.5% indicates that there were at least 363,000 current and/or future gay/lesbian/bisexualteens in the U.S. in 2000. Futhermore, the U.S. census estimates that the number of U.S. teens will increase over the next several decades, growing to 24.4 million in 2010 and 26.0 million in 2020. In short, millions of teens currently identify as GLBTQ or will as adults. "Table 1. Number of Children Under Age 18 in the United States and Children as a Percentage of the Population, Selected Years, 1950–2030." http://www.childtrendsdatabank.org/tables/53_Table_1.htm (accessed 7/20/05).

2. "Alabama Bill Targets Gay Authors," CBS Evening News April 27, 2005, http://www.cbsnews.com/stories/2005/04/26/eveningnews/main691106.shtml (accessed 5/10/05); "Lawmakers Threaten Library Funds Over Gay-Themed Kids Books," ChannelOklahoma.com, May 13, 2005, http://www.channeloklahoma.com/politics/4486200/detail.html (accessed 5/13/05). Further examples can be found on "Chronology of Anti-Gay Legislation and Actions" on Theocracy Watch website, http://theocracywatch.org/homo_chronology.htm (accessed 5/10/05).

3. Wall, Lucas. "ACLU Sues Klein School on Behalf of Lesbian Student." *Houston Chronicle,* 1/22/03. http://www.chron.com/cs/.

4. Ford, Michael Thomas. "Gay Books for Young Readers: When Caution Calls the Shots," *Publishers Weekly,* 241:24 (February 21, 1994).

5. Irvine, Martha, "Gay Teens' Lives Called More Risky," *The Sacramento Bee,* 5/5/98, p. A10.

6. Cockett, Lynn. "Entering the Mainstream: Fiction about Gay and Lesbian Teens," *School Library Journal,* 41:2 (February 1995), p. 32.

7. Sims Bishop, Rudine. *Shadow & Substance: Afro-American Experience in Contemporary Children's Fiction.* Urbana, IL: NCTE, 1982.

8. Jenkins, Christine. "From Queer to Gay and Back Again: Young Adult Novels with Gay/Lesbian/Queer Content, 1969–1997" *Library Quarterly* 68 (July 1998): 298–334. Her more recent study of this literature, "Desperately Seeking Community: Theorizing a Model for Young Adult Literature with Gay/Lesbian/Queer Content, 1969–2002" was first presented at the 2003 National Reading Conference Annual Meeting, Dec. 5, 2003, Scottsdale, AZ.

9. Watkins, M. "James Baldwin Writing and Talking." *New York Times Book Review.* 23:3 (September 1979), pp. 36–37.

• 1 •

Give Us Faces

In his *Notes Towards the Definition of Culture,* the poet and critic T. S. Eliot offered three "permanent" reasons for reading:

1. the acquisition of wisdom
2. the enjoyment of art
3. the pleasure of entertainment.[1]

In the case of young adult (YA) literature (which we define as books that are published for readers age twelve to eighteen, have a young adult protagonist, are told from a young adult perspective, and feature coming-of-age or other issues and concerns of interest to YAs), we would add a fourth reason to Eliot's list. In this quintessential literature of the outsider who is too often rendered invisible by society, there is also the need to see one's face reflected in the pages of a book and thus to find the corollary comfort that derives from the knowledge that one is not alone in a vast universe, that there are others "like me."

Novelist and essayist James Baldwin made this point more eloquently when he wrote, "You think your pains and heartbreaks are unprecedented in the history of the world, but then you read. It was books that taught me that the things that tormented me were the very things that connected me with all the people who were alive or who have ever been alive." [2]

In the decades since 1967, the year that S. E. Hinton's *The Outsiders* and Robert Lipsyte's *The Contender*—widely regarded as the first modern young adult novels—appeared, the literature has done an increasingly better job of including teens from varying racial, class, and cultural origins.

1

Yet, to many critics, these changes have been glacially slow, and certainly YA literature, taken as a whole, continues to focus primarily on characters and settings located solidly in white mainstream culture. Though it has been forty years since Nancy Larrick challenged the "all-white world of children's books" in her influential 1965 article in *Saturday Review*, the actual world in which U.S. teens live has changed far more in those forty years than the worlds portrayed in literature for young readers.[3] Nevertheless, this literature is—however slowly—growing more diverse and so is doing an increasingly better job of giving faces to teens from a range of races, ethnicities, cultures, classes, national origins, abilities/disabilities, and religious beliefs. And yet one group of teenage outsiders—GLBTQ youth—has been nearly invisible in YA fiction. As we will see, this situation, too, is gradually beginning to change for the better, but in the context of literary history, the homosexual as a character in American fiction (for both young adults *and* adults) has been a largely absent figure.

Why? Perhaps in part because homosexuality has been regarded, in Lord Alfred Douglas' words, as "the Love that dare not speak its name."[4] Thus, despite the fact that historians have documented the reality that a gay, largely urban culture existed in the U.S. as early as the 1890s, homosexuality as a public aspect of mainstream American life was largely invisible.[5] During the early decades of the twentieth century, this gradually changed as a geography of gay-friendly (or at least gay-tolerant) meeting places and establishments (neighborhood parks, hotels, bars, restaurants, and clubs) emerged in urban areas. During the 1940s this process accelerated for several reasons.[6]

First, as noted by historian Allan Berube, the massive enlistments and war time draft that accompanied America's entrance into World War II in late 1941 "relaxed the social constraints of peacetime that had kept gay men and women unaware of themselves and each other, 'bringing out' many in the process."[7] The burgeoning military brought together large concentrations of gay men and lesbians, "perhaps the largest concentration ever found inside a single American institution."[8] The resulting synergy sparked a new self-awareness on the part of gay men and lesbians as individuals and as a community.

Secondly, the publication of Alfred Kinsey, et al's well-known *Sexual Behavior in the Human Male* in 1948 revealed the startling fact that the sexual histories of one-tenth of American males included significant sexual experience with other males.[9] The book quickly became a best-seller and historian Charles Kaiser has argued that this event marked the point in time at which the existence of homosexuality was publicly acknowledged in the U.S.[10] The facts reported by what came to be known as "the Kinsey Report" contributed to what Martin Duberman calls "a critical mass of consciousness" that slowly began to be reflected in—among other venues—the literature of the time.[11]

EARLY HOMOSEXUAL FICTION FOR ADULTS

The late 1940s also saw the publication of two important adult novels with gay themes: *Other Voices, Other Rooms* by Truman Capote and *The City and the Pillar* by Gore Vidal. They are significant for two reasons. First, they were serious works of fiction by writers who would become vital forces in American literature. Second, they were issued by mainstream publishers: Random House and E. P. Dutton, respectively. Previously, as Joseph Cady notes, "while there was frank and affirmative gay male American writing from the century's start" (most of it now forgotten except by literary historians), "it was either published abroad or issued in this country by marginal publishers."[12] During the 1950s and early 1960s, other noted works of fiction with gay male characters appeared: *Giovanni's Room*, by James Baldwin (1956); John Rechy's *City of Night* (1963); and Christopher Isherwood's *A Single Man* (1964).[13]

Literature with lesbian content followed a somewhat different path. Radclyffe Hall's *The Well of Loneliness*, one of the first—and certainly the best-known–of the modern novels from a mainstream commercial publisher to include specific lesbian content, was published in England in 1928. It is the story of Stephen Gordon, a young woman of the English landed gentry who is a lesbian or (in the words of English psychologist Havelock Ellis, who wrote the book's preface) "a congenital invert." As she matures, her difference is noted by her mother with revulsion, by her father with love and pity, and by her governess with maternal warmth. As an adult, she is an intelligent and aloof outsider. When World War I breaks out, Stephen joins a battalion of female ambulance drivers and meets her soulmate, Mary. They live together for a time, but the story ends tragically when Stephen sends Mary away (and into the arms of a man) so that Mary can escape the stigma of lesbianism, while Stephen nobly resigns herself to a life of permanent loneliness.

The book was declared obscene in England because of its subject matter. Indeed, newspaper editor/reviewer James Douglas famously declared that he "would [rather] give a healthy boy or a healthy girl a phial of prussic acid than this book. Poison kills the body, but moral poison kills the soul."[14] *The Well of Loneliness* was published in the U.S. in late 1928. In the early months of 1929 it was challenged by the Society for the Suppression of Vice, brought to trial, and judged obscene. By the end of April, however, the ruling had been successfully appealed and the book became a best-seller. Other titles of that time with lesbian content, such as *Orlando* by Virginia Woolf, *The Lady's Almanack* by Compton MacKenzie, *Nightwood* by Djuna Barnes, and the avant garde poetry of Gertrude Stein, were considerably more artful and discrete, making them less accessible and interesting to many teen readers. Perhaps accordingly, it is *The Well of Loneliness* that is still cited by many women as the first novel they recall reading that included characters identified as lesbians.

In the 1950s, however, the appearance and subsequent popularity of adult lesbian pulp paperbacks were a boon to teen readers. Two paperback bestsellers—*Women's Barracks* by Tereska Torres in 1950 and *Spring Fire* by Vin Packer (a pseudonym for Marijane Meeker, who later became better known as YA author M.E. Kerr) in 1952—demonstrated that there was an eager audience for mass market novels with lesbian content. These were followed by a flood of pulp romances whose covers featured scantily clad women and titles like *Women Without Men, Twilight Girl,* and *Whisper Their Love.* Typical storylines featured naïve young women who are seduced by lesbians but finally won back to heterosexuality by men who could offer them marriage, a home, and children. If the lesbian character was actually a good person, she usually died before the end of the book. If she was evil, she might die or end up in a mental hospital, or she might head off to further conquests. There were, however, some books with happy endings—most notably Ann Bannon's five-book "Beebo Brinker" series (1957-1962) that begins with *Odd Girl Out,* a sorority house romance, and ends with *Journey to a Woman* in which two women, Beth and Beebo, find their soulmates in each other, plus *Beebo Brinker,* a prequel about the early life of the eponymous heroine.[15]

Despite their predictable plots and often-tragic endings, these books—widely available on paperback racks in drug stores and newsstands across the country—are often cited as having introduced isolated young lesbians to a world of possibilities in the lesbian communities that were slowly becoming visible in cities across the country. As Lillian Faderman reported her experience as a lesbian teen in 1956: "Almost as soon as I claimed that identity, being already enamored of books, of course I looked around for literary representations that would help explain me to myself. I did not have far to look, because the pulp bookracks at the local drugstores exhibited a dizzying array of titles like *Odd Girl, Twisted Sisters, Twilight Lovers, We Walk in Shadows,* and *Whisper Their Love.*"[16]

In the 1970s, with the rise of the Second Wave of feminism, small and alternative women's presses began publishing fiction with lesbian protagonists. One of the best-known products of the women in print movement was Rita Mae Brown's *Rubyfruit Jungle,* a lesbian coming-of-age novel published by alternative press Daughters Inc. in 1973. Although the book was originally published as an adult title, it was taken up by teen readers and has been a staple in the coming out narratives of adult lesbians ever since. And to bring the story full circle, Naiad Press, one of the most prolific women's publishers, reissued all of Ann Bannon's novels in 1983. This history of fiction with lesbian content as popular mass market paperbacks in the 1950s is a unique feature in the specific history of lesbian fiction, viewed separately from gay male fiction.

YOUNG ADULT FICTION: FIRST STIRRINGS

The new homosexual consciousness that appeared during and after World War II coincided with the first stirrings of "young adult literature." Two of the literature's best-known early practitioners, Maureen Daly and Madeline L'Engle, published their first novels in the 1940s. Daly's *Seventeenth Summer* appeared in 1942, while L'Engle's *The Small Rain* was published in 1945. Though both titles were published as adult novels, they were widely and enthusiastically read by YAs and, interestingly, both also included incidental treatments of homosexuality.

In *The Small Rain,* the teen protagonist, Katherine, is taken to a squalid gay bar where she encounters "a woman, or what perhaps had once been a woman. Now it wore a man's suit, shirt, and tie; its hair was cut short, out of a dead-white face glared a pair of despairing eyes."[17] The horrified pity of Katherine's response marks her as a naif among her more worldly friends and points up the finer nature of her character in contrast to the callous voyeurism of her companions.

In *Seventeenth Summer* the protagonist, Angie, and her boyfriend, Jack, go to a club to hear a musician who is portrayed as stereotypically gay: "With his eyes still closed, the colored man leaned back on the bench, way back, one hand limp at his side . . . 'Look, Jack,' I remember saying, 'He has red nail polish on! Isn't that funny—for a man?'"[18] Like Katherine's experience this brief incident underlines Angie's unworldly innocence as a girl from a small Wisconsin town unversed in the big city sophistication of this talented, but clearly alien, entertainer.

In J. D. Salinger's 1951 novel *Catcher in the Rye,* another brief homosexual encounter is reported. Like L'Engle's and Daly's, this novel was also published for adults but was claimed by succeeding generations of young adults as their own. Indeed, many would argue that if these books were first being published today, it would be as young adult titles. Salinger's protagonist, seventeen-year-old Holden Caufield, has a—to him—disturbing encounter with a favorite teacher when he stays overnight at the man's New York apartment:

> "What he [the teacher] was doing was, he was sitting on the floor right next to the couch, in the dark and all, and he was sort of petting me or patting me on the goddam head. Boy, I'll bet I jumped about a thousand feet. 'What're ya *do*ing?' I said.
>
> 'Nothing! I'm simply sitting here admiring—' 'What're ya *do*ing, anyway?' I said over again. I didn't know *what* the hell to say—I mean I was embarrassed as hell.
>
> 'How 'bout keeping your voice down? I'm simply sitting here—'
>
> 'I have to go anyway,' I said—boy, was I nervous! I know more damn perverts at schools and all, than anybody you ever met, and they're always being perverty when *I'm* around."[19]

These brief moments had little direct impact on the evolution of gay and lesbian literature published specifically for young adults; nevertheless, for some of their many YA readers the incidents/settings of these three novels may well have been their first exposure to homosexuality in literature. A more important treatment of this theme, in the context of a coming-of-age novel, was James Baldwin's *Go Tell It on the Mountain.* Published in 1953, it dealt authentically with its fourteen-year-old protagonist's attraction to a seventeen-year-old boy. Then, in 1960, John Knowles' *A Separate Peace* was published. Like the Daly, L'Engle, Salinger, and Baldwin titles, this novel was aimed at an adult readership but quickly became a YA classic. Though Knowles' book did not deal overtly with homosexuality, to sophisticated readers it clearly had a gay—though coded—subtext. And in a 1972 interview, Knowles acknowledged that his main characters, the two boys Finny and Gene, "were in love" (Cady, 37). Whether teens, then or now, perceive this is moot.

I'LL GET THERE. IT BETTER BE WORTH THE TRIP

However, by the end of the decade the subject would be treated more explicitly when, in 1969, the first young adult novel to deal with homosexuality was published: *I'll Get There. It Better Be Worth the Trip* by John Donovan. There is no simple cause-and-effect relationship between the fact that the publication of this book and the Stonewall Rebellion—a landmark in the gay civil rights movement—happened in the same watershed year, 1969, but both were products of the same social/cultural climate. The 1960s were years of turbulent social change, of political unrest, and of sexual revolution. The media—often the first to observe changes in popular culture—took note and, according to Martin Duberman, "the years 1962 to 1965 saw a sharp increase in the amount of public discussion and representation of homosexuality." (97) He cites, in particular, the proliferation of lesbian pulp novels and of motion pictures with homosexual content ("The L-Shaped Room," "Lilith," "Darling," etc.). There was a similar increase in the publication, for adult readers, of serious literary novels with gay/lesbian content, including James Baldwin's *Another Country* (1962), Mary McCarthy's *The Group* (1963), John Rechy's *City of Night* (1963) and *Numbers* (1967), Christopher Isherwood's *A Single Man* (1964), Sanford Friedman's *Totempole* (1965) and Gore Vidal's *Myra Breckenridge* (1968).

Meanwhile, in the field of books for young readers, the late 1960s saw the emergence of the first modern young adult fiction, i.e., novels of social realism with contemporary settings like *The Outsiders, The Contender,* and Paul Zindel's *The Pigman*. Not surprisingly for books aimed at teen readers addressing teen concerns, heterosexual sex was often a theme in these novels of the late 1960s. With the early exception of Henry Gregor Felsen's *Two and the Town,* published in 1952, which dealt with an unmarried teen's pregnancy, sex was a taboo topic in YA literature before the sixties. In 1966, Jeannette Eyerly's *A Girl Like Me* the unwed teenage friend of the protagonist becomes pregnant; in 1967 it's the protagonist herself, the eponymous heroine of Zoa Sherburne's *Too Bad about the Haines Girl.* The same year saw the publication of Ann Head's adult novel *Mr. and Mrs. Bo Jo Jones,* in which two teenagers, July and Bo Jo, are swept away by passion; she becomes pregnant and they elope. This novel appeared in paperback the following year and became a best-seller with young adults through teenage book clubs.[20]

Despite the increasing treatment of teenage heterosexuality in fiction and the increasing awareness of homosexuality in American culture, Harper & Row viewed the publication of Donovan's *I'll Get There* with considerable trepidation. William C. Morris, a vice president of Harper, recalled, "Everyone was very frightened. In fact we went to such great lengths to make it 'acceptable' to the general public that the book got more attention for the fuss we made than for anything that was in it."[21]

One of the "lengths" was the solicitation of a statement for the dust jacket from the acclaimed Dr. Frances Ilg, Director of the Gesell Institute of Child Development. In a letter to Ilg dated August 8, 1968, Ursula Nordstrom, director of Harper's Department of Books for Boys and Girls, wrote, "I do not need to tell you that the book will meet with considerable resistance with certain influential persons in the children's book field. Yet surely this is an experience many boys have and one that worries and frightens them badly. It seems strange that a curtain has been drawn over this entire subject in fiction for young readers. Our book will be the first." According to the critic Leonard S. Marcus, "FI (Frances Ilg) responded enthusiastically, providing a comment for publication."[22]

Here it is, as it appeared on the book's rear dust jacket flap: "A moment of sexual discovery is told simply but poignantly in the life of a thirteen-year-old boy, through his relationship with a friend of his own sex and age. It is how he absorbs this experience that becomes the key to what will happen next. Davy is able to face the experience and to make his choice."

I'll Get There was Donovan's first novel but he was no stranger either to writing or to books for young readers. A former attorney, Donovan was the Executive Director of the Children's Book Council, a position he held from 1967 until his death in 1993. He was also the author of a picture book, *The Little Orange Book,* and an adult play, *Riverside Drive.* In a query letter to Nordstrom, Donovan described his novel as being "about a kid with love problems." In her cordial reply, Nordstrom said she'd be "delighted" to read the manuscript, adding that she had been waiting "a long time" for a novel that included "buddy love problems."[22]

Davy Ross, the thirteen-year-old protagonist of Donovan's novel, has more problems than buddy love, as it turns out. The son of divorced parents, he has been living near Boston for eight years with his beloved grandmother who, as the novel begins, has just died. Davy is devastated and dubious about being sent to live with his mother in New York City. He has good reason. Their relationship is strained, to say the least. His mother has a problem with alcohol that causes erratic behavior and unpredictable mood swings. "She's either slobbering all over me or ready to boot me out of the house," Davy tells the reader (189). To make matters worse, she is less than overjoyed by the presence of Davy's pet dachshund, Fred ("Can't you keep the little bastard quiet?" [45]). Her animosity is exacerbated, the reader infers, by her jealousy of Davy's almost obsessive love for Fred who, following the grandmother's death, has become the emotional center of the boy's life.

Davy is also reunited with his remarried father on occasional weekend visits. Their relationship, though not without its awkward moments, is far less strained than that of mother and son. Nevertheless, Davy often feels more tolerated than loved and, in this regard, clearly identifies with Fred when he says, "When you make a dog like Fred part of your family, he is a full-time member, not just someone who will be around when you want him to" (45).

Soon enough, however, someone other than his dog will begin to matter to Davy: his new friend, Douglas Altschuler. Davy's mother has enrolled him in an Episcopal boys' school and Douglas occupies the seat in front of him in geography class. As we will see, private schools provide the setting for many of the homosexual novels in the early years of the genre—perhaps because, like English boarding schools, they offer a ready-made, same-sex environment for boys or girls away from home for the first time. It turns out that the boys have a great deal in common. Both have divorced parents and live with their mothers, and both have suffered a recent emotional loss; Davy has lost his grandmother, of course, while Douglas has lost his best friend to cancer. But for Davy perhaps the most important reason for friendship is that Altschuler shares his affection for Fred.

And it is Fred who, ultimately, provides the opportunity for the boys' first physical intimacy. It happens one afternoon after school. They are at Davy's apartment. Mrs. Ross, who works in an advertising agency, is not yet home from work. The two boys are lying on the living room floor where they have been playing with Fred. When the dog darts away, the two are left, face-to-face, eye-to-eye. Though Davy knows he should get up, he doesn't move. Neither does Altschuler. Tension begins to build when, suddenly, Fred jumps in between them, excitedly licking their faces. And then it happens: "I guess I kiss Altschuler," Davy reports, "and he kisses me. It just happens. And when it stops, we sit up and turn away from each other.

'Boy,' I say. 'What was that all about?'

'I don't know,' Altschuler answers."

Awkwardly, the two boys get up and, to break the tension, resume playing with Fred. Then Altschuler lunges at Davy with his fists up like a boxer and the two pretend to spar.

"We are two bantamweight tough guys," Davy says. "I mean very tough. I mean a couple of guys like Altschuler and me don't have to worry about being queer or anything like that. Hell, no" (143).

The boys avoid each other the next day and might have gone on avoiding each other forever if Davy's mother hadn't made plans for the weekend and—to Davy's consternation—invited Altschuler to spend the day . . . and the night.

Davy doesn't tell us anything about the day but the next morning he tells us that he has a new way of looking at Altschuler "because of what we did together last night."

He is no more specific than that. The catalyst for what they did was not Fred, this time, but the time-honored adolescent male discussion of girls "we had made out with." Davy insists to the reader that he feels there was nothing wrong with what the two did, but his words have the ring of false bravado.

In a letter dated August 5, 1968, Nordstrom wrote to Donovan of the work that was then still in progress, "I know you don't want to hit your readers over their heads, but we do think you can make it clearer, more vivid that David does suffer from considerable worry and guilt feelings" (Marcus, 258). There is no way of knowing what changes to the manu- script this may have inspired but there is no question that Donovan found a way to create a considerable burden of guilt for Davy to shoulder.

After a week of casual friendship the boys finally talk about what has happened, each acknowledging that he had lied to the other about hav- ing made out with girls and agreeing there is no reason they shouldn't be friends "like before" (156). They take Fred for a walk and return to the Ross apartment where, Davy tells us, "I give Altschuler a big dumb kiss.

He looks surprised. And so do I" (158).

What happens next seems a bit contrived. The boys decide to sam- ple some whiskey from one of Mrs. Ross's many bottles. They drink enough to become dizzy, sit down on the floor with Fred, and fall asleep with their arms stretched across each other's backs.

Mrs. Ross comes home from work, finds them there, and, pre- dictably (for her), has hysterics. Altschuler quickly leaves for home and after three cocktails and numerous tears, Mrs. Ross calls Davy's father, who comes over immediately. To give them privacy for what promises to be a serious talk, Mrs. Ross leaves the apartment, taking Fred with her. After acknowledging that the two "don't talk about personal things much, but sometimes it can't be avoided," Mr. Ross asks Davy if he has a crush on Altschuler. Davy immediately becomes defensive, "I'm not queer or anything, if that's what you think," he replies. Mr. Ross, though portrayed as being distant, is not insensitive. He moves quickly from the specific to the general, assuring Davy that many boys experiment but urging him not to "get involved in some special way of life, which will close off other ways of life."

"We only made out once," Davy protests (166). Mr. Ross laughs and the two continue their conversation until Davy becomes nervous about the length of time his mother and Fred have been absent. He goes to the window just in time to see Fred run around the corner with his mother, who has lost her hold on Fred's leash, in hot pursuit.

Davy is alarmed, since, as he tells his father, "Fred is never off his leash on the street."

The boy then runs downstairs, arriving on the street just in time to hear "a big thud. A terrible, unnatural yelping." Fred has been struck by a car and dies in Davy's arms. The boy is devastated and consumed by guilt over the cause and effect relationship he infers between his "making out" with Altschuler and Fred's death. "Nothing would have happened to Fred if I hadn't been messing around with Altschuler. My fault. Mine!" (172).

For six weeks Davy tortures himself with these guilty, self-flagellating thoughts. He avoids Altschuler as much as possible and is distantly polite when school brings them together. Gradually, however, Davy's anger at himself expands to include Altschuler. He rationalizes this by convincing himself that it was Altschuler's lying about having made out with a girl that "got us started . . . Fred died because of some stupid lies about making out." Davy continues his rationalizing by adding, "It certainly isn't in my nature to queer around. I never did it before. If it hadn't been for Altschuler, I would never have done it at all" (174).

Davy's anger continues to build until, following a school baseball game that has been won by Davy's home run, the two boys encounter each other in the locker room shower. Congratulating Davy on his "great hit," Altschuler pats him on the shoulder. Davy reacts angrily, saying, "I don't like to be touched."

Altschuler's reply is telling: "Since when?"

Davy blows up. "We're going to end up a couple of queers," he tells Altschuler hotly. "You know that, don't you? All that junk back there before Fred died. You know what happens, don't you?" (176–177).

A fight ensues and only stops when Davy's ear is so badly cut he has to be taken to a doctor. The episode is cathartic and several days later the two talk about what Davy calls "this queer business." Davy is anxious that Altschuler should know that he had never done anything like "that" before. Altschuler acknowledges that it had upset him but "it didn't feel wrong. Did it to you?"

"Look what happened," is Davy's terse retort. Altschuler wisely states that what happened to Fred had nothing to do with what they did, but Davy continues to insist that maybe it did. "Go ahead and feel guilty if you want to, I don't," the other boy replies. "I guess the important thing is not to do it again," Davy says, to which his friend replies, "I don't care. If you think it's dirty or something like that, I wouldn't do it again if I were you."

"Maybe," Davy concludes, "if we made out with some girls, we wouldn't have to think about, you know, the other" (188).

The book ends a bit anticlimactically with the two boys agreeing that they can "respect" each other. But it seems clear that, for both of these emotionally vulnerable kids from fractured families, getting there—to adulthood, presumably—will still be no easy trip.

Despite Harper & Row's pre-publication anxiety, most reviewers received Donovan's book warmly. Indeed, both the *New York Times* and *School Library Journal* named it to their annual best book lists. Paul Heins, editor of *Horn Book*, called the book's impact "shattering" and praised the protagonist's "frankness and intelligence."[23] Zena Sutherland, in *Saturday Review*, called it "as poignant and honest an account of an unhappy child as one could read."[24] And Lavinia Russ, writing in *Publishers Weekly*, praised it as "a perceptive, funny, touching story, a remarkable book."[25]

Surprisingly, while all the reviews note the homosexual encounter, not a single one mentions that this is the first time the subject has been treated in a book for this age group, though Alice Hungerford does acknowledge what she calls "the new sophistication in fiction," adding that this is "a very modern book which directs itself to the increasing maturity of younger readers."[26]

For the most part the reviewers interpret Davy's homosexual encounters with Altschuler as being little more than a routine rite of passage, a lonely boy's reaching out for friendship—indeed, the same interpretation Davy's father seems to apply. Heins calls it "a slight homosexual incident." *Booklist* magazine describes it as "a spontaneous act of sexuality" that is "tastefully handled."[27] *School Library Journal* calls the boys' physical encounters "childish caresses."[28] At the outset, John Weston's *New York Times* review appears to promise more insight. He begins by saying, "The contribution this book makes, giving reason why it should be available wherever young people read, is that it touches, with lyricism and simplicity, upon a spontaneous sexual relationship between two adolescent boys." But then he goes on to say that "such desires" are "something beautiful at the moment, but to be replaced in the natural course of life with interest in the other sex."[29] Which is to suggest, of course, that homosexuality is both unnatural and transient.

Only one reviewer, Martha Bacon, writing in the *Atlantic Monthly*, viewed homosexuality as a major theme of the book and was actively hostile to it. She writes, "The novel celebrates the child's homosexual encounter with a schoolfellow" (a very odd reading of the book!) and goes on to say, "the language of children is inadequate to [the loss of innocence] and the application of grammar school jargon to corruption and passion is neither natural nor comforting. . . . I am also inclined to think that a book focused on a love affair between schoolfellows might have just the opposite effect on this age group from that which the author intended. It would not meet the needs of the initiated and it might arouse in the unconcerned unnecessary interest or alarm or both."[30]

In fact, it is a gross overstatement to describe the relationship between the boys as "a love affair." Indeed, love seems not to come into it at all. What disturbs Davy is not his affection for Altschuler but the fleeting physical expression it is given. For Davy, being "queer" begins and ends with making out. And being "queer" is, indisputably, not a way anyone would want to be.

Writing twenty-eight years after the book's publication, David Rees, the British critic and novelist who was himself the author of several gay-themed young adult novels, commented on this aspect of the book. "John Donovan suggests that teenage homosexuality is so totally unacceptable, socially and psychologically, that any young homosexual is likely to have his fears and worries increased rather than reduced, and the prejudice of the heterosexual reader against homosexuals is reinforced."[31] This judgment may be a bit harsh, but we do agree it's hard to imagine any gay or lesbian teen finding much comfort or support in this novel.

Nevertheless, *I'll Get There. It Better Be Worth the Trip* remains tremendously important three-and-a-half decades after its publication, not only because it was the first book for young readers to deal with homosexuality, but also because it established—for good or ill—a model for the treatment of the topic that would be replicated in many of the novels that followed in the 1970s. The characters are male, white, and upper middle-class. The physical nature of what happens between them remains obscure. A cause and effect relationship is implied between homosexuality and being the child of divorced parents—more specifically, having an absent father and a disturbed and/or controlling mother. Homosexuality is presented both as a rite of passage experience with no long-term meaning or consequences (Davy's father tells him "a lot of boys play around in a lot of ways when they're growing up" [166].) and also as a matter of conscious choice.

Surely Donovan is not to be taxed too severely for this last, however, since he was simply reflecting the prevailing beliefs of the day. Note that Ilg in her dust jacket comment says as much, too: "Davy is able to face the experience and to make his choice."

In a 1976 document, "What To Do Until Utopia Arrives," drawn up by the American Library Association's Gay Task Force "to help librarians evaluate the treatment of gay themes in children's and YA literature," the following startling statement appears: "Librarians should be aware of the need for portrayals of growth and development of gay identity as *a valid life choice*" (emphasis added).[32] Choosing to act upon one's attractions to those of either sex is indeed a choice, but sexual orientation or identity—the emotions and attractions that inform that choice—is something more fundamental. Most distressing, however, is the close—even causal—connection Donovan's book makes between homosexuality and death. This equation haunted the early history of gay and lesbian literature, as we will see in the next chapter.

NOTES

1. Eliot, T.S. *Notes Towards the Definition of Culture*. In *Crosscurrents of Criticism: Horn Book Essays 1968–1979*, edited by Paul Heins. Boston: Horn Book, 1977.

2. Baldwin, James. "Talk to Teachers." *Saturday Review*. 21 (December 1963): 42–44, 60.

3. Larrick, Nancy. "The All-White World of Children's Books." *Saturday Review*, September 1965, pp. 63–85.

4. Douglas, Lord Alfred Bruce. *Two Loves*. 1894.

5. Robb, Graham. *Strangers: Homosexual Love in the Nineteenth Century*. New York: W.W. Norton, 2004.

6. Chauncey, George. *Gay New York*. New York: Basic Books, 1994.

7. Berube, Allan. *Coming Out Under Fire: The History of Gay Men and Women in World War Two*. New York: Free Press, 1990. p. 6.

8. Kaiser, Charles. "Life Before Stonewall." *Newsweek*, July 4, 1994.

9. Kinsey, Alfred C. et al. *Sexual Behavior in the Human Male*. Philadelphia: W.B. Saunders Co., 1948.

10. Kaiser, Charles. *The Gay Metropolis, 1940–1996*. Boston: Houghton Mifflin, 1997. pp. 52–56.

11. Duberman, Martin. *Stonewall*. New York: Dutton, 1993.

12. Cady, Joseph. "American Literature: Gay Male, 1900–1969." In *The Gay and Lesbian Literary Heritage*, edited by Claude J. Summers. New York: Henry Holt, 1995.

13. Haggerty, George E., ed. *Gay Histories and Cultures: An Encyclopedia*. New York: Garland, 2000.

14. Souhami, Diana. *The Trials of Radclyffe Hall*. New York: Doubleday, 1999. Quoted in http://www.galha.org/glh/181/souhami.html (accessed 3/34/05).

15. Keller, Yvonne. "'Was It Right to Love Her Brother's Wife So Passionately?': Lesbian Pulp Novels and U.S. Lesbian Identity, 1950–1965." *American Quarterly* 57 (June 2005): 385–410.

16. Faderman, Lillian, ed. *Chloe Plus Olivia: An Anthology of Lesbian Literature from the Seventeenth Century to the Present*. New York: Viking Penguin, 1994, vii., cited by Keller on p. 386.

17. L'Engle, Madeline. *The Small Rain*. New York: Vanguard. 1945.

18. Daly, Maureen. *Seventeenth Summer*. New York: Dodd, Mead, 1942.

19. Salinger, J.D. *The Catcher in the Rye*. Boston: Little, Brown, 1951.

20. Kraus, W. Keith. "Cinderella in Trouble. Still Dreaming and Losing It." *School Library Journal*. 21:18 (January 1975).

21. Ford, Michael Thomas. "Gay Books for Young Readers." *Publishers Weekly*. February 21, 1994.

22. Marcus, Leonard, ed. *Dear Genius: The Letters of Ursula Nordstrom*. New York: HarperCollins, 1998. 261; 257–258.

23. Heins, Paul. *Horn Book*. XLV:4 (August 1969).

24. Sutherland, Zena. *Saturday Review*. 52:59 (May 10, 1969).

25. Russ, Lavinia. *Publishers Weekly*. March 17, 1969.

26. Hungerford, Alice. *Book World. The Washington Post*. May 4, 1969.

27. *Booklist*. 65:1174 (June 15, 1969).

28. *School Library Journal*. May 15, 1969.

29. Weston, John. *New York Times Book Review*. May 4, 1969.

30. Bacon, Martha. "Tantrums and Unicorns." *Atlantic Monthly*. 224:6 (December 1969).

31. Rees, David. *Children's Literature in Education*. No. 25 (Summer) 1997.

32. American Library Association. Gay Task Force. "What To Do Until Utopia Arrives." In *Young Adult Literature in the Seventies: A Selection of Readings*. Edited by Jana Varlejs. Metuchen, NJ: Scarecrow Press, 1978.

The 1970s: What Donovan Wrought

$\mathcal{T}$he pioneering late 1960s work of S.E. Hinton, Robert Lipsyte, and Paul Zindel became the order of the day in the decade that followed, a period when so many of the grandmasters of the genre (Robert Cormier, M.E. Kerr, Walter Dean Myers, Richard Peck, Judy Blume, and others) launched their innovative writing careers. Indeed, many critics view the seventies as the first golden age of young adult literature, a time of creative prowess and prodigious production.

Unfortunately, the same cannot be said of GLBTQ literature for young adults, since the publication of Donovan's book did not exactly open the floodgates to a torrent of gay-themed novels. In fact, it would be three years before the next YA title to include gay content, Isabel Holland's *The Man Without a Face,* appeared in 1972. Only seven other novels with similar themes would follow during the entire decade of the seventies (an eighth title, David Rees' *In the Tent* was published in England in 1979 but would not appear in an American edition until 1985). And too many of these were marred by stereotypical characters and predictable plots centered on the inherent misery of gay people's lives.

In fact, these flaws were also characteristic of a kind of fiction that began appearing in the larger world of YA literature in the seventies. Quickly dubbed the "problem novel," this type of fiction was driven by its relentless focus on social issues that affect some contemporary teens; e.g., alcohol or drug abuse, teen pregnancy, parental divorce, etc. Highly didactic, these novels were notable for one-dimensional characterization, plot contrivance, and near total lack of art. Perhaps the most enduring example is *Go Ask Alice* (1971), the best-selling fictional memoir of a fifteen-year-old girl with low self-esteem who unknowingly imbibes an

LSD-spiked soft drink at a party and quickly spirals down to a life of drugs and depravity (including pot, speed, heroin, drug-dealing, and prostitution), and ultimately dies of a drug overdose. That homosexuality was viewed by many at that time as a social problem only exacerbated the tendency to regard literature with gay content as belonging in the "problem novel" category, which robbed homosexuals of individuality and perpetuated stereotypes.

In an insightful 1983 article titled "Out of the Closet But Paying the Price"[1] Jan Goodman listed ten such stereotypes:

1. It is still physically dangerous to be gay.
2. Your future is bleak if you are gay.
3. Gay people lead lonely lives, even if they're happy with each other.
4. Gay adults should not be around children because they'll influence them to be homosexual.
5. Something traumatic in a gay person's past makes him/her homosexual.
6. Gay men want to be women and lesbians want to be men.
7. SEX: Don't worry. If you do "it" once, you may not be gay. It may only be a phase.
8. Gay relationships are mysterious.
9. All gays are middle/upper middle-class and white.
10. As far as young children know, there's no such thing as a gay person. (13–15)

THE MAN WITHOUT A FACE

A number of these stereotypes marred Isabel Holland's *The Man Without a Face* (1972). Like Donovan's *I'll Get There,* Holland's book is told in the first-person voice of a male protagonist, fourteen-year-old Charles (Chuck) Norstadt. Like David Ross, Chuck lives in a home headed by his much-divorced mother. "Mother's hobby is marrying," he says acidly (11). His family also includes two stepsisters: "repulsive" Gloria, who is sixteen, and "okay" Meg, eleven. Chuck's father is long dead, and the boy has only shadowy memories of him. His only friend in the New England village where the well-to-do family is summering is his pet cat, Moxie.

As the only male in the house (aside from Moxie), Chuck feels he is "drowning in women" (15) and longs for the day Gloria will go away to boarding school. He is so counting on this that—an indifferent student himself—he has "more or less deliberately flunked" the entrance exam to what had been his own intended boarding school destination, St. Matthew's. "And that's that," his mother says when she gets the news, "not even trying to sound unhappy" (16). Chuck's explanation for her matter-of-fact attitude reads like foreshadowing: one of her ex-husbands has told her that boarding schools turn out a high percentage of homosexuals, "and mother has a thing about homos" (16).

Chuck realizes he is in serious trouble when Gloria blithely announces she has changed her mind about boarding school and plans to remain in her New York day school to be closer to her new boyfriend. "I nearly blew my lid," he fumes (8). Hastily, he writes to the headmaster of St. Matthews' and is told in reply that he may sit for the exam again at the end of the summer. At first relieved, Chuck is soon desolate, as he recognizes that he doesn't know where to begin a summer of remedial work.

"Good" sister Meg suggests an unlikely solution: that he find a tutor in the person of Justin McLeod, a local recluse known as "The Man Without a Face." The sobriquet derives from the fact that half of the man's face is a mass of scars. Because of his resolute aloofness, McLeod is also called "The Grouch." Though rumors are rife about him, at least one—that he was once a teacher—is promising. Chuck gathers every ounce of courage he can muster and approaches McLeod, who first rebuffs him ("No. Certainly not" [28].) but then relents, on one condition: "You'll have to do it my way, and that means the hard way" (35).

"I had found myself another Hitler," Chuck thinks ruefully, and some readers may agree. Though McLeod is intended to be a Romantic, even a Gothic figure (think Heathcliff with scars), he is also a bit of a martinet. Despite this—or perhaps because of it (there is a suggestion that Chuck welcomes the rigid structure the man enforces on his life)—the boy soon warms to his new teacher (who is, improbably, a former St. Matthews faculty member). Chuck thinks, "I'd never had a friend and he was my friend . . . and I trusted him" (128).

Chuck begins to wish the man were his father. But factored into this increasingly complex emotional equation is Chuck's growing awareness of his physical attraction to McLeod. When the man finally reveals the source of his scars—driving drunk, he had lost control of his car, which crashed, burning him and killing the boy who was riding with him—Chuck reaches out in sympathy to grasp his arm and is harshly rebuffed. The boy is incensed that he has been made to feel as if he were making a "pass."

Several weeks later the two go swimming and, afterwards, they sun together on a rock. Chuck once again finds himself attracted to the man. "I reached over and touched his side. The hot skin was tight over his ribs. I knew then that I'd never been close to anyone in my life, not like that. And I wanted to get closer" (120).

Nothing more happens but later that day, Chuck blurts out the question that has been bothering him, "Do you think I'm queer?" This would be a common question in early GLBTQ literature; Davy asks it in *I'll Get There*; Pete will ask it in *What's This About Pete?*, as will Tom in *Sticks and Stones*. While the catalyst for this question is often concern over a same-sex attraction, it can also be a manifestation of the pollution myth, i.e., if you have any sort of positive connection with a homosexual, you must be homosexual yourself. Regardless of the question's root, the inevitable answer in these early books is "No," which is what McLeod tells Chuck, adding rather glibly that everybody wants and needs affection. "Also, you're a boy who badly needs a father" (121).

All of this is prelude to what happens the night Chuck arrives home to discover Gloria and her boyfriend Percy having sex in his bed. Worse, he discovers that Percy has killed Moxie for soiling Gloria's bed (shades of Davy and Fred). Later that night, Chuck discovers a bundle of news clippings Gloria has heartlessly left for him. They reveal the truth about his late father who, it turns out, had died on skid row of chronic alcoholism.

Bereft, Chuck flees to Justin's house and finds him asleep in bed. McLeod wakes and in comforting the weeping Chuck, takes him into bed and holds him. And then it happens (yes, "it" again). "I didn't know what was happening to me until it happened," Chuck reports. The next morning McLeod has a one-sided conversation with Chuck who doesn't want to talk about "it." The man assures the boy that nothing of lasting significance has happened. "There's nothing about it to worry you. You reacted to a lot of strain—and shock—in a normal fashion" (148).

Chuck, however, refuses to be comforted and challenges McLeod about his own sexuality and, though the word "homosexual" is never used, the man acknowledges, "I've known what I was for a long time." The conversation ends awkwardly as Chuck's new stepfather (yes, his mother has married again) arrives to take him home.

Chuck retakes and passes the entrance exam and goes off to St. Matthew's, where he scarcely thinks of McLeod for two months until he has a dream in which his new stepfather—who, coincidentally enough, is also an old friend of McLeod's—explains that the real "man without a face" is not McLeod but, rather, Chuck's late father. For some reason this convinces Chuck he must see McLeod again but, alas, it is too late, for he has died of a heart attack, handily removing any possibility that the two will ever have to discuss their feelings. And, p.s., McLeod has left his entire estate to the boy. In death the man without a face becomes a martyred saint, with the apparent implication that the only good homosexual is a dead homosexual.

What is the reader to make of all this? Holland herself said she intended the novel to be a love story, "an unusual love story but, nevertheless, a love story,"[2] and most reviewers, who were lavish with their praise of this flawed novel, agreed. *Horn Book*, for example, said, "The author has delved into the joy and sorrow concomitant with love and growth."[3] But what does the book actually say about love? When events conspire to drive Chuck into McLeod's arms, the boy is horrified by what happens (as we read it, Chuck has a spontaneous ejaculation) and rejects the man—and his feelings for him. For his part, McLeod himself is made by the author to downplay the event ("there's nothing about it to worry you"), reinforcing the implicit message that Elizabeth Minot Graves states in her *Commonweal* review: "One act of overt homosexuality need not imply real homosexuality."[4] And, lest Chuck rethink his feelings, McLeod is now dead.

The symbolic treatment of McLeod's homosexuality—his horribly scarred face—is also unfortunate. Although certainly teens get information about homosexuality from a variety of sources, within the world of this book, the consequences of being gay include:

1. being hideously injured in a car wreck
2. becoming an embittered, tormented recluse
3. being rejected by a boy whom you have sought only to mentor, comfort, and reassure
4. exiling oneself to a life among strangers

   5. dying prematurely of a heart attack no doubt brought on by 1,
      2, 3, and 4

Talk about being "scared straight!"

To her credit, these negative consequences were not Holland's intended message. Indeed, in a *Horn Book* essay, she imagines herself writing to readers of the twenty-first century as follows, "You have to realize they had something in those days they called a taboo against any expression of love between members of the same sex. Yes, I know it's hard to believe, but without that there wouldn't even be a story to tell . . ."[2]

And yet, in reflecting the prevailing social attitudes of her time, the author nevertheless equates homosexuality with disfigurement, despair, and death, and her novel, along with Donovan's, reinforced some of the stereotypical thinking about homosexuality that became a fixture of GLBTQ literature.

To say, simply, that it was "physically dangerous to be gay" was not only a stereotype but also a bit of an understatement for these early novels, considering how many of the homosexual characters die. To be perfectly fair, death has always figured large in young adult literature of every sort. But, that said, death would again be the fate of another gay character in the third YA novel to deal with homosexuality, Sandra Scoppettone's *Trying Hard To Hear You*, which appeared in 1974. In this novel, however, it is not the protagonist who is wrestling with sexual identity but, rather, the protagonist's best friend. Scoppettone's novel is a first-person narrative told by sixteen-year-old Camilla (Cam) Crawford as she recalls the events of the summer of 1973, which led to her discovery that her best friend and neighbor, Jeff, is gay.

The two teens and the rest of their high school theater crowd are involved in staging a summer stock production of "Anything Goes" (an ironic choice, in retrospect). When Jeff is discovered kissing another boy, Phil, the two are subjected to a great deal of verbal abuse ("They're goddamn queers" [182]) and worse—they're almost tarred and feathered. Ultimately, Phil cracks under the pressure and, screaming at his tormentors that "being a fag was a choice—you know, he could be straight if he wanted to" (238). So he invites a girl on a date, they drink some alcohol, and in what was to become a cliché, the first of many in this genre, they both die in a car crash.

Writing some years later, Scoppettone defended this plot choice: "The ending of THTHY, in which one of the homosexual boys dies, was misconstrued by many people. Perhaps this was my fault; I should have made the reason for this clearer. My intention was to show that he died trying to be something he wasn't (heterosexual) and *not* because he was a homosexual."[5] Well, yes, but doesn't this invite the reader to conclude that the gay person is doomed both ways—either through being homosexual or through trying to deny his sexuality? This "damned if you do, damned if you don't" quandary was all too typical in the early days of this literature.

In her defense, however, Scoppettone does at least make a clear equation between homosexuality and love. Jeff says to Cam, "As long as people love instead of hate, what difference does it make who they love?" (208). And, later, Cam herself says to another character: "If two people love each other, they should be together, no matter what. Jeff and Phil love each other" (230). This statement evidences Cam's emotional growth, because she had originally been heartbroken to learn that Phil was gay, since she had a serious crush on him, becoming the first of what would be many straight girls who learn, to their sorrow, that boys they desire are gay. As another girl, Brie in Rinaldi's *The Good Side of My Heart,* wistfully observes, "All that handsomeness, all that masculinity, wasted. I wanted to cry" (272). Happily, though Phil dies, Jeff survives and heads off to college. At the book's end, Cam reports that Jeff is dating another boy "and he's planning to bring him home for Thanksgiving" (264).

Though well received by reviewers (*Booklist* called it "a teenage story of unusual depth for mature readers"[6]), Scoppettone's novel is, in some ways, even more clearly a snapshot in time of prevailing social attitudes toward homosexuality during the 1970s than either the Donovan or Holland books. It includes, for example, a rebuttal to the egregiously fallacious material about homosexuality contained in the then-popular book *Everything You Always Wanted to Know about Sex But Were Afraid To Ask* by Dr. David Reuben. A sample from his book: "Since ancient times they [homosexuals] found employment as professional torturers and executioners. More recently they filled the ranks of Hitler's Gestapo and SS."[7] As it happens, Cam's mother is a psychiatrist, and when the girl *finally* (on page 252 of a 264-page book) asks her mother about homosexuality, she replies: "Homosexuality—and that includes lesbianism—has been part of life as long as there have been people and it always will be. I don't think anybody quite understands why some people are and some people aren't. There are several schools of thought: some think it's environment, others think it's biological, still others think it's choice. The uninformed and the ignorant think it's evil or even a disease . . . Homosexuality and alcoholism are the two things that the medical and psychiatric professions know very little about. But I do know this . . . as long as you don't hurt anyone else, you have a right to be what you want to be."

In fact, it wasn't until two years *after* THTHY's publication that the American Psychiatric Association finally removed the classification of homosexuality as a mental illness, declaring "Although we can choose whether or not to act on our feelings, psychologists do not consider sexual orientation to be a conscious choice that can be voluntarily changed."[8]

In the final analysis, THTHY represented a cautious step forward in terms of its attitudes toward and treatment of homosexuality, though it also comes uncomfortably close to being a "problem novel" that suffers from the didacticism and melodrama typical of that genre.

Mary Sullivan's *What's This About Pete?*, published in 1976, suffers from some of the same flaws. Although protagonist Pete Hanson is fifteen years old, he appears to be far more child than teen due to his extraordinary naivete and the author's relentlessly prim, old-fashioned style, diction, and presentation of teen life (boys avidly read a magazine called "Ribald Capers," for example).

A sensitive "little guy," Pete likes "good-looking things" and enjoys doing "girl's work." No wonder his macho, motorcycle-riding father calls him a "pantywaist" and, when he discovers the boy has been helping his seamstress mother by sewing, angrily claims, "You been turning him into a queer behind my back." Pete is worried his father might be right about him. After all, hadn't he felt "a pleasant hum of recognition—a special awareness" the first time he saw the new guy, Mario? (7). "It was crazy, but there was no other way to say it. I love Mario, he thought," (34) and later, in a panic, he wonders, "Am I turning into a—a homosexual . . .?" (98).

His concern is exacerbated when "a pleasant young man" in a passing car offers him fifty dollars "if you'll come home with me" (104). Pete is so upset that he finally turns to the school's guidance counselor, kindly old Doc Logan, who tells him, "Just forget your worries about homosexuality—incidentally, many boys go through stages when they think they may be gay, only to outgrow it—just forget your worries and be yourself. Love girls, love boys—but love. It's an old cliche, Peter, but love is what makes the world go round" (115). Pete, his heart "positively light," is freed by this wisdom, freed not to love Mario, who is revealed to be "a lying swine," (120) but to love classmate Barbara, instead. And so, the book triumphantly concludes, "Tomorrow this gutsy little guy had a date with Barbara" (125).

The same year that *Pete* was published, a more successful novel—in literary terms, at least—also appeared. It was Rosa Guy's *Ruby,* which is historically important as the first YA novel to feature a lesbian relationship. A sequel to Guy's more celebrated *The Friends,* which has appeared on all five "best of the best" book lists prepared periodically by ALA's Young Adult Library Services Association (YALSA), this novel turns the focus from Phyllisia—the protagonist of the first of what would be three novels about the Cathys, a West Indian immigrant family—to her older sister, Ruby. Herself born in the West Indies (in Trinidad), novelist and dramatist Guy was founding president of the Harlem Writers Guild and was a pioneer in writing about the real-life circumstances of immigrants of color, as they carve out new lives in an often inhospitable, urban American environment.

Indeed, in *The Friends* both Cathy girls are routinely bullied and rejected because of their "foreignness." It is the younger, Phyllisia, who finds comfort and support in the friendship she forges with Edith Jackson, a classmate who would become the titular main character of the third novel. In the second novel, though, it is the desperately lonely Ruby who looks for heartsease in a friendship with another girl, the beautiful Daphne, and finds, instead, a love affair. "At last she had found herself, a likeness to herself, a response to her needs, her age, an answer to her loneliness" (46–47).

The answer proves to be a fleeting one. Although their relationship finds expression in physical intimacy, the strong-willed Daphne finally ends the relationship as part of her trajectory toward college and a middle-class future. And despite a seemingly full-hearted commitment to the relationship ("people don't leave people they love" [138]), Ruby—after an initial period of emotional turbulence—seems to recover with astonishing ease and the book ends with Ruby poised to resume a relationship with her former boyfriend Orlando. Since Ruby is portrayed as being heterosexual in both the books that precede and follow this novel about her, the reader is left to conclude, once again, that homosexuality is—as earlier novels of the '70s suggest—simply a rite of passage on the way to mature (read "heterosexual") adulthood. As reviewer Mary Hoffman put it, "Her lesbian experience is an interlude for her, not a major realization about her own sexual orientation."[9]

It is especially difficult to accept Ruby's affectional about-face since—unlike the young characters in the Donovan, Holland, and Sullivan books—she is eighteen years old, although it could be argued that her limited life experience due to her domineering father Calvin has left her emotionally younger than her chronological age. For the passive Ruby, her relationship with Daphne is something that happens to her—she is acted upon, but rarely acts on her own behalf, and there is scant evidence of any emotional growth on her part by book's end.

The Interracial Books for Children Bulletin criticized this aspect of the novel and also took it to task for reinforcing "sexist stereotypes about heterosexual males, heterosexual females and lesbians by implying that lesbians are 'masculine' types like Daphne, while 'feminine' types like Ruby are destined to 'go straight.'"[10]

The very next year, however, just as it looked as if there would be nothing but *Sturm und Drang* in YA literature with GLBTQ content, M. E. Kerr poked fun at prevailing gay stereotypes in her delightful novel *I'll Love You When You're More Like Me* (1977). This is also the first novel with this content that could be viewed as one of gay assimilation, as a secondary character, Charlie Gilhooley, is an openly gay teen who is the best friend and confidant of protagonist Wally Witherspoon. It is Charlie who wryly complains that since the movies and television have been showing great big tough gays, to get away from the stereotype effeminates, he's been worse off than ever before. "Now I'm supposed to live up to some kind of big butch standard, where I can Indian-wrestle anyone in the bar to the floor, or produce sons, or lift five-hundred pound weights over my head without my legs breaking" (41).

Charlie knows about stereotypes; he's been "out" since he was sixteen, when, Wally reports, "he started telling a select group of friends and family that he believed he preferred boys to girls. The news shouldn't have come as a surprise to anyone who knew Charlie even slightly. But honesty has its own rewards: ostracism and disgrace" (38). Apparently, these "rewards" begin at home, since Charlie's parents do not receive the news of their son's sexual preference with any degree of equanimity. His mother rushes to the local priest to try to arrange an exorcism for her boy while the father, "a round-the-clock, large-bellied beer drinker," breaks his son's nose.

But Charlie's homosexuality is not the theme of the novel or even an issue, since Wally remains a loyal and steadfast friend . . . though on one condition: "My own deal with Charlie was don't you unload your emotional problems on me, and I won't unload mine on you. We shook hands on the pact and never paid any attention to it. I went through a lot of Charlie's crushes with him. Charlie, in turn, had to hear and hear and hear about Lauralei Rabinowitz" (with whom Wally is hopelessly in love) (38).

Despite this—or perhaps because of it—Charlie remains well-adjusted, cheerful, and self-deprecatingly humorous, and a lively three-dimensional gay character at a time when young adult literature was portraying homosexual characters as guilt-ridden loners who are destroyed by self or society. The closest Charlie comes to death is his (ironic?) decision to work in Wally's father's funeral home business.

In her first YA novel to deal with homosexuality, Kerr—a winner of the 1993 Margaret A. Edwards Award for lifetime achievement in YA literature—quickly established herself as an innovator: the first to offer homosexuality in a humorous context; the first to offer a happy, well-adjusted gay character, and the first to integrate homosexuality into the larger context of a novel that explored other issues of establishing personal identity and being true to oneself. It's small wonder that Kerr has become one of the two or three most important YA writers to include significant gay/lesbian content in her fiction and no surprise at all that she also received the Bill Whitehead Award for Lifetime Achievement from the Publishing Triangle (a gay publishing organization) and the Robert Chesley Foundation in 1998.

The same year that *I'll Love You . . .* was published, a second, more traditional gay YA novel also appeared: *Sticks and Stones* by Lynn Hall. As its title suggests, this one is about the power of words—pejorative words, that is—and the negative consequences of being "out." When sixteen-year-old Tom Naylor and his divorced mother move from Chicago to tiny Buck Creek, Iowa, to open an antiques store, the boy is lonely, finding no one near his age who shares his interests (he's a gifted pianist with a quick mind). In fact the only persistent overtures of friendship he receives come from his obnoxious neighbor Floyd Schleffe. When Tom rejects those, Floyd retaliates by starting a rumor that Tom is gay. The situation is not helped when Tom finally finds a kindred spirit in Ward Alexander, a young Buck Creek native who has recently returned home after having been discharged from the Air Force. And there are rumors about Ward, too—that he wasn't discharged for "medical reasons" but for being gay.

Improbably, Tom remains entirely ignorant of these rumors as he begins to wonder why "something" is "wrong between him and the others at school" and why he feels ignored, even invisible, "as though he were in parentheses" (107). The situation comes to a head when the school principal summons Tom to his office to tell him that he will not be allowed to attend the state music finals because of parental complaints: "They don't want their sons making a two-day out-of-town trip with a young man who is a homosexual" (138).

Tom is stunned and understandably devastated. In the weeks that follow he comes down with a lingering illness (similar to the way Victorian melodrama characters might respond to adversity by going into a physical decline). When he does return to school, he is shunned by his classmates, and his life quickly becomes a living hell of isolation. But wait! There is worse to come: he tells his friend Ward what has happened, the older boy responds by confessing that he has lied about the reason for his military discharge. In fact, "I was discharged because of a 'homosexual involvement' with another guy in my barracks" (183). Once again stunned and devastated, Tom feels he's lost his last friend. "There were no more sanctuaries" (185).

But wait! There's worse still to come: Tom's isolation and accompanying paranoia so preoccupy him that he fails his semester exams. The principal calls Tom into his office again: this time to tell him that he will not have enough credits to graduate with his class. Moments after Tom receives this news, Floyd, who has missed the school bus, asks Tom for a ride home. A stunned and devastated Tom complies reluctantly, but in his eagerness to get rid of Floyd, he drives too fast, loses control of the car, and there is an accident. Floyd is killed and Tom wakes up in the hospital with an epiphany: "There's probably nothing wrong with my masculinity, only with my stupid head, for not being surer of myself" (187).

At just that moment, a visitor arrives: it is Ward, whom Tom has been studiously avoiding. But no longer. Now that he is sure of his "masculinity," he can reach for his friend's hand and utter the last line of the book: "Ward, I'm glad you came" (187).

Sadly, though Hall's intentions are obviously of the best, her book is typical of the issue-driven problem novels of the late 1970s and more specifically, YA fiction with GLBTQ content. Tom is too clueless, Ward is too decent, and Floyd is too villainous in his rumor-mongering and too pathetic in believing that he can win Tom's friendship by showing him his "dirty pictures, let him know I've never showed them to anyone else in my life. Then he'll know he's my best friend" (25).

Also, it is scarcely conceivable that Tom could remain ignorant of what is happening for so long, but so sadly predictable that he will reject Ward when his friend finally comes out to him. The inevitable car crash that gets Floyd permanently out of the picture, plus Tom's sudden mental health epiphany in the hospital, provide a deus-ex-machina ending that creaks with artifice.

And yet . . . it could have been much worse. Lynn Hall wrote to librarians Frances Hanckel and John Cunningham with the details of the book's creation: "One editor wanted me to kill Tom in a car accident." Happily she resisted that but was not able to fully realize her creative intentions. "I wanted Ward and Tom to love each other, to live happily ever after, and that was the way I ended it," she explained. "But the publishers would not let me do it. In their words this was showing a homosexual relationship as a possible happy ending and this might be dangerous to young people teetering on the brink. At least I held out for a friendship at the end, one which might or might not develop into something more, depending on the reader's imagination."[11]

Though the book was, for the most part, sympathetically reviewed, one critic, Lillian Gerhardt, was more frank and insightful when she wrote, "Although peer group gossip about degrees of masculinity or femininity will undoubtedly continue to make high school life hell for some people, these stock characters neither reflect nor illuminate the situation and the low-action plot fails as entertainment."[12]

Small-town attitudes and prejudices were also the subject of Sandra Scoppettone's second novel to deal with homosexual issues. *Happy Endings Are All Alike,* published in 1978, is set in the village of Gardner's Point, a hundred miles from New York City. In the very first sentence of the novel Scoppettone establishes the theme, "Even though Jaret Tyler had no guilt or shame about her love affair with Peggy Danziger, she knew there were plenty of people in this world who would put it down" (1). And so, as the omniscient narrator puts it, "The two girls didn't go around wearing banners but there were some people who knew." One of these is Jaret's mother, Kay, who—despite some early reservations about the truth—quickly assures her daughter, "If you're happy, that's all that counts" (9). Others—including Peggy's sister Claire, who refers to the girls' relationship as "deviant"—are . . . less sympathetic, to put it mildly. Since Claire is said to "represent society" (26), it is small wonder that the two girls "could imagine what would happen if it [their affair] were ever made public." "And they were right," the narrator concludes with ominous foreshadowing (11).

Their romantic relationship threatens to become a matter of public knowledge when Jaret is raped by a deranged teen stalker who has "accidentally" observed the two girls making love in their "secret place" in the woods. When Jaret decides to press charges, the local police chief urges her parents to drop the case, because "I guarantee you that this sort of deviant stuff doesn't go over too big in a nice little town like Gardner's Point" (168). Moreover, he tells them, Jaret's former boyfriend has told him that they had been intimate and thus she is not a virgin. What does all this mean? "Let me put it to you this way," the chief explains, "See, we have a hearing and the judge learns your girl's not a virgin and on top of that she's a les. Well, he's not gonna think much of her morals. I'm just trying to give you some friendly advice" (169).

Things go from bad to worse. When Jaret resolutely continues to press charges, Peggy, who doesn't want her private life to become public knowledge, ends their relationship. Fortunately, Peggy ultimately decides, "I don't want to spend the rest of my life being what other people want me to be" (201) and the two reconcile as the book closes. "They held each other tightly, knowing the future held many surprises, that nothing was guaranteed. And what if happy endings didn't exist? Happy moments did" (202).

Despite its tentatively hopeful ending, Scoppettone's second novel is deeply flawed. The linking of the girls' lesbianism with the rape is confusing; the rapist's inner thoughts are part of the narrative, but his motivation remains inexplicable; the book included much didactic exposition about the true meaning of rape and the victimization of women; and the principal antagonists—the police chief and Peggy's sister Claire–become almost allegorical in their relentless representations of misogyny and homophobia, respectively.

The sanctification of homosexuals and the corollary demonizing of homophobes has been a recurring problem throughout the entire history of GLBTQ literature, one that often, as in the case of *Happy Endings,* can undermine the believability of the entire story. Similarly, the cause and effect relationship between homosexuality and physical violence—even death—will continue. As late as 1997, for example, Jack Gantos' *Desire Lines* eerily echoes *Happy Endings* with its story of two teenage lesbians who—discovered by a boy in the act of making love—instantly enter into a murder-suicide pact as if this was an entirely normal and natural response to being outed.

Happily, though, this is not a problem in the second novel to appear in 1978, *Hey, Dollface* by Deborah Hautzig, in which the reader returns to the urban world of New York City and the corridors of a private school, where two new girls—Chloe and Val, the first-person narrator— meet and quickly become friends. The story that ensues is an exploration of their deepening relationship, with all its ambiguities, including those involving their mutual attraction. Both girls ultimately acknowledge having had sexual fantasies about each other, but they never act on them and, after a period of uneasiness, agree that, though they love each other, they are not lesbians. Neither the girls nor the reader, however, is quite sure precisely what their feelings might mean about their personal identities. As Val muses at book's end, "I've had time to think about the Chloe I knew then and all that she meant to me, but it's never been something I could define." And, "What we had was part of the truth, but only a part; the rest was a feeling too complicated and too strong to explain" (150). Chloe's take is more straightforward: "We don't have to fit into any slots, so let's stop trying" (150).

Because of this ambiguity, this suggestion that sexual identity may be mutable and not easily categorized, this notion that the heart does have its reasons that the mind may sometimes not know, *Dollface* may be the most sophisticated treatment of homosexuality we have yet encountered. Certainly it is one of the best written. The emotional tone is just right—often funny, sometimes sarcastic, and never cloying. As for the teenage characters, they are likable, multidimensional and—best of all— believable, perhaps because the author herself was only twenty-two when this book was published.

QUEER CONSCIOUSNESS / COMMUNITY

Of the nine YA novels with GLBTQ content published in the 1970s, only one—David Rees' *In the Tent*—contains any mention of a gay/lesbian community. Though it's not actively denied in the other novels, community simply does not exist. As a book that first appeared in England in 1979 but was not published in the U.S. until 1985, *In the Tent* straddles the two decades and foreshadows advances that would enhance the quality of America YA fiction in the years that followed. Until then, however, the "good" gay person in American YA had to isolate himself from others: both Justin in *The Man Without a Face* and Ward in *Sticks and Stones*, for example, are writers who lead deliberately sequestered lives in isolated houses full of books and solitude. There appears to be little if any social reward for coming out—"to thine own self be true" is all very well, but if the price is social isolation, is it worth it? The rewards—if any—are intellectual and moral rather than emotional. The lack of community is also underlined in both of Scoppettone's novels. In *Trying Hard To Hear You*, for example, Phil and Jeff are introduced as part of a close-knit community of peers—in this case a summer theater crowd of long-time friends—but when they fall in love, they face instant ostracism, and their former community becomes an actively hostile environment. The two of them cling to each other, but the newfound warmth of each other's company cannot withstand the cold isolation they face. Although they continue to have each other, they have *only* each other, and the resulting isolation leads, albeit indirectly, to Phil's death in the drunk-driving accident. Thus, the point is made that the closet is the price that the gay/lesbian character must pay in order to belong—and continue to belong—to his/her community of friends and family of origin.

The same fate befalls Jaret and Peggy in *Happy Endings Are All Alike* as the community the two have grown up in turns hostile when their relationship is discovered by Mid, Jaret's deranged rapist. And the police investigating the rape are confident that *they* know that the townspeople will turn against any lesbian–even a battered rape victim–in their midst, regardless of her former insider status as a popular girl and high school achiever.

Thus, in the context of the other books from the 1970s, Rees' *In the Tent* (1979) is all the more remarkable. Consider: as the story begins, Tim is a lonely teen who copes with his romantic feelings toward his straight friend Aaron through daydreams and self-isolation. Tim's isolation ends when he and another boy, Ray, come out to each other and become physically involved during the course of a camping trip. Ray tells Tim about a gay newspaper he's seen with an ad for a gay pub. Tim asks, "Why do you want to go there?"

'To meet others like us, of course. You can't live in a vacuum . . . We can't be the only two nice decent homosexuals in the world.'

'I suppose not.' He [Tim] had a cheering vision of hundreds of happy, uncomplicated people enjoying themselves together, sharing each other's lives. 'I suppose not'" (106).

Following the camping trip, the two actually do visit the pub. "Last night he and Ray had visited the gay pub. They had gone in with beating hearts and nervous shivers. It turned out to be rather an anticlimax: it was so ordinary. Nothing about the people in there, apart from some fragments of conversation they overheard, indicated that they were different from the rest of the world. . . . No one accosted them, though several people eyed them with a certain curiosity. There's nothing, he thought, to prevent him coming in again" (126). Tim is quietly thrilled with his new knowledge of and access to the gay/lesbian community in his own city, a discovery that—beyond his friendship with Ray—is his reward for coming out.

It is interesting to note that author David Rees, an openly gay man, was also a distinguished children's writer whose 1978 novel *The Exeter Blitz* had received the Carnegie Medal, Great Britain's equivalent to the Newbery Medal. It is also interesting, though not surprising, to note that an openly gay man was the only writer of young adult fiction in the 1970s whose book is such a solid representation of queer community. But still, the friendly English gay pub that Tim and Ray visit is not quite equivalent to a gay bar in the U.S., the former being a place where teens could linger, whereas the latter would be forbidden to minors.

In the Tent was also a significant contribution to the GLBTQ literature of homosexual visibility for YAs. In his struggle to come to terms with his sexuality and to come out, Tim's biggest problem is his Roman Catholicism and the attendant guilt he feels about his sexual orientation. Nevertheless, though Tim is only moderately attracted to Ray, he does find comfort in his embrace and the two become friends. And their relationship helps Tim to find self-acceptance. As he muses, "I'm coming to terms with it, slowly. The next few years will be the aftermath of civil war, mending the parts that bleed. Will I be happy? There's a chance even though growing up's so painful. There will be a time when it all slots into place, there must be. Then I shall be free; I've already chosen to be what I am, which is what I always have been" (127). It's important to note that this kind of choice is different from that which had been a fixture of

American novels. Tim is not choosing to be gay but, rather, to embrace "what I have always been;" i.e., homosexual. It's also noteworthy that Tim's friends—unlike many of the friends in American novels of the time—are quite accepting of his homosexuality. His parents are a different story—next to his religion, his biggest problem is coming out to them.

The biggest problem for the American reader, however, may well be Rees' inclusion of a parallel story, told in flashbacks, of the 1646 siege of Exeter, which is designed to expand, metaphorically, Tim's struggle with his sexuality, which—as noted above—is described as a "civil war." Reinforcing this is the fact that Ray's family comes from Spain, having fled to England to escape the Civil War there. This attempt to integrate two metaphorically similar but narratively different stories is an ambitious literary device that is more confusing than illuminating, particularly to U.S. readers unfamiliar with British history.

YA NOVELS AND THE (HETERO) SEXUAL REVOLUTION

As we have noted, the treatment of sexual activity in these novels of the seventies was, at best, obscure—indeed, an erotic encounter between two people was usually described simply as "it." In *The Man Without a Face*, for example, Chuck enigmatically explains, "I didn't know what was happening to me until it had happened" (147). Of course, one argument made against including sexual explicitness in YA novels was that it is merely voyeuristic. Real life voyeurism is inappropriate, to say the least, but no matter how realistic a work of fiction may be, the reader is in a different relationship with a text than the observer is with the people observed in one's immediate surroundings. Teens who pick up a book are often readers with questions, and as instructors know, when potential learners ask their own questions, they listen to the answers. Given the choice between learning about sex via media (texts, films, video, etc.) or via lived experience, mediated information is certainly physically and emotionally safer. In considering sexually explicit texts from this perspective, actively preventing teens from reading them seems an at best foolish—and at worst dangerous—enterprise. But the concern remains that sexually explicit texts encourage readers to "try this at home" (or, more likely, in the car). Perhaps this is precisely why many teens *want* to read about sex—not because they are looking for titillation but because they are looking for information that they would actually prefer *not* to experience first hand—or at least, not yet.

It was the sexual and political revolutions of the sixties, including the advent of the gay rights movement, that made it possible for publishers to experiment, however cautiously, with producing fiction that included the topic of homosexuality, while at the same time expanding their previously timid treatment of other aspects of human sexuality. Judy Blume's ground-breaking novel, *Forever*, the first to include detailed scenes of explicit sexual activity between two (straight) teens, was published in 1975. At the time many assumed that it portended an avalanche of sexually explicit novels for teen readers. Instead, *Forever* has remained a high-water mark in terms of the inclusion of sexual detail in young adult fiction. With few exceptions, YA books published before, during, and after 1975 have adhered to the conventions of mainstream television serials, which generally place physical intimacy at the end of scenes where a couple's embrace and kiss are followed by a convenient fade-out.

Nevertheless, YA literature of the seventies often focused less on the sexual act per se than on the unintended—but seemingly inevitable—consequences of it: unwanted teenage pregnancies. Once books with sexual content began to appear, young readers seemed to have an insatiable appetite for them. Indeed, as early as 1970 four of the top five books sold to students through the Xerox Educational Publications teenage book clubs were about sex and pregnancy (1). Of course, the sex remained resolutely of the hetero sort but the consequences often involved the same social opprobrium or consequential death that the homosexual sort did, though in this case the cause of death was abortion, which had emerged as a subject of the genre in 1969 with the publication of Paul Zindel's *My Darling, My Hamburger*.

CRITICAL WRITING

As noted earlier, beyond the reviews of individual titles, there was little critical writing about GLBTQ literature published during the 1970s. The single exception we have found is an article by two librarians, Frances Hanckel and John Cunningham, both of whom were active in

ALA's Gay Task Force and who later co-authored the first YA nonfiction book about homosexuality, *A Way of Love, A Way of Life: A Young Person's Guide To What It Means To Be Gay.*[13] Their essay, "Can Young Gays Find Happiness in YA Books?" appeared in the March 1976 issue of *Wilson Library Bulletin* and celebrated the appearance of four "pioneering efforts on a controversial theme;" the four being *I'll Get There, Man Without a Face, THTHY,* and *Sticks and Stones.* In their discussion, Hanckel and Cunningham fault these four titles for two principal reasons, which we have also noted. The books suggest that (1) "Being gay has no lasting significance" (i.e., it's a phase) "and/or (2) costs someone a terrible price" (532). As for the latter point, the authors reasonably ask, "In an open democratic society, why must minorities be expected to withstand extraordinary pressures?" (534). Thirty years later that question has yet to be answered. But as for the former point (the "transitory" nature of homosexuality), many may find the words of the authors' argument outdated. They write, "This may be fine reassurance for insecure straight youths but it cheats the ones who want to be gay by presenting such experiences as "phases" instead of the first step toward a valid choice" (533).

However, given the social opprobrium—and worse—that GLBTQ youth have been subjected to, it seems unlikely that any teen would "want" to be gay. And, again, it also unquestioningly accepts the notion that being homosexual is a matter of conscious choice. These reservations aside, it is hard to dispute Hanckel and Cunningham's conclusions. "Where is there honesty and realism in approaching the gay experience?" they ask. And, "Where is there a life-affirming hope for a young person who knows or suspects he or she is homosexual?" (534). For answers to these questions readers would have to wait until the next decade. And, some would claim, they are still waiting.

GAY AND LESBIAN NOVELS OF THE 1970s

(Note that we are using the following abbreviations: HV stands for "Homosexual Visibility;" GA stands for "Gay Assimilation;" QC stands for "Queer Consciousness/Community;" "Gay" refers to novels with male GLBTQ content; "Lesbian" refers to novels with female GLBTQ content.)

1972

Holland, Isabelle. *The Man Without a Face*. Lippincott. 159 pages.

> HV. Gay. A confused and hostile boy is mentored by the disfigured, gay, Mr. Rochester-like Justin McLeod. First novel to include what became a near-obligatory death of the gay character. Filmed in 1993 minus its gay content.

1974

Scoppettone, Sandra. *Trying Hard To Hear You*. Harper & Row. 264 pages.

> HV. Gay. Cam discovers her best friend, Jeff, is gay—and so does everyone else in their high school theater crowd. First novel to include the death of a gay character in an automobile accident.

1976

Guy, Rosa. *Ruby*. NY: Viking. 186 pages.

> HV. Lesbian. The story of a brief but passionate romance between the shy and self-effacing Rudy and the brash and confident Daphne. The first YA novel with lesbian content, though the homosexuality is presented as a passing phase. Also the first (and one of the few) to feature African American characters.

Sullivan, Mary W. *What's This About Pete?* Nelson. 125 pages.

> HV. Gay. Young Pete, who enjoys doing "girl's work" like sewing and helps out in his mother's bridal gown business, is afraid he might be gay. He isn't.

1977

Hall, Lynn. *Sticks and Stones*. Follett. 220 pages.

> HV. Gay. Tom learns his new best friend Ward is gay, and a false rumor spreads that the two are lovers. After a period of alienation, the obligatory car crash resolves their problem by killing the rumor-monger and bringing Tom to his senses.

Kerr, M.E. *I'll Love You When You're More Like Me*. Harper & Row. 160 pages.

> HV. GA. Gay. The straight protagonist's best friend, Charlie Gilhooley, is gay. The first GLBTQ title to approach its subject with some refreshing humor. "Honesty has its own rewards: ostracism and disgrace."

1978

Hautzig, Deborah. *Hey, Dollface*. Greenwillow. 151 pages.

> HV. Lesbian. Val and Chloe—two new girls at an elite New York City high school—meet and quickly fall in love. Or are they "just good friends?"

Scoppettone, Sandra. *Happy Endings Are All Alike*. Harper & Row. 202 pages.

> HV. Lesbian. Jaret and Peggy are girlfriends but when Jaret is raped by a deranged teen stalker, the prospect of a criminal trial that will out them tests the strength of their relationship.

1979

Rees, David. *In the Tent*. London: Dobson Books. (Boston: Alyson, 1985). 208 pages.

> HV. QC. Gay. Tim is the gay protagonist struggling to come to terms with both his sexuality *and* his Roman Catholic guilt. Originally published in England, this is the most thoughtful treatment of homosexuality produced in its time and the first to include elements of gay community.

NOTES

1. Goodman, Jan. "Out of the Closet But Paying the Price." *Interracial Books for Children Bulletin*. 14:3&4, 1983.

2. Holland, Isabelle. "Tilting at Taboos." In *Crosscurrents of Criticism: Horn Book Essays 1968-1977*. Edited by Paul Heins. Boston: Horn Book, 1977, 143.

3. *Horn Book*. 48:375 (August 1972).

4. Graves, E.M. *Commonweal*. 97:157 (November 17, 1972).

5. Scoppettone, Sandra. "Some Thoughts on Censorship" in Feehan, Patricia E. and Pamela Petrick Barron. *Writers on Writing for Young Adults*. Detroit: Omnigraphics, 1991.

6. *Booklist*. 71:340 (November 15, 1974).

7. Reuben, David, M.D. *Everything You Always Wanted To Know about Sex But Were Afraid To Ask*. Philadelphia: David McKay, 1969.

8. Huegel, Kelly. *GLBTQ: The Survival Guide for Queer and Questioning Teens*. Minneapolis: Free Spirit Publishing, 2003.

9. Hoffman, Mary. "Growing Up: A Survey." *Children's Literature in Education*. 15:3, 1984.

10. Williams, Regina. "Ruby." *Interracial Books for Children Bulletin*. 9:2 (1977).

11. Hanckel, Frances and John Cunningham. "Can Young Gays Find Happiness in YA Books?" *Wilson Library Bulletin* 50 (March 1976): 7.

12. *School Library Journal* 97 (Nov. 15, 1972): 3813.

13. Hanckel, Frances and John Cunningham. *A Way of Love, A Way of Life: A Young Person's Guide to What It Means to be Gay*. New York: Lothrop, Lee and Shepard, 1979.

· 3 ·

The 1980s:
Annie on My Mind and Beyond

The decade of the eighties saw an appreciable acceleration in the pace—if not necessarily the quality—of GLBTQ publishing. The increased numbers were immediately evident, with three titles published in 1980 and thirty-seven more in the next nine years—four times the number in the seventies. Ironically the increasing visibility of GLBTQ characters and issues coincided with a period of otherwise reactionary change in the larger world of young adult literature, as the pendulum swung from the seventies emphasis on realistic—i.e., hard-edged—YA fiction to a renascence of fifties-style romance. However, with the notable exception of *Annie on My Mind* (1982), romance remained largely absent from GLBTQ fiction. Unfortunately, of the forty GLBT titles published in this decade, only seven would offer notable contributions to the field in terms of thematic innovation or literary quality: *Annie on My Mind* by Nancy Garden; *Dance on My Grave* by Aidan Chambers; *Night Kites* by M. E. Kerr; *The Arizona Kid* by Ron Koertge; *Weetzie Bat* by Francesca Lia Block; *Jack* by A. M. Homes, and *In the Tent* by David Rees (its first U.S. edition appeared in 1985).

Also worth noting is the overall homosexual gender segregation in the entire body of literature, which became increasingly evident in the eighties as the number of titles grew. In reality, it is not uncommon for teen gay males and teen lesbians to be friends, but in YA fiction with GLBTQ content, gay males and lesbians lead very separate lives. If a novel features a gay male character, it is a safe bet that there will be no lesbian characters—and vice-versa. Thus, for better or worse, these books can be readily sorted according to their male or female gay/lesbian content (see Appendix C). Of the nine titles published in the seventies, there were three (33%) with lesbian characters and six (67%) with gay male characters. Of the forty titles published in the eighties, ten (25%) included lesbians and thirty (75%) included gay males. With the rise of the Second Wave of feminism and an increased social visibility of women, including lesbians, one might expect the gender bias in this body of literature to have become less pronounced over time. But clearly, this was not the case. Regardless of these changes, however, homosexual visibility (i.e., coming out and related issues) remained the single most important focus of GLBTQ literature in the 1980s.

Though the titles of the eighties varied widely in literary quality, many do remain historically important for having introduced new themes, types, and approaches that would become characteristic of this developing genre. Indeed, our chief focus in this chapter will be on those books that were—for their time—innovative.

GAY/LESBIAN PARENTS

For example, in the very first year of the decade Norma Klein's *Breaking Up* became the first YA novel to feature a gay parent. Throughout her career Klein, the author of nearly two-dozen novels for young adults, was an innovator. Her first book for young readers was the ground-breaking *Mom, the Wolfman and Me* (1972), a story told in the voice of eleven-year-old Brett, a girl who has been raised by her single mother and has never met her biological father. He is, in fact, unaware of her existence. But Brett's "problem" is not her fatherlessness—how can you miss what you've never had?—but rather the possible changes in her hitherto pleasant and predictable life when "the wolfman" (Brett's friendly nickname for her mother's boyfriend, who owns an Irish wolfhound) moves in with them. Thirty years later, this seems a bit tame, but at the time many adults were shocked to encounter—in a book intended for children—a happy, well-adjusted child of a never-married mother.

In the years before Klein's untimely death in 1989, she became an increasingly vocal advocate for making the sometimes uncomfortable truths of teen lives visible on the page, once writing, "What is shameful in life is concealment and distortion and evasion, not truth" (231).

In *Breaking Up*, Alison lives in New York City with her older brother, her mother, and her mother's partner Peggy. When Ali and her

brother spend the summer in California with their newly remarried father, it becomes evident to Dad that Mom and Peggy are more than "just
good friends." Ali muses, "I thought about Mom and Peggy. It did seem
strange in a way but not *that* strange. Maybe it was because Mom is such
a regular sort of person, not that far-out or weird in any way, so it seems
like anything she would do seems okay. I wonder if Mom loves Peggy
more than she used to love Daddy when she loved him" (180–181). In
fact, the father's reaction is far less salutary than Ali's. "Everything about
this is odd," he says (95) and later tells his daughter, "You're old enough
to realize that raising children in a household with two homosexual
women isn't exactly some kind of ideal" (102).

"If Mom is gay," Ali asks, "how come you married her?"

"She wasn't when I married her," he replies (142).

Despite her father's continuing—and often bitter—reservations as
he initially threatens Ali's mother with the prospect of a really nasty custody battle, he finally agrees to permit his daughter to return to New
York to live with those "two homosexual women." Ali reports, "The odd
thing is, nothing seems very different. I thought now that I know about
Mom and Peggy, I would notice things I hadn't before but I don't" (163).

Klein returned to this theme in her 1988 novel *Now That I Know*.
Once again a teenage female protagonist learns that a parent is gay,
though this time it's the father. And thirteen-year-old Nina does not react as well as Ali. "In a sadistic way I wanted to hurt him. I felt like he'd
hurt me" (78). Later, she adds, "I hope he and Greg" [his lover] "die in
their sleep" (83). Ultimately, however, Nina comes around, helped in part
by learning that the brother of her new boyfriend, Damian, is also gay
and by her cathartic confession to her father that she is afraid he will get
AIDS. The father's answer—intended by Klein to be reassuring—is actually a dangerous bit of misinformation. "Neens," he says, "the sad, dull
fact is that I'm a monogamous guy. I was with Jean [his ex-wife] and now
I am with Greg" (162). What isn't mentioned, of course, is Greg's sexual
history and the fact that the father is not only having sex with his partner but also—in effect—with everyone else his partner has ever been intimate with. Aside from this misinformation—and the improbable fact
that in both books the straight parent is astounded to learn that his/her
former spouse is homosexual—Klein's examination of gay parents is
sympathetic, though the situation is treated, as one of several "problems"
or "issues" the protagonist must resolve.

Happily, love is much more clearly an integral part of the same-sex relationships that parents launch in the two other novels from the eighties that explore this subject: George Shannon's *Unlived Affections* and A. M. Homes' *Jack,* both published in 1989. In the former, Willie—an eighteen-year-old boy who has been raised by his recently deceased grandmother—discovers a cache of letters written by his father, whom he has never known, to his mother, who died when the boy was two. Reading them, Willie discovers his father was gay. "I can't love you the way you should be loved by a husband," he writes to his wife, "I love you, you have to believe that, like a friend, my best friend, but not like a lover. I love men" (67). Later, his father writes, "I finally told Evan that I loved him and hoped he had feelings for me . . . Being with him feels so bright and alive, so safe and warm that making love *is* the truest thing to do no matter what anybody else says" (108–109). Realistically speaking, his enthusiastic revelation might seem a bit *too* honest to put into a letter to the woman who is still his wife, but it serves to educate the reader. As for Willie, his initial reaction is to mutter "damn queers," but he immediately repents and is glad "no one had heard him . . . Willie had lived too much of his father's life through the letters to dismiss him like that" (108). The boy ultimately comes to terms with his new knowledge, telling his girl friend, "He loved my mom but he was . . . gay." And there is a suggestion, at book's end, that he will seek out and get to know his father.

The latter novel (i.e., *Jack*) is not only one of the most substantial treatments of having a gay parent in the body of the literature, it is also one of the most engaging novels. Amazingly, it was written when Homes was a young adult herself.[1] Finished in 1985, the book didn't see print for four years, however, because "more than one publisher wondered how to position this novel." The author had no doubts, though, telling *Publishers Weekly,* "It's a novel for everybody." Ultimately Macmillan would publish it as a YA title and Vintage would publish it in paperback as an adult title. (The same thing happened seven years later when Simon & Schuster published Michael Cart's gay coming-of-age novel *My Father's Scar* as a YA novel and St. Martin's subsequently re-issued it in paperback as an adult book.) In fact, like Francesca Lia Block's *Weetzie Bat,* which was published the same year, *Jack* is one of the first crossover novels, those books with intrinsic multi-generational appeal that became a fixture of YA literature in the mid- to late-'90s.

It is also squarely in the tradition of J. D. Salinger's *The Catcher in the Rye*, for the eponymous protagonist, Jack, who tells the story in his own first-person voice, sounds not unlike Salinger's Holden Caufield, only younger, less disturbed, and (arguably) nicer. Jack is also a character who evokes different responses from this text's two authors: Michael finds him likeable, even charming; Christine sees him as an irritating loudmouth, whom Holden would have scorned.

Jack is fifteen when his divorced father rows him out into the middle of a lake to tell him . . . something. "As soon as we were out there in the middle of nothing, he started getting the look fathers get when they're about to say something they know is gonna make you lose your lunch" (18). Jack doesn't receive the news of his father's homosexuality gladly. "It makes me sick, seriously," he tells his mother's live-in boyfriend Michael, "My father's a fucking faggot." Michael, an appealingly laid-back ex-hippie replies, "Jack, just because your father is gay is no reason for you to be dramatic. It doesn't mean anything."

Jack: "They're queer [his dad and his dad's lover]. I mean, it's not the normal thing."

Michael wisely replies, "Who's to say what's normal?" (28–29).

Word about Jack's father soon gets out and the boy discovers that someone has painted the word "faggot" on his locker. Worse, other kids soon start calling him "fag baby." Jack, who finds this maddening but not life-threatening, is somewhat mollified when he discovers that his new girlfriend Maggie also has a gay father (this sounds contrived but, as Homes artfully presents it, it's not). The boy's appreciation of his gentle father is also heightened when he discovers that the straight father of his best friend is a wife-batterer.

What makes this book so memorable is that it tells the truth with welcome humor and without melodrama. With the exception of the brutish wife-batterer, there are no villains here, just human beings who are trying to find out who they are and how to cope with what they find. The characters are complex and sympathetic, and they react in believable, authentically human ways. Moreover, the author shows the impact of the father's being gay not only on Jack but on his whole family. The book is definitely more than a one-issue novel.

Another of the most engaging books of the eighties featured not a homosexual parent but an uncle. Given the stereotypical place in popular culture of the gay uncle about-whom-we're-not-supposed-to-speak, it's surprising that it was not until 1988 that a homosexual uncle should have appeared as a character in a YA novel. Fortunately the uncle in Ron Koertge's *The Arizona Kid* is anything but a stereotype. In this memorable novel, sixteen-year-old Billy heads to Tucson, Arizona, to spend the summer with his Uncle Wes, his father's brother, whom he's never met but has long known is gay. Nevertheless, Billy—straight and from a small town in the Midwest—has reservations about living with "somebody who was really different from me. Somebody who was homosexual. Believe me, I hadn't told anyone in Bradleyville High School. They just wouldn't have understood." (13) Arriving in Arizona, Billy quickly realizes he's not in Missouri any more. "In Bradleyville, most people thought gay men were diseased Commies and here my uncle got his picture in the paper." (44)

It turns out that Uncle Wes, who, Billy says, "might have been the best-looking guy I'd ever seen outside of the movies," is a prominent local citizen and an AIDS activist. The two hit it off immediately, though Billy still has to get past some stereotypical thinking. When Uncle Wes fixes him breakfast, the boy thinks, "I wanted to ask him if he could cook because he was gay or if he was gay because he could cook. But that seemed stupid, barely a notch above, 'Hey, so how's it feel to be queer, huh?' Dad had said to just be cool about it" (14). And Billy does a good job of that. When an obnoxious fellow employee at the racetrack where Billy works jeers, "You've got a gay uncle—what does that make you?" Billy coolly replies, "His nephew" (39).

As this implies, though Tucson may not be Bradleyville, it is not without prejudice and the threat of homophobic violence. When Uncle Wes is involved in a public healing service for AIDS patients, for example, a carload of men follow him home, throw a beer can at his house and taunt him with cries of "You fucking faggots" and "You dirty cocksuckers."

"Another opening, another show," Uncle Wes calmly says to Billy as he closes the door on them (71). AIDS is presented as a fact of life—and death, as one of Uncle Wes's friends dies in the course of the book. And Wes responds to the news of his friend's death by getting drunk and vomiting—to Billy's bemusement.

"I hate for you to see me like this," the man groans.

"I'm just surprised you throw up like everybody else," Billy replies. "Knowing you, I thought it'd come out gift-wrapped" (107).

Uncle Wes is himself sexually active (a first time an adult gay character is depicted thus) but is careful to practice safe sex and tells Billy, who is falling in love with Cara Mae, that safe sex is a must for him as well. But this is presented as an integral part of the story, non-didactically and with humor. When Uncle Wes comes home from a date, for example, Billy asks, "Will you not get mad if I ask you something?"

Uncle Wes: "Who knows."

Billy: "Do you kiss these guys?"

Uncle Wes: "Sometimes."

Billy: "Yuk."

Uncle Wes: "Do you kiss Cara Mae?"

Billy: "Well, sure."

Uncle Wes: "Yuk" (151).

Compassionate, principled, and funny, Uncle Wes is a memorable character and just like anybody else—only handsomer, smarter, funnier, and more successful. More importantly, though, he is a happy, fulfilled human being, though often heartsick, like all men of compassion and conscience, about the ever-present specter of AIDS. He is, in short, what has been all too absent from GLBTQ literature to this point: a viable role model for young homosexuals and, come to think of it, for all young people.

GAY EDUCATORS AND MENTORS

The second year of the decade saw another innovation when Gary Bargar introduced the first working gay teacher to YA literature in his novel *What Happened To Mr. Forster?* (1981) (former teacher Justin "Man Without a Face" McLeod, remember, is "retired" when we meet him). Since teachers are typically among the first non-familial adults most young people encounter, it's surprising that they did not figure in GLBTQ fiction until the 1980s when, in addition to *Mr. Forster,* four other novels would include homosexual educators as characters (*Call Me Margo, Annie on My Mind, Just the Right Amount of Wrong,* and *Big Man and the Burn-Out*).

Set in Kansas City in 1958, Bargar's novel is the story of an effeminate sixth-grade boy named Louis, who is called "Billy Lou" by his Aunt Zona, with whom he lives, and by everyone at the Louisa May Alcott Elementary School. Well, everyone but his new teacher, Mr. Forster, who calls him Louis and helps him develop his talent as a writer. Unfortunately Mr. Forster, a "high church Anglican," antagonizes a number of parents because of his liberal attitudes, and when people learn that he lives with his "best friend," a whispering campaign ensues and Mr. Forster is "called away." Louis is devastated when a classmate, Veronica, explains, "Mr. Forster wasn't 'called away,' he was fired. And everybody knows why" (152). Even Louis's best friend Paul sighs, "Well, God, Louis. Okay, Mr. Forster is a nice man. He's even a pretty good teacher, as teachers go. But after all, he *is* a queer" (168).

Reluctant to accept this, Louis visits his ex-teacher, who acknowledges that he is, indeed, homosexual. "But how can you just quit teaching?" the boy demands.

"Oh, Louis," the teacher replies, "Sometimes we have to do things we don't want to do. Of course, I don't want to quit teaching. But in this situation I have no choice. The decision has been made for me" (162).

Unfortunately, the homosexual teacher as a victim or martyr who quietly accepts his or her fate has become something of a fixture of YA literature. Even in Nancy Garden's otherwise exemplary *Annie on My Mind*, two teachers are fired when it is revealed they are lesbian lovers and, instead of contesting their termination, they go gently into that good night of early retirement. This compromises their viability as otherwise sympathetic role models, but it also reflects the very real problems that gay teachers faced in the 1980s—and which many gay teachers continue to face today. For example, in 1984 David E. Wilson, a teacher at Kirkwood Community College in Cedar Rapids, Iowa, published an article titled "The Open Library: YA Books for Gay Teens" in *English Journal*. The article was a sympathetic but hardly incendiary call for more novels that "gay young adults" can look to, "hoping to find answers and positive role models."[2]

Two years later, Wilson published a second article in *EJ* in which he described the consequences of the first.[3] "My phone rings. It's the principal of the private high school where only two weeks earlier I had accepted a teaching position. I hadn't yet signed a contract. 'I have to inform you that the job is no longer available,' he says. 'I'm sorry but we won't be needing your services'" (46). Subsequently he pursues two other job offers. "Both schools—which formerly courted me—now refuse to write or take my calls. Finally, an administrator from one confides in a mutual friend, 'We'll never touch him after that article'" (47).

A year earlier, the editors of the *Interracial Books for Children Bulletin* noted (perhaps wryly?) that Jan B. Goodman, the author of the article cited in Chapter Two and a teacher in the Boston area, "in a sudden burst of lesbian pride and affirmation has decided to sign her actual name to this article instead of her usual pseudonym."[4]

Former school librarian Christine Jenkins recalls a similar incident. Her story:

"I came out in 1975 and began working as an elementary school librarian in 1976. It's sometimes hard to remember just how scary it could be to be a gay/lesbian adult working with children at that time, but this was when Anita Bryant's "Save the Children" campaign in Miami was in full swing and it seemed likely that California's Briggs Initiative, which would have barred gays and lesbians from working in the public schools, would pass. (In fact, Bryant's efforts to overturn Miami-Dade County's anti-discrimination ordinance were successful; in 1998—21 years later—the Miami-Dade County board again approved an anti-discrimination ordinance, which remains in place. The Briggs' Initiative failed to pass by a wide margin.)

As a professionally active librarian, I was a reviewer for the *Interracial Books for Children Bulletin*. A friend and I self-published *A Look at Gayness*, an annotated bibliography of materials (books, articles, and recordings) with gay/lesbian content suitable for young people. The *Bulletin's* editors approached us about creating a similar annotated bibliography of recommended books for an upcoming theme issue of the *Bulletin* on homophobia. Although I was very pleased to be asked, I was ambivalent about claiming authorship in print. On the one hand, being asked to share my expertise in this way was a feather in my professional cap. On the other hand, I worried that I would in effect be "outing" myself as a lesbian working with children, which could be problematic (to say the least!) for some parents and community members. My dilemma: should I publish under my own name or a pseudonym? I went to my principal for advice. I wasn't officially out to her but I knew she was a good liberal and a warm-hearted human being. She was entirely comfortable with my "secret" and said she would do all she could to protect me if trouble arose but cautioned that she couldn't guarantee that her efforts would be successful. I finally decided to use "C. A. Jenkins" and my principal smiled when I told her I was going to publish under my own name—this was clearly what she'd hoped I would decide. Her affirmation meant a lot to me and happily, none of her or my fears were realized. For the time being I remained more or less closeted at school but had taken a successful first step toward openness. Five years later when I published an article on YA fiction with GLBTQ content in *Out/Look: A Gay & Lesbian Quarterly*, I used my full name.

Other gay and lesbian educators have wrestled with similar dilemmas regarding openness, as Rita M. Kissen demonstrated in her thoughtful—and sometimes heartbreaking—1996 book about "the real lives of gay and lesbian teachers." Its title? *The Last Closet.*[5]

The danger of being a gay teacher is dramatically illustrated in Alice Childress' 1989 novel *Those Other People* in which a young and closeted gay teacher is blackmailed and finally resigns his position (see below for a further discussion of this book). Another negative depiction of gay educators is found in Judith St. George's *Call Me Margo*, (1981) which presents the dismal case of Miss Frye and Miss Durrett, lesbian teachers who are two halves of a former couple and definitely not people one would want teaching children of any age. One, a tennis coach, is friendly and attractive but abuses her position of authority to get close to girls; the second, an English teacher, is a disagreeable bully described by the narrator with a mixture of pity and disgust as being "very crippled. In fact, she wore braces on both her thin, misshapen legs and large orthopedic shoes" (33). Not since *The Man Without a Face* has sexual identity been branded with such an unfortunate symbolic presentation.

In light of this, the presence in Clayton Bess' 1985 novel *Big Man and the Burn-Out,* of an openly gay male teacher, who not only doesn't lose his job but is presented as a hero, may seem almost like wish fulfillment. However, in this story of a boy named Jess who is struggling to find his sexual identity, the presence of a positive adult role model, whose homosexuality is not an issue but is simply presented as part of his larger identity, is a refreshing change and a template for the future treatment of such characters. As an early example of gay assimilation literature, it is the first of several GLBTQ YA novels in which the reader is provided with more insight about a character's sexuality than is the protagonist him/herself.

OTHER GAY/LESBIAN ADULTS

Five other homosexual adults appear in novels of the '80s. In Elizabeth Levy's *Come Out Smiling* (1981), the gay character is a counselor/riding instructor at a posh girls' summer camp. In *Just the Right Amount of Wrong* (1982) by Larry Hulse, not one but two adults are secretly gay: the school principal and the local sheriff (who murders the principal to protect his secret!). In Madeleine L'Engle's *A House Like a Lotus* (1984), the young female protagonist's mentor, Maximiliana (Max), is a lesbian. And in Carolyn Meyer's *Elliott and Win* (1986), a possibly gay man serves as an Amigo (read: Big Brother) to a fatherless boy. Only two of these characters—Elliott and Max—are at all memorable.

Fourteen-year-old Win's first meeting with his new Amigo Elliott begins inauspiciously as Elliott serves him a kid-unfriendly lunch of gazpacho followed by a dessert of cheese and walnuts. Win is dismayed to learn that Elliott—a confirmed bachelor, gourmet cook, and opera lover—hates baseball and organized sports and (to Win's horror) doesn't even *own* a television set. But is Elliott really gay? There is no doubt in the mind of Win's cretinous friend, Paul, who warns, "You hang around with a faggot, people are going to start thinking you're a faggot, too. What do you think a confirmed bachelor is, anyway?" (27–28).

Of course, in an act of convenient authorial contrivance, it is not Elliott but Paul's divorced father who is revealed as being gay. As for Elliott, his sexual identity is never specified, the point of this well-intentioned but didactic book being that it shouldn't make a difference. And it shouldn't, but it would have helped if Elliott weren't the most annoyingly self-important adult figure this side of Justin McLeod.

And then there is Madeleine L'Engle's *A House Like a Lotus*. The protagonist narrator is Polly, the sixteen-year-old daughter of Meg and Calvin O'Keefe, whom readers may have met as the protagonists of L'Engle's Newbery Award-winning *A Wrinkle in Time*. Although intelligent and mature, Polly is suffering the pangs of adolescent gawkiness and feels "out of it" with her high school peers. Then along comes Maximiliana, a world-famous painter friend of the O'Keefes, who lives nearby with Ursula, her companion of thirty years (and a world-famous brain surgeon). Max takes Polly under her wing, and her friendship gives Polly confidence and self-appreciation. But Max appears ill and is in fact dying. She has kept her condition a secret, but Polly guesses the truth. And Max has another secret as well—she and Ursula are lovers. The story then veers into a Southern Gothic tale of passion and betrayal: Max uses alcohol to dull her physical pain, and one dark and stormy night she makes a drunken pass at Polly, who flees barefoot into the rain and injures her foot. When Polly heads to town to get her foot taken care of, she ends up at the very hospital built by Max's lecherous father and named for Max's delicate sister who died young from the pneumonia she contracted while fleeing (barefoot, no doubt) into the rain to avoid her father's sexual advances . . . and so on. In the end Max makes elaborate amends and Polly is finally able to accept Max as the flawed-but-beautiful person she is. The author advocates tolerance, at least up to a point (as Polly's father Calvin declares, "I thought it was now agreed that consenting adults were not to be persecuted, particularly if they keep their private lives private" [111]), but her portrayal of gayness is an odd one indeed. Max explains to Polly that she herself is a lesbian because she couldn't forgive her father for her sister's death. And Ursula is a lesbian because she is a brain surgeon (no, really—"Ursula is the way she is. She's competed in a man's world, in a man's field. There are not many women neurosurgeons" [120]). But Max—with her midnight black hair and silver gray eyes outlined in kohl—is unquestionably an intriguing character, and readers may well remember this charismatic mentor long after they've forgotten the unlikely plot and Polly's irritating penchant for demonstrating her "amazing innocence" (120)—and her heterosexuality—at every turn.

GLBTQ YOUNG ADULTS

Of the nearly sixty homosexual—or more often, questioning—characters in the novels of the eighties, thirty-six are young adults. But of that thirty-six, only ten are protagonists, the balance being friends (twenty-one), boyfriends (four), or older brothers (two). This trend of placing a certain distance between the teen protagonist and the story's GLBTQ content serves to both broaden *and* narrow the scope of GLBTQ YA literature. On the one hand, this distance allows a YA novel (which is, after all, a story told from a teen perspective) to include gay/lesbian characters of various ages, backgrounds, and relationships to the protagonist. On the other hand, this has meant that most of the teen protagonists in the novels of the 1980s have been heterosexual, so the reader is usually seeing the gay/lesbian character at a remove from the protagonist. What these numbers seem to suggest is that it was much easier (safer?) for authors in the eighties to write about homosexuals who were adults or, if young adults, ones who were secondary characters. This distancing may also further isolate GLBTQ teen readers (though, in this chronological context, one might as well drop the "B" and the "T" altogether, since bisexuality would not be treated until M. E. Kerr's 1997 novel *"Hello," I Lied* and transgender issues would not be addressed until the 2004 publication of Julie Anne Peters' *Luna*). One is tempted to suggest that the "L" could be dropped, too, since after 1984, only three adolescent characters are lesbians (and one of those is secondary). And in the eight novels published between 1980 and 1984 that did, even marginally, deal with female sexuality, only one, *Annie on My Mind*, treated it positively.

Six of the eight books are so similar they might be carbon copies. The six—*Bouquets for Brimbal* (1980) by J. P. Reading, *The Last of Eden* (1980) by Stephanie Tolan, *Crush* (1981) by Jane Futcher, *Come Out Smiling* (1981) by Elizabeth Levy, *Call Me Margo* (1981) by Judith St. George, and *Flick* (1983) by Wendy Kesselman—feature upper middle-class white girls, most of whom attend posh private schools (or, in the case of the Levy novel, a posh summer camp). And in virtually all, the treatment of sexuality is foggy once it proceeds past the first kiss. While this lack of sexual detail is evident throughout most YA literature, fictional gays and lesbians seem to have *extremely* limited sex lives. Too, the consensus seems to be that homosexuality is a phase, a crush, a passing fancy. As a "wise" teacher tells Michelle ("Mike"), the protagonist of *The Last of Eden,* who has had a crush on another girl, Marty, "The only thing we know for certain is that some kind of homosexual experience, sometimes it's physical, sometimes psychological, is natural—'normal,' Mike—during adolescence. It's a part of figuring out who you are, a first step with someone like yourself, before you take the chance of reaching out to the other sex" (151–152).

Typically the girls who are undergoing these rite-of-passage experiences are deeply conflicted about their feelings. Jenny Mandel in *Come Out Smiling,* for example, is appalled to discover that her camp counselor Peggy, on whom she has a major crush, is a lesbian. "Did this whole thing mean I was a lesbian?" she agonizes. "It might be normal to have crushes, but it was definitely not normal to have a crush on a lesbian. I had to be queer. I could see my whole life ahead of me. I'd never get married. I'd die all alone. Maybe I would kill myself instead" (126). Jinx, in *Crush,* frets, "Maybe everyone was partly queer and just didn't call it that. They called it having a crush" (255).

Jinx's crush is on Lexie Yves, a manipulative beauty who charms and seduces her, but then slides out of trouble with school authorities by blaming the two girls' escapades on Jinx's "unnatural" affection for her. Unfortunately, Lexie's "pretty poison" temptress persona sets the pattern in these books for the worldly and seductive young women who lead their naïve and trusting friends astray. Like Daphne in Rosa Guy's *Ruby*, they are domineering, self-absorbed, and cruelly capricious in dispensing their emotional largesse. Consider the eponymous Flick in Wendy Kesselman's novel, who might be Lexie's even more evil twin. She summarily dumps Nana—the one and only protagonist in this suite of novels who actually considers herself a lesbian. Bereft and all alone at novel's end, Nana masochistically muses, "I close my eyes and a longing sweeps over me. And I think of Flick, as I know I shall always think of her, the night we leaped down the dune and dove into the sea, the night she found a long gray stick and wrote our names deep in the sand" (136).

But what does it actually mean to be a lesbian—aside from being left to drown in a sea of loneliness? Jinx, who has been ordered to see a psychiatrist, reports, "It has to do with sexual feelings. If you have SEX-UAL feelings for a girl, then it's more like being lesbian." This simplistic equation of homosexuality and the physical act of sex is reinforced by the fact that the three adult lesbians in these books—Miss Frye and Miss Durrett in *Call Me Margo* and Maxamiliana in Madeleine L'Engle's *A House Like a Lotus*—are depicted as being sexual predators.

And it is neatly summarized in this typical exchange from J. P. Reading's 1980 novel *Bouquets for Brimbal*. Macy and her boyfriend Don are talking about Macy's discovery that her best friend, Annie Brimbal, is a lesbian. Don asks, "You can't feel being gay is 'wrong' or 'bad,' can you?"

"I don't know," Macy replies. "I've never really thought of it in terms of actual people. Or as if it were love, a deep feeling, you know? I just think about sex and being 'queer.' Loose-jointed decorators and big butchy girls with mustaches who wear leather jackets. I've just never thought of 'gay' in terms of caring" (164). So what, in the context of these six novels, does it mean to be a lesbian? Apparently it is simply a matter of same-sex physical intimacy, as there is little same-sex emotional intimacy happening anywhere that the protagonist—and by extension the reader—can see it.

Happily, a vastly more balanced and emotionally eloquent definition would be offered by Nancy Garden in her 1982 novel—and now acknowledged classic—*Annie on My Mind*. Liza Winthrop and Annie Kenyon are seventeen when they first meet at New York's Metropolitan

Museum of Art. Though the girls feel an instant kinship, the evolution of that bond into expressed feelings of love takes place gradually, naturally, and plausibly—even to the uncertainty the first time they kiss. Liza—who is the first-person narrator—describes her feelings: "It was like a war inside me; I couldn't even recognize all the sides. There was one that said, 'No, this is wrong; you know it's wrong and bad and sinful,' and there was another that said it was happening too fast, and another that just wanted to stop thinking altogether and fling my arms around Annie and hold her forever" (93). Happily, Liza's heart wins this tug of war and she stammers, "Annie, I think I love you." And immediately she thinks, "the moment the words were out, I knew more than I'd ever known anything that they were true" (94).

But does this mean she's homosexual? At first, Liza is uncertain. She's never consciously thought about being gay, though it turns out Annie has and, sensing Liza's confusion, writes her a letter saying that it wouldn't be fair to influence her, to try to push her into something she doesn't want, concluding, "Liza, if you don't want us to see each other anymore, it's okay" (104). Happily, this noble self-sacrifice is unnecessary, for Liza *does* want to see Annie again and the two girls begin a relationship that Liza thinks of as "magical"—"and a big part of that magic was that no matter how much of ourselves we found to give each other, there was always more we wanted to give" (108).

The one thing, however, that is not acknowledged at this point is a sexual dimension to the relationship. Gradually this adds a layer of unspoken tension to their interpersonal dynamic, causing the two to become awkward and restrained around each other. Ultimately—and believably—it leads to an emotional confrontation in which Annie tells Liza that she's making her afraid "because you seem to think it's wrong or dirty or something" (121).

Liza denies this but she can't stop thinking about her confusion as she confronts the power of her feelings for Annie. "You're in love with another girl, Liza Winthrop," she tells herself, "and you know that means you're probably gay. But you don't know a thing about what that means" (143). Looking for knowledge, she reads the entry for "Homosexuality" in her father's encyclopedia and is incensed when she realizes that "in that whole long article, the word 'love' wasn't used even once. That made me mad; it was as if whoever wrote the article didn't know that gay people actually love each other" (143). And so when the two finally do become intimate, the experience transcends the purely physical; it is an act not only of consummation but also of bonding that is almost spiritual as Liza describes the 'wonder of the closeness:' "We can be almost like one."

Seeing these words, the reader will remember what Liza has said earlier, recalling the first time they had kissed: "Have you ever felt really close to someone? So close that you can't understand why you and the other person have two separate bodies, two separate skins?" (91).

Annie's particularized treatment of falling in love is so effectively drawn that it can easily be generalized or extrapolated to the hetero-sexual experience of first love. And indeed, with the exception of Mau-reen Daly's *Seventeenth Summer* (1942), it's hard to recall a more nu-anced picture of the gradual deepening intimacy of teens falling in love than *Annie on My Mind*. We've given so much attention to describing the evolution—and complex nature—of the relationship between Liza and Annie because most readers find it the most enduringly important aspect of the book. Garden herself agrees with this assessment. In an e-mail to Michael Cart she wrote, "It's the emotional content of *Annie* that still speaks to readers."[6]

Other aspects of the book have not endured quite so well. Those who have read the novel will know that, in a scene that now seems a bit contrived, Annie and Liza are discovered in bed together by a teacher from Liza's school. Worse, the discovery takes place in the home of two female teachers from the school who turn out to be lesbian partners. Liza survives a disciplinary hearing, but the two teachers do not. They are fired and, as noted earlier, do not contest their dismissal. Also, the por-trayal of the antagonists—the headmistress, Mrs. Poindexter, and her ad-ministrative assistant Ms. Baxter—seem one-dimensional and many of the scenes involving them are tinged with melodrama.

Nevertheless, the characters of Liza and Annie and the wonderful integrity of their relationship have made the book one of the few en-during classics of GLBTQ literature. It was the principal reason that, in 2003, Garden received the American Library Association's prestigious Margaret A. Edwards Award for Lifetime Achievement in Young Adult Literature. The award citation noted, "Garden, in writing *Annie on My Mind* also has the distinction of being the first author for young adults to create a lesbian love story with a positive ending."[7]

Just as Annie and Liza have discovered much about themselves through reading ("I felt as if I were meeting parts of myself in the gay people I read about," Liza notes [144]), so, too, generations of gay, lesbian and questioning teenagers have discovered themselves and the truth about homosexuality by reading Garden's novel. "Don't let ignorance win," one of the two lesbian teachers tells Liza. "Let love" (232). Garden has made such a victory possible. One cannot think of higher words of praise.

Male teens would have to wait until the very end of the decade for a book that treated male partners with such large-hearted acceptance. Francesca Lia Block's *Weetzie Bat* (1989) was that novel and the partners were Dirk and Duck. Dirk's coming-out to his best friend Weetzie is beautiful in its simplicity and breathtaking in the sweetness of its spirit of acceptance.

> "I'm gay," Dirk said.
>
> "Who, what, when, where, how—well, not *how*," Weetzie said. "It doesn't matter one bit, honey-honey," she said, giving him a hug.
>
> Dirk took a swig of his drink. "But you know I'll always love you the best and think you are a beautiful, sexy girl," he said.
>
> "Now we can Duck hunt together," Weetzie said, taking his hand." (9)

Duck-hunting, in Block's wonderfully inventive argot, is searching for your soul mate. It's just one of the many delights of this punk fairy tale that Dirk's duck should turn out to be a boy who is actually named "Duck." In like fashion, the romantic "secret agent lover man" that Weetzie seeks turns out to be a rakish film-maker with green eyes, a slouchy hat, and a trench coat. His name? What else? "My Secret Agent Lover Man."

Dirk and Duck will be featured players in the four cinematic novels that follow about Weetzie and her very nontraditional, extended family of musicians and filmmakers, and Dirk will even have a novel, *Baby Bebop,* all of his own. But that will not happen until the next decade; further discussion of Block and her novels will be covered in the next chapter of *this* book.

But to return to the eighties: while the decade—as previously noted—saw the appearance of twenty-seven gay male characters in YA novels, only eight of those are protagonists (and four of *those* appear in novels first published in England). Of the nineteen gay male non-protagonists, eight are adults, two are the protagonists' older (but still young adult) brothers, and the nine remaining are friends or boyfriends of the protagonist(s). Again, as was the case with lesbian characters, this suggests that distance remained the order of the day, an obligatory comfort factor that didn't necessarily serve either the characters in or the readers of these novels terribly well. However, a case could be made that having a heterosexual protagonist observing a homosexual character does make the book more accessible to straight readers who might balk at being asked to identify with a gay or lesbian protagonist. When the observing is done with insight and affection—as in the case of the several novels by M. E. Kerr that employ this device—such books can be useful.

But what of the four gay male protagonists in U. S. novels who were dealing—or attempting to deal—with the immediacy of their own sexual identity? In the case of Neil, the eighteen-year-old protagonist and narrator of Frank Mosca's *All-American Boys* (1983), there is no doubt. In the very first sentence of the novel he declares, "I've known I was gay since I was thirteen" (7). How does he react to this? With startling aplomb: "According to one of the lousy books I read back then, I'm supposed to tell you it came as some sort of huge shock that sent me into fits of suicidal depression. Actually, it was the most natural thing in the world. I thought everyone was" (7). Fortunately, for him, he doesn't share this discovery with anyone, since, when he gets to high school the next year, he encounters a group of "queer bashers" and—in the interest of self-preservation—dives headlong back into the closet.

The agony of coming out becomes the theme of this book when Neil meets Paul, whose family has just moved to town (where would young adult literature be without the obligatory new kid in town?), and the two fall in love. Paul is more candid about his sexuality than Neil, whom he criticizes for his "closet mentality." Neil's prudence would seem to be justified, however, when the gang of gay bashers attacks Paul and nearly beats him to death. At this point the novel turns into a revenge fantasy. Neil has a black belt in kung-fu and when *he* encounters the gang, the tables are turned. Many sympathetic readers will derive some guilty pleasure from seeing bullies get their own back, but one hopes that, on mature reflection, they will reject violence as a strategy for coping with yet another dispiriting and dehumanizing example of gay-bashing. That aside, it is refreshing to see a protagonist who realizes his sexual identity at such an early age and accepts it without guilt or self-hatred. Unfortunately, although both Paul and Neil are sweet and likable characters, the novel is one of the most didactic of the eighties, an unfortunate characteristic of many of the novels—like this one—then being published by Alyson, a small, independent publisher specializing in gay and lesbian literature.

A second Alyson novel from the eighties is Don Sakers' *Act Well Your Part* (Alyson 1986), the story of Keith, the new boy in school (and the protagonist this time) who falls in love with an "older man," Brian, who is a senior (Keith is a junior). Brian returns his feelings and the two become partners. For the most part, the other students are surprisingly accepting of this but, then, they are part of the Drama Club.[8] Keith's mother is also the most amazingly accepting parent thus far encountered in this chronology. "Good heaven's, son, you don't think I love you any less? Of course not. I don't care who you're attracted to—you're still the same boy you've always been" (100). While this may be more wish-fulfillment than reality, it is refreshing to see a parent in a YA book from the eighties who doesn't respond to a teen's being gay by kicking him out of the house or calling an exorcist. Otherwise, this—like the Mosca novel—is a gracelessly written and didactic exercise. Like *All-American Boys,* Sakers' book was marketed as an adult title, though *School Library Journal* reviewed both as young adult titles. One doubts that very many libraries would have purchased these two books, however, since they were published as paperback originals and their pulp-novel covers were targeted at an adult trade bookstore market.

A third novel with a gay protagonist, B. A. Ecker's *Independence Day* (1983), was also published as a paperback original. The story of Mike, a high school soccer player, it is one of the first gay sports novels. The only other gay sports novel of the 1980s, *Counter Play* by Anne Snyder and Louis Pelletier (1981), was also published as a paperback original. Both of these novels treat homosexuality positively, but neither is an enduring work of literature. Though out of print for years and almost impossible to find today, the books—like many paperbacks of that period—sold briskly and, in fact, *Counter Play* was turned into a made-for-television after-school special, *The Truth about Alex*, starring Scott Baio. Nevertheless, it wasn't until the 1990s that a gay sports novel, Diana Wieler's *Bad Boy* (1992), was published as a hardcover and was targeted at the library and school market.

Meanwhile, the fourth novel of the 1980s to feature a gay protagonist was Scott Bunn's problem novel *Just Hold On* (1982), the melodramatic story of two teens: Charlotte, who is being molested by her doctor father, and Stephen, whose doctor father is a hopeless alcoholic. The over-the-top melodrama is unfortunate, since the book's treatment of Stephen's emerging homosexuality is actually fairly positive (if one overlooks that fact that his father dies of a heart attack on the morning after Stephen and his friend Rolf finally consummate their relationship!). And Stephen's antic best friend, Wharton, is one of the most accepting characters in all of GLBTQ literature. Discovering that his friend is gay by finding him in bed with Rolf, Wharton—after a moment's consideration—says, "Rolf, I guess you're an okay person, since Stephen obviously likes you . . ." Wharton sat down on the chair and stared back and forth from Rolf to Stephen. "Obviously likes you," he repeated, then looked to the ceiling, "That's for sure . . ." (135). Ultimately Stephen and Rolf will wind up taking an apartment in New York with Wharton and his girlfriend, though the precise nature of the relationship between Stephen and Rolf by that time is frustratingly ambiguous.

Equally ambiguous—and annoying—is the undefined relationship of Eric, the nineteen-year-old protagonist of Emily Hanlon's *The Wing and the Flame* (1980), and his best friend Chris. Told in flashbacks, the story is principally that of Eric's relationship with Owen Cassell, an eccentric, seventy-one-year-old sculptor whom Eric's father suspects of being a pedophile. The man is not, but this plot point does introduce the element of homosexuality, though when Eric and his friend Chris finally have a moment of intimacy (on page 127 of a 147-page novel), it catches the reader and, apparently, Eric by surprise. "Why can't we just be friends?" he asks, sounding remarkably like Val in *Hey, Dollface.* "Just ordinary friends like everyone else has friends?"

Subsequently, the author writes, "He knew his feelings for Chris hadn't changed." (And now he begins to sound like Jinx in *Crush.*) "The difference was those feelings had a name now—a name which caused him to fear what he loved most about their friendship—the joy he felt from their closeness. He was held back by his fear of what loving Chris meant. Gay, queer, fag—the words loomed threateningly before him" (131–132). Sensing Eric's distress, Chris—who, like Davy's friend Altschuler, has no such conflicted feelings about his homosexuality—nobly says, "Don't you see, Eric? It doesn't ever have to happen again" (131). And the two remain friends. There's nothing wrong with that outcome, but it seems fairly likely that Eric, too, is gay but simply doesn't want to confront this fact. And both Chris—and the author—give him a free pass: the author by changing the subject and Chris by sacrificing himself—or at least his feelings.

The temptation to deny oneself, either by discounting one's same-sex attractions (like Eric or Tom Naylor or Davy Ross), or by denying one's own emotional needs (as Chris and Ward and Altschuler do), is, of course, a recurring theme in gay and lesbian literature. It is all part of the larger issue of—first—discovering one's sexual identity, then—second—struggling to come to terms with it and then—third—sharing the truth about oneself with others.

The impact on others of the decision to deny the truth and to choose to live what is, in effect, a lie is demonstrated in the several novels we have examined in which parents belatedly come out of the closet. But it also figures in two novels from the '80s in which girls discover that their boyfriends are gay: Hila Colman's *Happily Ever After* (1986) and Ann Rinaldi's *The Good Side of My Heart* (1987). Both of these not terribly good novels are weakened by the fact that the female characters— Melanie in the former and Brie in the latter—seem almost impossibly naïve in not seeing what a current-day reader will have readily discerned: the homosexuality of the respective boyfriends. Nevertheless, the pain the girls feel on discovering the truth is real and even poignant, though Brie's initial reaction, at least, is irritating as well: "All that handsomeness, all that masculinity wasted. I wanted to cry" (272). Melanie reacts in a similar manner: "He couldn't be what he had said. He was tall, handsome, *manly*—he was nothing like anyone who was odd or queer, nothing like the man who had the interior design shop in the village who everyone said was gay" (102). Her erstwhile boyfriend will lecture her, later, about this attitude: "We're people like everyone else—and we're men, too. All kinds of men—weak, strong, big, little, even great athletes" (121). As one might infer from these quotations, both of these books also suffer from didacticism, plus the "sad-eyed loner" phenomenon that is frequently used in YA novels as an indication of a male character's homosexuality.

The Good Side of My Heart by Ann Rinaldi is, however, interesting for a second reason: it is the first to feature religion as a major theme (though this had been a minor theme in Bargar's *What Happened To Mr. Forster?,* in which conservative religious beliefs are a contributory reason for the teacher's firing). In the Rinaldi title, Brie's older brother, Kevin, is a Roman Catholic priest, whose reaction to the news that her boyfriend is gay is to explain the Church's position on homosexuality, noting that if the homosexual isn't practicing his sexuality, there is no sin. The brother, who is in the midst of a crisis involving his vocation, acknowledges that he doesn't agree with the Church's position, since he has "trouble with denying a person their sexuality if they're made that way" (244). Of course, this is academic, since Josh has already told Brie that he is celibate, "You know, like your brother" (222). Brie doesn't tell Kevin this and his ultimate advice to her is the hoary truism "Hate the sin and love the sinner."

As confusing as this is in summary, it's exponentially more confusing in the prolix pages of the book. What is clear, however, is that homosexuality is once again being defined not as a complex aspect of self-identity but, rather, as a physical act, which may—or may not—be sinful.

The reductive treatment of homosexuality and personal denial reaches its acme—or nadir, depending on one's point of view—in Alice Childress' novel *Those Other People* (1989), a story that is told from multiple points of view, including that of seventeen-year-old Jonathan, who is portrayed as a stereotypically self-hating homosexual. Deeply closeted and proud of it ("*in* and proud?"), he decides to delay going to college for a year because "being gay was slowly becoming uncomfortable," and when he does go to check out a college, he is appalled by "signs and posters all over campus" about "sexual stuff. Gay rights discussion! Lesbians united. Bisexual society" (13). So he moves to New York, instead, (there's no homosexuality there!) and gets a gay roommate, Harp, who pressures him to come out. Harp orchestrates a gathering of gays at their apartment and tells Jon beforehand, "You'll meet a pitifully over-swish Nellie." (19). Of course, when Jon, at the meeting, protests that he doesn't want to come out ("Hell, it's my closet, I can live in it if I want to" [19]), "that Nellie was the only one who spoke up for me." Later, Jon thinks, "I was not then, and am not now, comfortable with who and what I am" (75). When Harp drunkenly outs him to his parents, Jon's mom thinks, "Our first hope is that we're dealing with a passing phase." Finally, Jon is forced to come out because he is being blackmailed. As a result, he resigns from the temporary teaching position he has taken and moves back home to his parents. Though the ethicality of outing closeted homosexuals, even for political reasons, is dubious, this may be the only novel in which being an out gay is presented as something to be actively deplored. As a result, the novel seems anachronistic; worse, it is replete with one-dimensional characters and some of the most unfortunate homosexual stereotyping in the literature.

Homosexuals are not the only characters in GLBTQ literature who are self-hating, as demonstrated in three novels by Barbara Wersba: *Crazy Vanilla* (1986), *Just Be Gorgeous* (1988), and *Whistle Me Home* (1997). Wersba writes very much in the tradition of J. D. Salinger and John Donovan, with a soupçon of Paul Zindel. Five of her sixteen YA novels—including *Whistle Me Home*—have been selected as ALA Best Books for Young Adults.

In *Crazy Vanilla,* the first—and definitely the best—of these novels, the protagonist is Tyler, a fourteen-year-old boy and aspiring nature photographer who falls in love with Mitzi, a brash, cosmically wise fifteen-year-old girl who shares his interest in photography. Tyler's adored older brother, Cameron is estranged from their father as a result of one too many arguments about Cameron's being not only gay, but a gay interior designer. Tyler and his brother continue to see each other, but when Cameron falls in love and moves in with Vincent, a handsome Italian interior decorator, Tyler distances himself from Cameron. Canny Mitzi sees what's going on: "You've decided to cut that poor guy right out of your life, simply because of Vincent. You want to pay him back for being in love" (143). At book's end, Mitzi abruptly moves to Santa Fe with her nomadic hippie mother and Tyler finally picks up the phone and calls his brother, presumably to begin a process of reconciliation.

In Wersba's two other novels, the protagonists are—like Melanie in *Happily Ever After* and Brie in *The Good Side of My Heart*—straight girls who fall in love with gay boys, but with far less favorable outcomes. In *Just Be Gorgeous,* the girl is sixteen-year-old Heidi, who loses her heart to Jeffrey, a flamboyantly gay, twenty-year-old street performer, who lives in an abandoned building and dreams of getting his big break on Broadway. When this doesn't happen, Jeffrey—to Heidi's dismay—decides to accept an offer from a somewhat older gay couple to move with them to Hollywood. Bleakly, Heidi thinks, "So once again I realized that there was a special club on this earth called 'being gay' and that I was not a member" (145). (This may be one of the only times in YA literature when a straight character expresses a desire to be gay!)

Wersba returned to this theme in the 1990s in *Whistle Me Home*, the story of Noli, a girl who falls in love with the new boy in her English class, only to reject him ("You dirty faggot!") when she learns he is gay. This story is described more fully in Chapter 4.

THE ADVENT OF AIDS

The decade of the eighties was notable for the appearance of AIDS (Acquired Immune Deficiency Syndrome), which emerged—like a demon from the darkness—in 1981. Though in the early years of the disease its chief victims were homosexuals, hemophiliacs, and others who acquired it through tainted blood, AIDS also spread to the heterosexual population, including both men and women. The disease finally received widespread public recognition with the 1985 announcement that the well-known actor Rock Hudson was, in fact, dying of AIDS.

Though teenagers—gay and straight—were definitely at-risk from the beginning, AIDS was not mentioned in young adult fiction until 1986, when M.E. Kerr courageously wrote her haunting novel *Night Kites*. She acknowledged in her 1993 Margaret Edwards Award acceptance speech that she felt she was committing a form of professional suicide by writing the book, since the disease in her novel is sexually transmitted to a young *gay* man, not to a straight hemophiliac who had received tainted blood or to a heterosexual drug abuser who had used an infected needle. Why her concern? Let Kerr herself answer that question: "It seemed to me that *not* to have a homosexual be the AIDS sufferer would be a way of saying I'll recognize the illness but not those who have it . . . a sort of don't ask/don't tell proposition, where the reader can know the nature of the plague, without having to deal with those personalities who threaten the status quo."[9]

The AIDS-infected, status-quo threatening character in the Kerr novel is Pete, the twenty-seven-year-old brother of the teenage protagonist, Erick. Pete discloses both his homosexuality and his HIV-positive status to his family at the same time, a devastating one-two punch that was not an uncommon pattern then . . . and now. Erick is surprised, since his brother is nothing like "poor Charlie Gilhooley" (the novel is set in Seaville, New York, as was Kerr's earlier *I'll Love You When You're More Like Me;* obviously Charlie, whom we met in that novel, is still the town's "resident gay"). Pete tartly asks, "Do I get extra points for not looking it [gay]?" (94). Surprise aside, Erick accepts his brother's homosexuality with—for a male teen—refreshing equanimity, telling their father, "It's just another way of being. It's not a crime; it's not anything to be ashamed about" (91). The father's reaction is more typical of the time: he insists this be kept a secret from everybody outside the immediate family. Ultimately, of course, the secret will leak out and, as a result, Erick's girlfriend will leave him. To his great credit, Erick doesn't blame Pete; indeed, his illness has brought the two brothers closer together than ever before. The book ends on a bittersweet note with the two brothers discussing—in the context of something Pete has written—the end of things, a tacit acknowledgement that AIDS, at that time at least, was virtually always fatal.

Following the publication of *Night Kites,* the silence that had surrounded the disease gradually became less pervasive, as AIDS began to be mentioned in passing, usually in the context of fear or the need to practice safe sex; nevertheless, it would receive major thematic or topical treatment in only three other YA novels published in the eighties. In Gloria Miklowitz's *Good-Bye Tomorrow* (1987), the HIV-positive character is a heterosexual teenage boy who has been infected by a blood transfusion. In Ron Koertge's already-discussed *The Arizona Kid*, the PWAs (people with AIDS) are all gay adults. Lastly, in Francesca Lia Block's *Weetzie Bat,* the disease is present but never referred to by name, a device that, in a way, makes it an even darker, more menacing presence. AIDS becomes a factor late in the novel when Duck, Dirk's lover, disappears, leaving a note saying that his friend Bam-Bam is sick, and asking the plaintive question, "Even though we're okay, how can anyone love anyone when you could kill them just by loving them?" (80).

Bereft, Dirk goes on a quest to find his friend, whom he finally locates in San Francisco. Duck asks, "How did you find me?" And Dirk tellingly replies, "I don't know. But you are in my blood" (85). AIDS, of course, is transmitted by the exchange of body fluids, including blood. To invoke the word "blood" in this context is to remind the reader that love, too, is in one's blood and therefore is as essential to life as blood, even though, as Dirk reflects, "Love is a dangerous angel. Especially nowadays" (84).

We will return to this topic in the next chapter. But the reader will find an even more comprehensive discussion and analysis of AIDS literature in Virginia A. Walter and Melissa Gross's *HIV/AIDS Information for*

Children: A Guide To Issues and Resources[10] and in Gross's subsequent journal article "What Do Young Adult Novels Say about HIV/AIDS?"[11]

BOOKS FROM BRITAIN

Another 1980s innovation was the appearance of American editions of GLBTQ books that had first been published in England. Three British writers—David Rees (whose *In the Tent* is discussed in the previous chapter), Aidan Chambers, and Jean Ure—emerged as significant figures in the 1980s. Of the three, Chambers is the writer of the greatest lasting importance; indeed, his later novel, *Postcards from No Man's Land*, which also explores considerations of sexual identity, was awarded both England's Carnegie Medal and the American Library Association's Michael L. Printz Prize as being the book "that best exemplifies literary excellence in young adult literature."

Rees, however, was the first of these to write about the subject of homosexuality. Like Chambers, Rees was both a novelist and a literary critic. Before his death in 1993 from AIDS, he published nearly two dozen works of fiction for both adult and young adult readers. This habit of writing for two different readerships has resulted in some confusion over which of his four novels about homosexuality were actually written for adolescents. In our estimation only two, *In the Tent*, (discussed in the previous chapter) and *The Milkman's on His Way* (1982) were intended by the author to speak to this readership. The others—*Out of the Winter Gardens* (1984), and *The Colour of His Hair* (1989)—have been regarded as adult titles. They are significant, however, for their inclusion of teen characters and elements of gay community.

Aidan Chambers' *Dance on My Grave* was first published in the U.S. in 1982. The author's intentions to experiment with his narrative strategies and techniques are announced on the title page in the form of the book's extravagant subtitle: *A Life and a Death/In Four Parts/One Hundred and Seventeen Bits/Six Running Reports/and Two Press Clippings/with a few jokes/a puzzle or three/some footnotes/and a fiasco now and then/to help the story along.*

Dance on My Grave is the history of the friendship of two boys, Hal, the narrator, and Barry, who will die in a motorcycle accident, but not before the two boys have become lovers. The title is a reference to a pact they make before Barry's accident: the survivor must dance on the other's grave. This Hal does and is discovered in the act, which is regarded as grave desecration. He is arrested and brought to court, where the judge orders him to be counseled by a social worker. The worker's findings are presented as the "six running reports" of the subtitle. As for the one hundred and seventeen bits, they refer to Hal's brief, first-person chapters that comprise the bulk of the narrative and are, indeed, divided into four parts. The book is bracketed, front and back, by two newspaper clippings with the respective headlines, "Grave Damage" and "Youth's Pact 'To Dance on Friend's Grave.'" All of these disparate bits, pieces, and occasional oddments come together in a cleverly coherent structure that might be called "assemblage," though Chambers himself has referred to his technique as "collages of different ways of telling."[12]

Whether assemblage or collage, the technique reveals not only a great deal about the author's cerebral approach to narration but also about his protagonist, Hal. Barry recognizes that Hal is obsessed with understanding: "That's what you always want, isn't it? To understand." (152) Hal's way of achieving understanding is akin to Chambers': he must translate his experiences into story. (Chambers says, "Until we have re-formed our lives into story-structured words, we cannot find and contemplate the meaning of our lived experiences." [112]) In order to effect that re-formation, Hal conveys a sense of circling events, examining and re-examining them by evoking memories. His life *and* his words seem to be an exercise in continuous circumambulation, his circles becoming ever tighter until, finally, he arrives at the essential eureka moment of understanding.

In the meantime his style of storytelling remains consciously self-conscious, hence, that long, almost whimsical subtitle. His style extends to his manner of speaking, which his social worker describes, thus: "Throughout the conversation he avoided questions he didn't like by giving flippant replies—sometimes genuinely funny." Like many teenagers, Hal uses humor as a distancing device. And this accounts for the jokes, puzzles, footnotes, and self-conscious reference to "a fiasco now and then."

If *Dance on My Grave* is a story of Hal's obsessive need to understand, it is also about his obsessions with friendship and death, both of which are realized in the person of Barry. Barry's death has been criticized as being another example of the "punishment" of homosexuals that was epidemic in the early years of the genre. But this is simplistic. Hal's obsession with death predates his friendship with Barry, who, at one point, says to his friend, "You have death on the brain" (86). This obsession begins when Hal is thirteen and is taken to visit a family grave (a scene that is echoed, some years later, in Chambers' novel *Postcards from No Man's Land*). Barry's life and death become an organic, even inevitable part of the evolution of Hal's obsessive interest in death—and, indeed, in friendship, in memory and in the past, a connection that is made when he and Barry go to see a production of *Hamlet*. Barry comments on the sadness of Hamlet's inability to remember his father; Hal, knowing that Barry's own father is dead, realizes his friend is talking about himself, but the reader will understand that this exchange also refers to the ultimate death of Barry and Hal's reaction to it.

The complexity of the novel extends to its treatment of homosexuality, which seems to be an admixture of love and sex, of power and submission, of obsession and compulsion, of elation and despair, of one thing and another, of certainty . . . and uncertainty. "Maybe I loved him," Hal muses. "How do you ever know?" Clearly, the heart *does* have its reasons that the mind cannot know.

In the richness of its content, in its use of ambiguity and symbol, in the maturity of its uncertainty, *Dance on My Grave* was a significant advance in the evolution of GLBTQ fiction for young adults. It was the first literary novel about homosexuality that, in its artistic ambitions and achievements, remained unrivalled until Francesca Lia Block's *Weetzie Bat* and Chambers' own later novel *Postcards from No Man*

GAY ASSIMILATION

The third English writer under consideration, Jean Ure, wrote two gay-themed novels that found American publication in the 1980s: *You Win Some, You Lose Some* (1984) and *The Other Side of the Fence* (1986). Her books are two of the few examples of gay assimilation titles published during the 1980s. Michael judges the first novel to be the more successful of the two, while Christine prefers the second. *You Win Some, You Lose Some* is the story of seventeen-year-old Jamie, who drops out of school to pursue his dream of becoming a dancer. Ure examines the stereotypes that surround this calling; most people presume that Jamie's desire to dance must mean he's gay (or, in the characters' patois, a "gawker"). In fact, he's not but his flatmate, Steven, is and makes no secret of his desire to have sex with Jamie. This is one of the only YA novels in which a common stereotype—the homosexual who tries to seduce heterosexuals—is depicted, though in an almost casual manner that Jamie clearly finds more humorous than threatening. Ure's light touch in dealing with issues of sexuality in this novel are a welcome relief from the *Sturm und Drang* of so many other titles from this period.

Ure's *The Other Side of the Fence* includes both homosexual visibility and gay assimilation. Its protagonist Richard, eighteen, is kicked out of the house when his odious father discovers the son's homosexuality. On his own and without any means of support for the first time in his heretofore privileged life, Richard picks up a homeless hitchhiker, Bonny, and the two find an abandoned house and move in together. Bonny has just been ditched by her loutish boyfriend, so Richard's polite and unassuming manner are understandably attractive to her. Richard can see she's interested but cannot, at first, bring himself to tell her he is gay. The reader may infer that the fence that divides the two is that of sexual orientation but there is also the matter of class and circumstance: Richard is a child of privilege; Bonny is from a working-class background. On the one hand this is one more YA novel depicting a straight girl's falling for a gay boy. On the other hand, both Bonny and Richard are able to acknowledge the mutual support they have provided for each other, and the two finally part amicably as friends as they each return to improved versions of their pre-runaway lives. Bonny spends most of the book on an ultimately successful quest to find her former foster family who turn out to be a lesbian couple, a fact that is presented but not commented upon.

Norma Klein's third novel of the '80s, *My Life as a Body* (1987), is another novel of gay assimilation in which protagonist Augustine's best high school friend is Claudia, who "claims she's known since she was five that she was gay"(5). Later, when she goes to college, Augie's best friend will be Gordon ("I knew he was gay. But everyone here seemed pretty up-front about the gay thing" [178]). Both Claudia and Gordon are notable for their "directness," their "cut-the-crap kind of honesty" (178), traits they share with their creator. In this book, as in other works by Klein, characters are defined or evaluated in part on the basis of their sexual activity and by how liberated their thinking about it is. Augie, who has a sexual relationship with a physically disabled male classmate in high school and with one of her male professors in college, embodies this attitude when she thinks, "I learned that you can make love with someone you're fond of without 'falling' or being in love. There didn't seem to be any price tag, no talk of future, of promises, of ultimate decisions" (243).

Marilyn Si   tooth
(1983) is anothe   www.ppnne.org | 1-866-476-1321   '80s.
Becky, the prota   Iemi
(short for Neher   Mid-
summer Night's]   cters
they play in act   ng a
problem that m   ome
cast members tl   and
Craig, must con   ; is a
quietly engagin;   Iemi
(who finally re   ;ood
friends") and th   their
respective obsta   ving
weathered some

QU

Although young adult novels published in the 1980s include significantly more evidence of queer community than those of the 1970s, isolation is still common. Many of the places where readers find hints of a fictional gay community are off-stage and often in the past. This has been particularly true for YA novels depicting HIV or AIDS. In M.E. Kerr's *Night Kites,* for example, Erick's older brother Pete, who has lived in New York City after college, returns to the family home to die. The reader learns that Pete's life in New York included work as a teacher and writer and much socializing with other gay men in bars and at parties. Pete tells his younger brother about the thrill of moving to New York City after graduating from college: "When I saw all the gay bars and discos here, I just wanted to dance and drink and play" (96). But all of that is in the past and none of it is visible to Erick or the reader.

The gay community is also definitely located in the past in David Rees' *Out of the Winter Gardens* (1984), in which sixteen-year-old Michael gets to know his gay father, whose absence from Michael's childhood was due to his mother's refusal to allow contact between them (also the theme of Sonya Sones' much later novel *One of Those Hideous Books Where the Mother Dies*). When Michael arrives for his first visit, his father's partner immediately moves out, and the father is certain that he will spend the rest of his life alone. But he reminisces wistfully about their years together, full of "parties and mutual friends, holidays in California and the Greek islands, dancing at discos" (54). But it's all in the past.

In addition to gay male loners (*all* single GLBTQ adults in *all* of these books are male), there are also gay/lesbian couples, but most are portrayed as a singular unit with no connections to other gay/lesbian people. In Madeleine L'Engle's *A House Like a Lotus* (1984), for example, Max and her partner Ursula live in an isolated mansion on the unpopulated end of a remote island. The adult lesbian couple in Catherine Brett's *S.P. Likes A.D.* (1989) is another singular unit, though in this case they live openly as a couple in an urban setting among (straight) friends and colleagues. Likewise, although Liza and Annie (in Nancy Garden's *Annie on My Mind*) are becoming aware of a larger gay/lesbian community as they read *Patience and Sarah*—a lesbian love story—and hunger for more evidence of kindred spirits, when Ms. Stevenson and Ms. Widmer (the lesbian teachers at Liza's school) are fired because of their relationship, they make their final appearance in the novel as they prepare to move from their long-time home in New York City. Despite the fact that they have lived in the city for more than twenty years, the partners are pictured in an apartment full of cardboard boxes but devoid of other people. How realistic would it be for an intelligent and sociable lesbian couple to have lived in Brooklyn Heights for two decades and to have no friends to help them pack? In this case, the community that Liza and Annie were so heartened to read about in New York's gay newspapers is no longer in evidence when it's time to help the teachers move.

Like Liza and Annie, some GLBTQ characters see no queer community in their present lives, but staunchly—or wistfully—hope that there will be a queer community in their future. For example, in Hila Colman's *Happily Ever After* (1986), Melanie believes that she and her childhood sweetheart Paul will eventually become lovers. As noted earlier, when Paul comes out to her, she feels a personal sense of loss as her dream of marriage falls apart. She and Paul talk about the future, and she asks him if he is thinking about college. He says, "I want to go to a place that has a gay group on campus." Melanie's heart thumped—"Why?"

"Why not? I feel so darn alone—I want to be with other guys like myself. It's natural, isn't it?"

"I thought you wanted to keep it secret. . . ."

"Around here, yes. But not outside, not forever" (131).

To Paul, his vision of future happiness is closely linked to his finding a community. Melanie, however, views Paul's gayness as a tragic disability as she mournfully tells him, "'Paul, I hope you will be happy.' 'Don't cry for me,' he said gently. 'I know it's not going to be easy. But I'm not alone. I'll find someone someday'" (168). Alas, if "someday" happens, it will be well after the close of the book.

Other novels of the 1980s provide the protagonist—and the reader—with tantalizingly brief glimpses of Queer Community. In Barbara Wersba's *Crazy Vanilla* , for example, when protagonist Tyler phones his gay older brother Cameron to talk, the brother and his lover are in the midst of "having a few friends over for cocktails" (128). This brief telephone conversation is the closest the reader gets to Cameron's world. And at that point, Tyler finds the distance between his family's Long Island suburb and New York unbridgeable.

Wersba provides another snippet of gay community in her 1988 novel *Just Be Gorgeous*. As noted, Heidi, a straight teen, befriends Jeffrey, a gay street kid who lives in an abandoned building and supports himself by tap-dancing to show tunes on street corners. Although his day-to-day life in New York City is precarious, Jeffrey's stubborn faith in his own future as a star impresses Heidi, who is deeply skeptical of her own ability to succeed at any endeavor. Their friendship is the mutual attraction of two loners who each find a supportive listener in the other. Heidi is drawn to Jeffrey for his openness to friendship and self-confidence in the face of a series of obstacles. "It doesn't matter what people think of you—it only matters what you think of yourself" (63). As also noted earlier, Jeffrey eventually makes other friends, Peter and Eugene, a gay couple whose couch becomes his temporary bed. Jealous of the friendship, Heidi—invited to their apartment for dinner—is prepared to dislike them but finds them both articulate and likeable. "I could not hate them—but at the same time, something told me that they were replacing me, that they were providing Jeffrey with the one thing I could not give him: a home" (146). The book ends as Jeffrey drives off to Los Angeles—and a new life—with his gay friends.

Several novels of the 1980s depict gay bars, but there is little evidence of the friendliness of Tim and Ray's gay pub from *In the Tent*. For example, in Snyder and Pelletier's *Counter Play* (1981), Alex self-identifies as gay but has never met any other gay people. One night he visits Kelly's Place, a gay bar, steeling himself by thinking, "This was his future, these people, his kind. . . . Alex looked at the dancers. Men with men. Some in leather jackets, some with tank tops, most virile, very masculine-looking. A few tables of obviously straight couples, men and women, ogled the dancers, laughed somewhat furtively behind their hands, whispered, gawked" (94). While not frightening, this image of gay community is hardly inviting.

Mike, the protagonist of B.A. Ecker's *Independence Day* (1983), has known he was gay since he was fifteen but has told no one. When he and his best friend take a weekend trip to New York City, he marvels as they walk down a Greenwich Village street: "There are many men walking these streets holding hands. No one is looking at them. They share secrets and laughter together and it makes me feel good to watch them. I have the feeling of home in this place. This is where I want to live; where I'll be judged on other things besides my sexual preference" (106). Later that evening he walks into a gay bar, sees men standing around a piano singing, and spots the friend who told him about the bar. "I feel better than I have in the past year. I feel like I belong. . . . It's been a strange night. I feel that the old me has died and left everything behind him. Where do I fit into all of this? Will my life be spent in hallways with quick, furtive kisses and hugs? Or will I someday be comfortable enough with the knowledge of who I am to be able to love in the open?" (111). That night he dreams he is knocking at the door of his home, but his family won't let him in. For Mike, finding a community could mean losing his family.

This juxtaposition of gay community and family as polar opposites is another common element in YA books with gay/lesbian content. In David Rees' *The Milkman's on His Way* (1982), a gay teen, Euen, lives a lonely life as a townie in a resort village, where he waits with waning patience for the end of his schooling and the beginning of adulthood and his future as a gay man. When he encounters a group of men on holiday at the beach, he can see for the first time what a world of out friends would look like. Although the visitors soon return to London, Euen is reassured by this evidence that he, too, will find kindred spirits when he finally leaves home, which is, indeed, the case.

In Mosca's *All-American Boys,* Neil and Paul socialize with an older gay couple, are invited to the men's anniversary party, and discover an active gay-lesbian center at the college they attend. In two 1988 books, Norma Klein's *Now That I Know* and Ron Koertge's *The Arizona Kid,* straight teen protagonists attend parties hosted by their gay father and uncle, respectively. In both cases, the narrators are the youngest people there—and while they are made welcome, the queer community they visit is adults only.

Lastly, just as *In the Tent* was a 1970s text that was a harbinger of the 1980s, so might Francesca Lia Block's *Weetzie Bat* be viewed as a preview of the more GLBTQ community-friendly 1990s, for Weetzie's friends Dirk and Duck meet, fall in love, and construct a community of their own in L.A. composed of friends of various backgrounds and sexualities. Though, as previously noted, Duck panics in the face of AIDS and flees to San Francisco, he is followed by Dirk, who finally tracks him down in a gay bar, where he spots him across the dance floor:

"Who was that beautiful blonde boy? Love is a dangerous angel, Dirk thought. Especially nowadays. It was Duck. Out of all the bars and all the nights and all the people and all the moments, Dirk had found Duck." (84–85).

Tenderly reunited, the two return to a "purple, smoggy L.A. twilight," take their places in the circle of their loved ones around the dinner table "lit up and golden like a wreath of lights," and are embraced by the people who are both their chosen family *and* community (87–88).

GAY AND LESBIAN NOVELS OF THE 1980s

(Again, "HV" stands for Homosexual Visibility; "GA" stands for Gay Assimilation; "QC" stands for Queer Consciousness/Community; "Gay" refers to novels with male GLBTQ content; "Lesbian," to novels with female GLBTQ content.)

1980

Hanlon, Emily. *The Wing and the Flame.* Bradbury. 160 pages.

>HV. Gay. During his fourteenth summer, Eric and his long-time friend Chris befriend a reclusive 71-year-old sculptor who lives nearby. As the summer progresses, the boys' relationship becomes physical—and a bit mystical—in a story told largely in flashbacks by the now nineteen-year-old narrator.

Klein, Norma. *Breaking Up.* Random House. 224 pages

>HV. Lesbian. Fifteen-year-old Alison spends the summer with her father and his new wife, but then gets caught in a custody battle when her father learns that her mother and another woman are more than "just good friends." The first young adult novel to include a gay parent.

Reading, J. P. *Bouquets for Brimbal.* Harper & Row. 186 pages.

>HV. Lesbian. Macy Beacon and Annie Brimbal are long-time best friends, but their relationship is strained during months in summer stock theater when each has her first serious romantic relationship: Macy with a man and Annie with a woman.

Tolan, Stephanie S. *The Last of Eden.* Warne. 154 pages.

>HV. Lesbian. Michelle "Mike" Caine, 15, enters Turnbull Hall, a girls' boarding school, and anticipates an edenic environment of warmth and camaraderie. She develops a close friendship with Marty, her artistically gifted but unstable roommate. Several crises— and a classmate's failed suicide attempt—later, Marty leaves Turnbull, and Mike is relieved to learn from her English teacher that same-sex attractions are a normal stage on the way to heterosexual adulthood.

1981

Bargar, Gary W. *What Happened To Mr. Forster?* Clarion. 169 pages.

>HV. Gay. Louis Lamb begins sixth grade determined to become a Somebody with his classmates. Mr. Forster, his kind-hearted and perceptive teacher, helps make this happen, but—in a story set in Kansas in 1958—Mr. Forster is fired for being gay. The first YA novel with GLBTQ content to feature a working gay teacher.

Futcher, Jane. *Crush.* Little, Brown. 255 pages.

>HV. Lesbian. Jinx Tuckwell is a senior (class of 1965) at an exclusive girl's boarding school when she becomes attracted to Lexie Yves, a

wild and beautiful classmate with a taste for crazy escapades. To no one's surprise, Lexie leads the willing Jinx astray, and in doing so, manages to get both of them expelled from school. Jinx is left wondering what happened and why, so she sits down to write this story.

Levy, Elizabeth. *Come Out Smiling*. Delacorte. 186 pages.

HV. Lesbian. Fourteen-year-old Jenny is happy to be spending the summer at Camp Sacajawea, but she is disturbed to learn that Peggy, subject of Jenny's longtime unspoken crush, and another counselor are in a lesbian relationship. Does the intensity of her feelings for Peggy mean that Jenny is a lesbian, too?

St. George, Judith. *Call Me Margo*. G.P. Putnam's Sons. 173 pages.

HV. Lesbian. Margo, fifteen, is a new student at the Haywood School—yet another girls' boarding school. Margo is initially lonely but when Miss Frye, the school's attractive tennis coach, gives her support and encouragement, Margo's game and self-confidence blossom. But even these positive developments are called into question when Margo learns that Miss Frye and Miss Durrett (her unpleasant and disabled English teacher) are not only lesbians, but former lovers as well.

Snyder, Anne and Louis Pelletier. *Counter Play*. New American Library/Signet (reissued in 1987 as *The Truth About Alex*). 166 pages.

HV. Gay. High school star quarterback Brad, seventeen, discovers his best friend and pass receiver Alex is gay. Brad adjusts to this news but then learns that his friendship with a "queer" will cost him a West Point appointment and that sometimes doing the right thing can be very difficult indeed. The first gay sports story.

1982

Bunn, Scott. *Just Hold On*. Delacorte. 160 pages.

HV. Gay. A somewhat gothic story of two troubled teens, Charlotte and Stephen, who are both saddled with highly dysfunctional fathers: Charlotte's is molesting her, while Stephen's is drinking himself to death. And yes, Stephen's father coincidentally dies of a heart attack the morning after his son has sex with another boy.

Garden, Nancy. *Annie on My Mind*. Farrar Straus & Giroux. 234 pages.

HV. Lesbian. A classic work that tells the exquisitely nuanced story of Annie and Liza, two high school girls who meet and fall in love. When their relationship is made public, a homophobic school board mistakenly assume that the girls have been led astray by two of Liza's teachers, who are a lesbian couple. "'Don't let ignorance win,' said Ms. Stevenson. 'Let love.'" The first GLBTQ love story with a positive ending.

Hulse, Larry. *Just the Right Amount of Wrong.* Harper & Row. 215 pages.

HV. Gay. Set in a little Kentucky town in 1958, this disturbing novel features the new school principal, a likeable bachelor, and the good old boy sheriff, an unlikable bachelor. When small-town gossip threatens to reveal their secret affair, the treacherous sheriff murders the trusting principal. Told through the eyes of thirteen-year-old Jerry, the inadvertent witness to the whole sorry mess.

1983

Chambers, Aidan. *Dance on My Grave.* Harper & Row. 253 pages.

HV. Gay. Originally published in England, this interesting, ambitious novel charts the evolution of Hal and Barry's romance, which ends tragically with Barry's death in a motorcycle accident.

Ecker, B. A. *Independence Day.* Avon/Flare. 205 pages.

HV. Gay. Sixteen-year-old Mike realizes he's attracted to his best friend and soccer teammate Todd. When Mike finally comes out to his friend, Todd (who is straight) offers to help Mike come out to his parents, and the two take a field trip to New York City's Greenwich Village so that Mike can start getting to know his future community.

Kesselman, Wendy Ann. *Flick.* Harper & Row. 136 pages.

HV. Lesbian. Nana, a shy loner, spends the summer at her school's riding camp and falls in love with Flick, a charming temptress. To no one's surprise but Nana's, Flick seduces and dumps her, but at the end of the story, Nana still maintains a wistful longing for the heartless Flick.

Mosca, Frank. *All-American Boys.* Alyson. 116 pages.

HV. QC. Gay. Neil falls for Paul, the new boy in town, and the feeling is mutual. When Paul is hospitalized due to being fag-bashed by homophobic classmates, Neil exacts a hard-hitting revenge and teaches them a lesson: never bash a gay teen whose boyfriend has a black belt in karate. The book's revenge fantasy elements are partly redeemed by the inclusion of elements of gay community.

Singer, Marilyn. *The Course of True Love Never Did Run Smooth*. Harper & Row. 246 pages.

> HV. GA. Gay. Becky and her best friend Nemi (short for Nehemiah) are part of a high school theater production of *A Midsummer Night's Dream*. As the show moves toward opening night, various cast and crew members find their true loves, including Richie and Craig, (aka Oberon and Demetrius) and (predictably) Becky and Nemi. As in the play itself, every couple's story has a happy ending.

1984

L'Engle, Madeleine. *A House Like a Lotus*. Farrar, Straus Giroux. 307 pages.

> HV. Lesbian. Gawky seventeen-year-old Polly finds a mentor in Maximiliana Horne, a beautiful, rich, and terminally ill painter who lives nearby with her partner Ursula, a world-famous neurosurgeon. One night, however, Max gets drunk on the alcohol she uses to dull the pain of her illness and makes a pass at Polly. Several months later, Polly finally decides to reconcile with the dying Max.

Ure, Jean. *You Win Some, You Lose Some*. Delacorte. 182 pages.

> GA. Gay. First published in England, this is the story of sixteen-year-old Jamie, who moves to London in hopes of entering ballet school, which means—according to his mates—that he must be gay. He isn't, though his gay roommate Steven cheerfully tries to convince him otherwise.

1985

Bess, Clayton. *Big Man and the Burn-Out*. Houghton Mifflin. 197 pages.

> HV. GA. Gay. Jess is attracted to an older boy, Meechum (the burn-out of the title) who has difficulty with authority figures and is well on his way to failing eighth grade....again! Their English teacher Mr. Goodban, who is gay and lives with his male partner Vic, is impressed by Meechum's writing talent and helps him turn his academic and emotional life around.

1986

Colman, Hila. *Happily Ever After*. Scholastic Point. 154 pages.

> HV. Gay. Melanie has known since she was in second grade that she would grow up to marry Paul—until he tells her he's gay. After

some initial estrangement, the two reconcile and their friendship is actually strengthened through the new honesty between them.

Kerr, M. E. *Night Kites.* Harper & Row. 216 pages.

HV. Gay. Erick's older brother Pete, a teacher and science fiction writer who has been living in New York, comes home to tell his family the devastating news that he is gay and has AIDS. When Pete's condition becomes public knowledge, Erick is shunned by his friends, rejected by his girlfriend, and must face the impending death of Pete. The first young adult novel to deal with the disease.

Meyer, Carolyn. *Elliott and Win.* McElderry. 187 pages.

HV. Gay. Win is disappointed when he meets his new Amigo (read "Big Brother") Elliott, who hates team sports, loves opera, and does not even *own* a television set. Elliott fits a number of gay stereotypes, but his orientation is never made explicit, and Win learns that friendship is more important than fitting a traditional masculine mold.

Sakers, Don. *Act Well Your Part.* Alyson. 181 pages.

HV. Gay. Keith wonders if he will ever fit in at his new high school, but when he joins the Drama Club he meets an attractive boy and the two fall in love. But when they decide to attend the school's Winter Dance together, their relationship becomes public, which some of their friends find troubling.

Ure, Jean. *The Other Side of the Fence.* Delacorte. 164 pages.

HV. Gay. Eighteen-year-old Richard leaves home after a quarrel with his parents and picks up hitchhiker Bonny, a tart-tongued working-class teen who is also running away. Their unlikely friendship is based on honesty, which in turn helps both deal with their reasons for running away. For Richard, this means confronting his parents' disapproval of his sexual orientation. First published in England.

Wersba, Barbara. *Crazy Vanilla.* Harper & Row. 178 pages.

HV. Gay. Tyler Woodruff's singular passion for nature photography helps him cope with the estrangement he feels from his family: his father (who believes photographing birds is for sissies), his mother (who is an active alcoholic) and his older brother Cameron (who has been banished from the family for being gay and becoming an interior decorator). His friendship with a fellow nature photographer, the brash and outspoken Mitzi Gerrard, helps him reconcile with Cameron.

1987

Klein, Norma. *My Life as a Body*. Knopf. 256 pages.

HV. GA. Gay and Lesbian. Shy and intelligent Augie (short for Augustine) falls in love with Sam, a boy who is disabled as a result of an auto accident. As Sam slowly recovers, their relationship begins to change. Augie's best friends are an out lesbian and an equally out gay male college classmate ("everyone here seemed pretty up front about the gay thing."). The first YA novel to feature both gay and lesbian characters.

Rinaldi, Ann. The Good Side of My Heart. Holiday House. 284 pages.

HV. Gay. Sixteen-year-old Brie is devastated when she learns that Josh, the good-looking boy she is in love with, is gay. Her brother, the priest, tells her to "hate the sin but love the sinner," and Brie finally finds it in her heart to be friends with Josh.

1988

Klein, Norma. *Now That I Know*. Bantam. 165 pages.

HV. Gay. Nina's parents have been divorced for years and she is happy with their joint custody arrangement until her father tells her that he is gay and that his boyfriend (whom she previously liked) will be moving in with him. Her initial response is rejection, but with the help of her new boyfriend, whose brother is gay, she eventually reconciles with her father—and his partner.

Koertge, Ron. *The Arizona Kid*. Joy Street Little, Brown. 228 pages.

HV. GA. Gay. Billy, sixteen, is spending the summer with his gay Uncle Wes, who is also an AIDS activist. Wes' self-acceptance and his warm regard for his nephew come through strongly, as does life in a gay community that is facing the AIDS crisis. This book is one of the first YA novels to include gay "camp" humor.

Wersba, Barbara. *Just Be Gorgeous*. Zolotow/Harper & Row. 156 pages.

HV. Gay. Heidi, sixteen, is a lonely private school student who learns "how the other half lives" when she meets—and falls for—Jeffrey, a flamboyantly gay street kid. He's out to her from the beginning, but still, it hurts when he makes gay friends and there is no longer a place for Heidi in Jeffrey's new life.

1989

Block, Francesca Lia. *Weetzie Bat.* Zolotow/Harper & Row. 88 pages

> HV. Gay. This punk fairy tale set in contemporary Los Angeles features Weetzie, a straight girl with a bleached-blond flat-top and pink Harlequin sunglasses; Dirk, a gay boy with a shoe-polish-black Mohawk and a red '55 Pontiac; and their extended family of parents, children, friends, and lovers. When Dirk comes out to Weetzie, her salutary reaction—"It doesn't matter one bit honey-honey" accompanied by a hug—is ground-breaking. "Love is a dangerous angel."

Brett, Catherine. *S.P. Likes A.D.* The Women's Press. 119 pages.

> HV. Lesbian. Thirteen-year-old Stephanie Powell is aware of—and confused by—the crush she has on Anne Delaney, a classmate she barely knows. Stephanie's world includes an older lesbian couple, a gay art teacher, and her good friend Devi, who is unfazed by Stephanie's same-sex attraction even as she asks "Why Anne Delaney? She's sort of a jerk."

Childress, Alice. *Those Other People.* Putnam. 186 pages.

> HV. Gay. Jonathan, seventeen, is gay and happily in the closet while he works as a high school computer teacher. When Jonathan inadvertently witnesses a popular male teacher molesting a female student and his former boyfriend threatens to out Jonathan to his school administration if he testifies against the teacher, Jonathan must decide how to do the right thing.

Homes, A. M. *Jack.* Macmillan. 208 pages.

> HV. Gay. When his divorced father tells Jack that he is now in a committed relationship with another man, Jack is furious, but eventually comes around, helped in part by the fact that his girlfriend also has a gay father. Jack narrates this wryly humorous and realistic treatment of his journey from anger to acceptance.

Shannon, George. *Unlived Affections.* Zolotow/Harper & Row. 135 pages.

> HV. Gay. Willie believes that his father is dead but when his grandmother dies, he discovers a cache of letters written by his father to Willie's mother, who died when he was two. Through reading the letters, Willie learns some unsettling truths, including the fact that his father was gay.

NOTES

1. "Flying Starts," *Publishers Weekly.* December 22, 1989.

2. Wilson, David E. "The Open Library: YA Books for Gay Teens." *English Journal.* 73:2 (November 1984).

3. Wilson, David E. "Advocating Young Adult Novels with Gay Themes." Reprinted in *The Education Digest.* 52:2 (October 1986).

4. Goodman, Jan. "Out of the Closet, But Paying the Price." *Interracial Books for Children Bulletin.* 14:3&4. 1983.

5. Kissen, Rita M. *The Last Closet: The Real Lives of Lesbian and Gay Teachers.* Portsmouth, NH: Heinemann. 1996.

6. Garden, Nancy. E-mail to co-author, September 14, 1999.

7. 2003 Margaret A. Edwards Award Winner, Nancy Garden. http://www.ala .org/yalsa/booklistsawards/margaretaedwards/maeprevious/2003nancygarden.htm

8. Perrotti, Jeff and Kim Westheimer. *When the Drama Club Is Not Enough.* Boston: Beacon Press, 2001. (The omnipresence of drama and acting in YA GLBTQ novels was wryly alluded to in the title of this informative study of Massachusetts' groundbreaking Safe Schools Program.)

9. Kerr, M.E. "1993 Margaret A. Edwards Award Acceptance Speech." *Journal of Youth Services in Libraries.* 7:1 (Fall 1993).

10. Walter, Virginia A. and Melissa Gross. *HIV/AIDS Information for Children: A Guide to Issues and Resources.* NY: H.W. Wilson, 1996.

11. Gross, Melissa. "What Do Young Adult Novels Say about HIV/AIDS?" *Library Quarterly.* 68:1 (January 1998).

12. Chambers, Aidan. "Ways of Telling." In *Booktalk: Occasional Writing on Literature and Children.* NY: Harper & Row, 1985.

· 4 ·

The 1990s: Was More Less?

$\mathcal{A}$s we have seen, GLBTQ literature for young adults—like the larger body of young adult literature to which it belongs—does not exist in a vacuum. Though there is a tendency to "ghettoize" it, GLBTQ literature remains a reflection of trends in the larger world of publishing (for both teens *and* adults) and of prevailing cultural, social, economic, and political attitudes. Thus, one can read this literature to learn something of the contemporaneus society's views on and responses to homosexuality—or at least to learn what publishers believe, however correctly or incorrectly, will appeal to teen readers.

For example, pivotal scenes in two novels, both published in 1990, illustrate the broad range of coming-out narratives and of attitudes toward GLBTQ people and their lives that would be represented in the literature published throughout the nineties. They also reflect the wide spectrum of attitudes toward GLBTQ people in the larger society. In the first, Joyce Sweeney's *Face the Dragon*, Paul comes out to his best friend Eric as they walk on a deserted beach:

> "I'm different from you . . . [Paul said] For a while I wasn't even sure about this, but lately, and especially after last night . . . I'm just not very interested in . . . girls."
>
> It was so sudden, Eric didn't get it. "Well, you probably . . ." Then he did get it. "What do you mean?" he asked warily.
>
> Paul wouldn't look at him now. "You know what I mean."
>
> "You're crazy. I've known you all your life. I'd know if you were like that."
>
> "How would you know? If I never said anything, you wouldn't know. You just said you didn't have a clue how I felt about that stuff.

Well, now I'm telling you. When I think about that stuff, I think about . . . the wrong people. . . ."

"Well, if I were you, I'd try to keep my options open. I'm saying it because you're talking about something that's risky and dangerous and makes your whole life a million times harder than it has to be. So if there is a way out, I think you should look for it." (102)

Eric's response to Paul makes it clear that the isolation Paul feels is based on an accurate reading of his peers' probable responses to his coming-out. No wonder all of his statements are negative and/or coded. He states what he isn't rather than what he is: he's "not very interested in girls," he thinks about "the wrong people." Eric is more forthright when he says he'd know if Paul were "like that," and follows this up with his own positive images (not favorable, but describing homosexuality by what it *is* rather than what it *isn't*). But his images are all gloomy stereotypes based on common images of gay men during the early years of the AIDS epidemic. Eric, the instant expert, declares that homosexuality is risky, dangerous, and will make Paul's life "a million times harder that it has to be," and urges him to turn himself into a heterosexual. And finally, though this is clearly a coming-out scene, Paul and Eric somehow manage never to utter the "G" word, much less the "F" word, the "H" word, or the "Q" word.

In Paul Robert Walker's *The Method*, the fifteen-year-old protagonist Albie participates in an intensive high school summer workshop in the techniques of method acting (yes, this is another gay-themed novel set in the theater), where he meets a new friend, Mitch. Toward the end of the book, Mitch takes Albie to a gay pride parade and from there to a crowded gay restaurant, where Mitch comes out to Albie over chocolate sodas. Albie reacts with laughter, to which Mitch responds:

"I'm sorry that it makes you nervous, Albie. But I want you to know. I'm gay. I'm queer. I'm a faggot. I'm a homosexual. This is not a joke. This is my life."

Albie . . . turned toward Mitch and asked, "Why are you telling me this?"

"I need to."

"How do you know? I mean, about being . . . you know . . . gay?"

"I know. Believe me. Albie, there's something I want to ask you, and I want you to be completely honest. Will you do that? Are we still friends?"

> Albie reached out and covered Mitch's hand with his own. "You know we are." (137–138)

In a refreshing contrast to *Face the Dragon*'s Paul, Mitch simply tells Albie he's gay, and when Albie responds with nervous laughter, Mitch restates "I'm gay" and follows this with a list of the other descriptors, negative, positive, and neutral, commonly used to describe gay people. Mitch is going to make *sure* that Albie understands him in whatever language Albie uses. The other clear contrast between these two scenes is in their settings. Paul and Eric walk on a lonely beach, a setting that reinforces the lonely life that Paul has led, and apparently will continue to lead in the future. For Paul there is no one, no community, no friends with whom he can be honest. He is an archetypical homosexual as sad-eyed loner. Mitch, on the other hand, has taken Albie to a gay pride parade and then to a gay restaurant. They are literally surrounded by gay people and Mitch is not declaring his loner-hood, but is instead showing Albie where he *does* belong. And Albie responds by making affectionate but nonsexual physical contact with Mitch, which is the most direct way he can demonstrate his okayness with Mitch's gay identity.

Unfortunately, the images of GLBTQ people in many of the YA novels published to date are limited and/or stereotypic—definitely more like the pain-filled outsider Paul than the refreshingly confident Mitch. Whether such negative depictions are preferable to invisibility is subject to debate but, happily, some books have included realistic GLBTQ characters who are integral to the plot and whose stories even provide the novel's central narrative.

THE NEGATIVE SIDE OF SEXUALITY— STRAIGHT *AND* GAY

When YA literature of the sixties and seventies portrayed heterosexual intimacy between teens, the health consequences were predictable. Even if the sexual act occurred only once, girls almost inevitably got pregnant. They then had several options: if the pregnant girl were a secondary character, she would often simply disappear from the story. If she had a steady boyfriend, the two might get married, to the chagrin of all, including themselves. If she had no steady boyfriend, the girl might get an abortion, which was likely to leave her either dead or permanently barren. There are, of course, exceptions to these fictional scenarios, but the majority followed the course(s) described above.

As for same-sex sexual activity, the most frequent unintended health consequence of it in YA novels of the 1980s and the 1990s was, of course, AIDS, which—in these novels—only males contracted. However, no matter how widespread or unremitting the disease at that time, AIDS-related literature has remained a very modest sub-genre of GLBTQ literature. As previously noted, only three novels (out of 40) from the eighties (*Night Kites, The Arizona Kid,* and *Weetzie Bat*) dealt with the subject in any way. In the nineties, only thirteen novels (out of 70) included *any* character who was HIV-positive or had AIDS. Since then, with the exception of Alex Sanchez's *Rainbow Boys* (2001) and *Rainbow High* (2004), the subject has scarcely been mentioned, despite the fact that AIDS remains an epidemic problem among young people. In fact, according to the Advocates for Youth web site "half of all new HIV infections occur in people under age 25."[2] Yet of these AIDS-related titles from the nineties, only one—*My Brother Has AIDS* by Deborah Davis (1994)—features a young adult as the infected character. And among *all* the AIDS-related titles within this body of YA literature, the character who is HIV-positive or has AIDS is never the protagonist. Judging from these novels, teen readers could assume that AIDS only infects adults—usually uncles or teachers.

Another negative aspect of sex, the sexual act as violence or as an abuse of power, was first addressed in 1976 in Richard Peck's influential young adult novel about heterosexual rape, *Are You in the House Alone?* Two years later, Sandra Scoppettone's *Happy Endings Are All Alike* depicts the rape of a young lesbian by a deranged young man who insists that seeing Jaret and her female partner make love drove him to beat and rape Jaret. This could be seen as another example of a girl's being punished for being sexually active: if she can't get pregnant from the sex she is having, she gets raped instead. Sexual abuse in the form of forced (i.e., nonconsensual) gay sex was the subject of Catherine Atkins' novel *When Jeff Comes Home* (1999). Four years later the subject of same-sex rape was first addressed in Kathleen Jeffrie Johnson's *Target* (2003). Another form of sexual abuse, incest, was off-limits to YA authors for years. It was subtly included in Scott Bunn's *Just Hold On* (1982) as the probable cause of Charlotte's eventual mental breakdown (see Chapter Three), but it was not introduced as the central focus of a YA novel until Hadley Irwin's *Abby, My Love* (1985). Several other novels on this subject—including Ruth White's *Weeping Willow* (1992) and Francesca Lia Block's *The Hanged Man* (1994)—have since appeared; in every case the stories have focused on a girl and an abusive, older male relative.

When we turn our attention to the world of young adult literature as a whole, it's evident that the decade of the nineties was one of profound change. Though pronounced near death by most observers at the beginning of the decade, the form made a remarkable recovery and by 1995 was entering a period of expansion, creative growth, and literary sophistication that has continued to the present day.[3] Among the indicators of YA literature's artistic maturity was the 1999 establishment of the Michael L. Printz Award by ALA's Young Adult Library Services Association (YALSA). Like the Newbery and Caldecott Awards, the Printz Award is based on literary merit and is a solid acknowledgement that young adult literature has finally come of age *as literature*. The expansiveness of the book categories eligible for the Printz reflect not only the new maturity of the literature but also the many innovations that are enriching its content. For example, the eligibility of books first published in other countries signals the expansion of the YA field beyond U.S. borders to all English-language titles, while the specifically stated eligibility of poetry, short story collections, and graphic novels demonstrates the creative reach of young adult literature into forms and genres beyond that of contemporary realism.

GLBTQ NONFICTION

GLBTQ YA nonfiction has been a bit slower to emerge than fiction. The first YA nonfiction book about gay/lesbian life, Frances Hanckel and John Cunningham's *A Way of Love, A Way of Life* (Lothrop, Lee, & Shepard) didn't appear until 1979, ten years after *I'll Get There*. Since then, however, progress has been made. The number of nonfiction titles gradually increased throughout the 1980s, but the real blossoming of the form came about in the 1990s.

YA nonfiction books with GLBTQ content fall into two principal categories: (1) informational/advice books aimed at teen readers and (2) first- and third-person accounts of the lives of GLBTQ teens and adults.

A Way of Love, A Way of Life fell into the first category, as did another of the earliest, the first U.S. edition of *Young, Gay, and Proud!* edited by Don Romesburg (Alyson, 1980), a text that was originally published in Australia. U.S. editions continued to be revised and republished, with the fourth and (thus far) final edition of *Young, Gay and Proud!* appearing in 1995. More recent informational/advice titles from both mainstream and alternative presses include: *Passages of Pride: Lesbian and Gay Youth Come of Age*, by Kurt Chandler (Times Books, 1995); *Joining the Tribe: Growing Up Gay and Lesbian in the '90s* by Linnea Due (Anchor, 1995); *The Journey Out: A Guide for and about Lesbian, Gay and Bisexual Teens* by Rachel Pollack and Cheryl Schwartz (Viking, 1995); *The World Out There: Becoming Part of the Lesbian and Gay Community* by Michael Thomas Ford (New Press, 1996); *Free Your Mind: The Book for Gay, Lesbian, and Bisexual Youth—And Their Allies* by Ellen Bass and Kate Kaufman (HarperCollins, 1996); *Growing Up Gay in America: Informative and Practical Advice for Teen Guys Questioning Their Sexuality and Growing Up Gay* by Jason Rich (Franklin Street Books, 2002); and *GLBTQ: The Survival Guide for Queer and Questioning Teens* by Kelly Huegel (Free Spirit Publishing, 2003).

The second category of nonfiction features first- and third-person narratives that focus on one or more GLBTQ individuals' lives. The first-person narratives include interviews, memoirs, and autobiographical accounts of the lives and experiences of GLBTQ youth and adults. The earliest teen-focused autobiography/memoir was the widely read *Reflections of a Rock Lobster: A Story About Growing Up Gay*, by Aaron Fricke (Alyson Publications, 1981), the teen who successfully challenged his high school for the right to bring a same-sex date to the prom. The earliest autobiography/memoir anthology was Ann Heron's *One Teenager in Ten: Writings by Gay and Lesbian Youth* (Alyson, 1983), which was later revised and re-titled *Two Teenagers in Twenty* (Alyson, 1995). Roger Sutton's more diverse and authoritative book, *Hearing Us Out: Voices from the Gay and Lesbian Community* (Little, Brown, 1994), featured photos and interviews with gay/lesbian people representing a range of ages, backgrounds, and experiences. More recent titles in this category include *The Shared Heart: Portraits and Stories Celebrating Lesbian, Gay, and Bisexual Young People*, Photographs by Adam Mastoon (HarperCollins, 1997), *In Your Face: Stories from the Lives of Queer Youth* by Mary L. Gray (Harrington Park Press, 1999), and *Revolutionary Voices: A Multicultural Queer Youth Anthology,* edited by Amy Sonnie (Alyson, 2000). Nearly all of these titles feature photographs of GLBTQ youth, thereby literally giving faces to this previously invisible group.

Third-person accounts (i.e., biographies) are also included in this category. Biographies of GLBTQ public figures have tended to leave their subjects' sexual orientation hidden from history and from their readers. This is not to say that the subject's gay identity should or would overshadow all other aspects of the subject's life, but all too often well-known figures who were openly gay have had their lives "tidied up" or have been identified as bachelors or spinsters who were either too busy with their accomplishments to have time for romance or were in lifelong mourning for an early lost love (of the opposite sex). A vivid illustration of this phenomenon can be found in a comparison of two Chelsea House biographies of the out gay writer James Baldwin. The first, *James Baldwin,* by Lisa Rosset (1989), is part of the publisher's Black Americans of Achievement series and describes Baldwin's life with no mention of his same-sex romantic relationships. The second, *James Baldwin,* by Randall Kenan (1994) is part of the publisher's series on Lives of Notable Gay Men and Lesbians. The information included is roughly the same, but intertwined with the account of Baldwin's life and career is his story of coming out as a gay man, his several significant romantic interests, and the various impacts that his gay identity had on the other events in his life. For teen readers looking for information about possible role models, a complete picture of a biographee's life is preferable to the evasions, omissions, and misdirected emphasis that have characterized so many biographies of GLBTQ subjects until recent years.

As this body of nonfiction literature grew, authors and publishers began looking beyond the gay/lesbian audience to a larger audience that would include heterosexual YA readers as well. No longer did publishers make the assumption that books with gay/lesbian content would be of interest only to gay/lesbian readers, but instead published titles that addressed gay-related topics in history, psychology, law, and medicine and assumed a readership not limited by sexual orientation. Thus, beginning in the mid-1980s, other types of information texts for teens on GLBTQ topics began to appear: books about the gay rights movement, such as Elaine Landau's *A Different Drummer: Homosexuality in America* (Messner, 1986), Sabra Holbrook's *Fighting Back: The Struggle for Gay Rights* (E.P.

Dutton, 1987), Diane Silver's *The New Civil War: The Lesbian and Gay Struggle for Civil Rights* (Franklin Watts, 1997), and Marilyn Tower Oliver's *Gay and Lesbian Rights: A Struggle* (Enslow Publishers, 1998). There were also factual books about homosexuality, such as Margaret O. Hyde and Elizabeth H. Forsyth's *Know about Gays and Lesbians* (Millbrook Press, 1994), and books such as Susan and Daniel Cohen's *When Someone You Know is Gay* (M. Evans, 1989), designed to help straight teens understand the gay/lesbian people in their lives. Information books on sexuality aimed at YA readers also slowly began to include information about same-sex attractions Sometimes title changes of new editions of standard works reflected changes in perspective over time. For example, the first (1993) and second (1999) editions of Eric Marcus's *Is It a Choice? Answers to 300 of the Most Frequently Asked Questions About Gay and Lesbian People* were addressed to both gay and straight readers. The most current third (2000) edition is addressed more specifically to a straight audience, its title having been changed to *What If Someone I Know Is Gay? Answers to Questions About Gay and Lesbian People* (Price Stern Sloan, 2000). No longer are GLBTQ readers (plus the occasional current events debater or report writer) assumed to be the primary audience for these books. There are now titles aimed at straight teens who want to learn more about homosexuality. But this does not mean that GLBTQ teen readers are invisible; instead, there are now increasing numbers of titles addressed specifically to them.

YA nonfiction with GLBTQ content has also included several gay-themed memoirs written in graphic novel format, such as Howard Cruse's *Stuck Rubber Baby*, an account of growing up gay in the American South during the Civil Rights Movement (Paradox Press, 1995); Judd Winick's memoir of his friendship with AIDS activist Pedro Zamora, *Pedro and Me: Friendship, Loss, and What I Learned* (Holt 2000); and Ariel Schrag's stories of her high school years as a lesbian in *Definition*, *Awkward*, and *Potential* (Slave Labor Graphics, 1997, 1999, and 2000, respectively). The popularity of the graphic novel format (a descriptor that has come to include both fiction and nonfiction) with teen readers began to take off in the nineties and the audience and demand for books using this narrative format continues to grow. If/when the next edition of this text is published, there is little doubt that the chapter on the 2000s and beyond will include many books for teens in this format.

GLBTQ YA FICTION IN THE 1990s

The decade of the '90s was one of expansion for GLBTQ young adult fiction, too, though this expansion was more in volume than in creative or thematic innovation. The number of GLBTQ fiction titles published, for example, nearly doubled: seventy-five titles (seventy novels and five short story collections) appeared in the nineties, and seven of these (10%) originated in other countries. Thus, the rate of publication for these novels went from an average of four titles per year in the eighties to seven titles per year in the nineties.

However, the gender imbalance in the books' content did not shift appreciably from the eighties to the nineties, nor did the novels' rigid gender segregation. Books included *either* gay male *or* lesbian content; only rarely did both appear in the same story. And if a book was either/or with regard to gay males or lesbian characters, the gender was typically male. As noted earlier, of the forty books published in the 1980s, twenty-nine (73%) included gay male content and eleven (28%) included lesbian content. Of the seventy GLBTQ YA novels of the nineties, 48 (69%) included gay male content, 18 (26%) included lesbian content, and only four titles (6%) included both gay males and lesbians.

The proportion of books having a GLBTQ protagonist relative to books with GLBTQ secondary characters increasingly favored those with secondary characters. During the eighties, sixteen (40%) of the titles included GLBTQ protagonists and twenty-four (60%) included GLBTQ secondary characters. During the nineties, nineteen (27%) of the titles included GLBTQ protagonists, fifty (71%) included GLBTQ secondary characters, and one title (1%) had two narrators, one gay and one straight.

In terms of creative or thematic innovation, the principal focus remained stuck on homosexual visibility, i.e., the voluntary or involuntary coming out of a character. Who comes out, under what circumstances, and with what consequences remained the substance of the story. And while there is some latitude for variety in this, there is also an inescapable air of sameness, a problem that has dogged GLBTQ literature since its beginnings. Of the seventy novels published in the decade of the '90s, fifty-one were titles of "homosexual visibility" that dealt, in one way or another, with coming-out issues. Twenty-three contained some elements of "gay assimilation" (i.e., the stories are about or include people who "just happen to be gay"). Only eleven included any depictions of "queer consciousness" or "queer community."

As in previous decades, the numbers of titles published fluctuated from year to year, going from three titles in 1990 to thirteen titles in 1999. (See Appendix D for a chronological list of titles.) Because there is not sufficient space in this chapter to focus on each of the seventy novels published during the nineties, we will highlight and examine the most significant titles in each of our three framework categories, beginning with homosexual visibility.

HOMOSEXUAL VISIBILITY

During the first half of the 1990s, one of the most common methods of outing—or revealing a character's sexual identity—was the discovery that the (invariably male) character had contracted AIDS from having had unprotected sex with a male partner. As noted above, this happened in thirteen novels but in only one (*My Brother Has AIDS*) is the character a young adult, and in none of these is the PWA (Person with AIDS) the protagonist. Also, in only one—Theresa Nelson's moving novel *Earthshine* (1994)—is the PWA openly gay from the novel's outset.

As noted earlier, in only twenty of the seventy novels is the GLBTQ character who comes out—to him/herself and/or to the world—is the protagonist. In all of the rest (i.e., fifty), the character is a member of the "supporting cast," usually a friend or relative of the protagonist. This removal of the homosexual character from center stage is also a feature of titles in our other two framework categories, gay assimilation and queer consciousness. As we have noted, this shift in the book's narrative distance with regard to gay/lesbian content—i.e., away from gay/lesbian protagonists and toward gay/lesbian secondary characters—was a trend that "continued and actually intensified" through the nineties.[4] Did this strengthen or did it weaken the genre? The answer—not to be unduly coy—is "yes."

If one key function of this literature is to give faces to GLBTQ youth, increased narrative distance may blur the portrait. Placing an intermediary heterosexual character between the reader and the gay/lesbian character can reduce the likelihood of reader's identification with that character. On the other hand, the presence of a heterosexual protagonist may well provide an easier point of access to the story for straight readers, who are also an important audience for these stories. And in terms of verisimilitude, the presence of secondary gay characters could seem to positively reflect the growing awareness of the universal presence of gay/lesbian persons in society. The bottom line is that more GLBTQ books than ever appeared in the 1990s, but overall the gay/lesbian characters moved farther from center stage.

Coming-out stories featuring gay secondary characters were published throughout the nineties. This chapter began with a descriptive comparison of two of them: Joyce Sweeney's *Face the Dragon*, in which Paul comes out to protagonist Eric on a deserted beach; and Robert Paul Walker's *The Method*, in which Mitch comes out to protagonist Albie in a gay restaurant. Although both were published in 1990, the former is one of the dreariest coming out scenes in this entire body of literature, while the latter is one of the most affirming.

Indeed, Albie's ready acceptance of Mitch's identity is as reassuring to gay readers as Weetzie's response to the news that *her* friend Dirk is gay. In critical terms, although homosexuality is only a sub-plot, its inclusion in the context of a coming-of-age novel that involves emerging sexuality is entirely appropriate and unforced. In addition, both *Weetzie* and *Method* present a fairly diverse range of gay/lesbian characters who are depicted with affection, humor, and accuracy. In contrast, *Dragon's* Paul is one more sad-eyed loner. While the loner role is played by teens of all sexual orientations at various points in their teenage years, such a consistently one-note portrayal of gay male teens has become a cliche in YA fiction. And where are all the sad-eyed loner lesbians?

Other nineties novels that address the homosexuality of secondary characters who are friends of the protagonists include: Jesse Maguire's *Getting It Right* (1991); Diana Wieler's *Bad Boy* (Delacorte 1992); Chris Lynch's *Dog Eat Dog* (1996); Barbara Wersba's *Whistle Me Home* (1997); Stephen Chbosky's *The Perks of Being a Wallflower* (1999); Phyllis Reynolds Naylor's *Alice on the Outside* (1999); Laura Torres' *November Ever After* (1999); and Lois-Ann Yamanaka's *Name Me Nobody* (1999). They range in treatment from the very good (*Perks*) to the very bad (*Whistle*).

The Perks of Being a Wallflower has become something of a YA cult classic since it was published in 1999 as a paperback adult title. An epistolary novel, it is the haunting story of a deeply troubled but precocious

fifteen-year-old boy named Charlie who writes letters about his freshman year in high school to someone who is identified only as "Dear
Friend," a recipient who could well be the reader him/herself. During
that eventful year, Charlie is befriended by two seniors, Samantha and
Patrick, who are step-siblings, and the two become Charlie's best friends.
When Charlie attends a party and discovers Patrick kissing another boy,
he (accurately) concludes that Patrick is gay, a fact that clearly does not
affect Charlie's warm feelings for his friend. Patrick is aware of this,
telling him appreciatively, "You see things. You keep quiet about them.
And you understand" (37).

Indeed, Charlie is wonderfully understanding. When Patrick is de-
spondent over the imminent break-up of his already shaky relationship
with his boyfriend Brad, Charlie continues to be there for him. At one
point Patrick says to Charlie, "It's too bad you're not gay." And Charlie's
response? "You know, Patrick? If I were gay, I'd want to date you."

"I don't know why I said it," he adds in an aside to the reader, "but
it seemed right" (137). Later, when Patrick becomes the object of a gay-
bashing (instigated by the closeted Brad), Charlie—who has learned to
fight from his older brother, now a football star at Penn—rushes to his
friend's defense, heedless of his own physical vulnerability as one against
many. And still later, when the traumatized Patrick gets drunk, kisses
Charlie, and then immediately apologizes—more than once—Charlie's
reply is "No, really. It was ok."

"Then," Charlie writes, "he started crying. Then he started talking
about Brad. And I just let him. Because that's what friends are for"
(160–161). This attitude of generous and full-hearted acceptance of a
friend's difference is, of course, the nonpareil of hoped-for responses.

An entirely different reaction is found in *Whistle Me Home*. This
slender (108 pages) 1997 novel is by Barbara Wersba and features a troubled girl, Noli. At seventeen, she has "a little problem with alcohol" and
a big problem with her mother, whom she hates. Oh, yes—she also has a
problem with shoplifting. But these problems pale into insignificance
early on, when she sees TJ, a new boy in town (Sag Harbor, New York),
and falls instantly in love with him. "The boy is beautiful—with the face
of an angel and the body of an athlete. His thick curly hair is longer than
any boy's in the room. And he is wearing an earring." TJ's physical presence is alluring, but what sends Noli head over heels is his announcement

in English class that, over the summer, he has read a biography of Gerard Manley Hopkins, and then, at the teacher's invitation, he shyly (but brilliantly) reads aloud one of Hopkins' poems.

Noli is captivated. As the omniscient narrator describes it, "The idea that *anyone*—and especially somebody new—could get up in class and read the work of a nineteenth-century priest . . . this idea is dizzying to her."

"'He was famous for something called sprung rhythm,' TJ says quietly. 'Hopkins, I mean.'"

By this point (page 11) many readers may wonder if TJ's playing against male gender stereotypes and his stance as high school aesthete signals that he is gay. But Noli is clueless. The two become friends, and she discovers that TJ prefers that he and she dress alike "in stonewashed jeans, boots, heavy jackets, and wool caps" (60). When Noli is (understandably) mistaken for a boy, she says, "God! I really must grow my hair longer, TJ. And wear dresses."

"Forget it," he answers. "You're fine."

When the two finally try to have sex, TJ is unable to become aroused. And "at last she says the words that must be said—and her voice breaks a little as she says them. 'You're gay aren't you?'" (72). He bursts into tears and Noli is initially sympathetic, but when the two begin to talk and TJ admits that he has had earlier "experiences" with males, Noli becomes upset.

> "What do you do with these people?" she asks.
>
> [TJ responds] "That's none of your business. I'm sorry."
>
> And that's when she explodes—all of her goodwill disappearing (73).
>
> "Who am I supposed to be?" she demands, "an experiment that will turn you straight?
>
> God! What a coward you are. . . you chose me because I look like a boy."
>
> "Not true. I love you."
>
> "*Do not use that word to me!*" she screams. "You dirty faggot" (74).

Needless to say, this ends their relationship.

Some months later the two encounter each other on the street and have an awkward conversation. Frustrated by Noli's continuing coldness, TJ demands, "Can't we be *friends*? Do we have to throw the whole thing away?" (104).

"'I'm sorry, TJ Baker,' she replies, 'but I cannot be your friend.' Yes, she says silently, that's it. I need to be free of you so I can find *me*" (105).

And she turns on her heel and walks away. Well, the reader may think, at least she didn't call him a dirty faggot this time, I *guess* that's an improvement. Yet the characters are so uniformly unsympathetic, the reader may not really care whether or not any of them finally find themselves.

In the novels discussed so far, the focus is on the impact that coming out can have on friendships. What about the impact on families? To answer that, we return to 1991, when two supporting gay characters whom the reader already knows to be partners—Dirk and Duck, first encountered in 1989's *Weetzie Bat*—re-appear in *Witch Baby*, the second of what would ultimately be five novels in Francesca Lia Block's "Dangerous Angels" series about her "slinkster cool" characters. The protagonist of this novel, however, is not Weetzie but rather her young "almost" daughter Witch Baby, who—during the course of the novel—outs Dirk and Duck to Duck's unsuspecting mother, Darlene. Certainly some readers may take exception to Witch Baby's action, but her motivation is pure—if somewhat naïve. She loves both Dirk and Duck and identifies with their outsider status, since she herself feels that she doesn't belong anywhere. "What time are we on and where do I belong?" she plaintively wonders at the novel's outset.

Her rationale for outing the two is complicated: part of it has to do with her wanting Dirk and Duck to know that she understands them better than anybody else; another part is her belief in the beauty of their love and her wanting others to share this belief. "They love each other more than anyone else in the world," she tells a startled Darlene (47). Though a period of emotional turbulence follows in the wake of WB's announcement, rapprochement arrives by the end of the novel. Indeed, Duck's mother, Darlene, thanks her, saying, "You knew more about love than I knew. You helped me get my son back again." Duck agrees: "Without you," he tells WB, "we [he and his mother] might never have really known each other." (99) Being honest about one's sexuality is presented as being a good, even necessary thing that brings families together.

A second important novel involving the outing of a secondary character who is also a family member is A. M. Jenkins' *Breaking Boxes* (1997). In this novel, which has strong echoes of S.E. Hinton's *The Outsiders*, two brothers—sixteen-year-old Charlie and twenty-four-year-old Trent, sons of a long-gone father and a mother who drank herself to death—are living on their own. Trent goes to college part-time and works in a bookstore to support himself and Charlie. Trent is gay, a fact that Charlie has known since he was "ten or eleven" and accepts completely. He is also aware that Trent keeps this part of his life "compartmentalized" in order to spare Charlie the perceived stigma of living with a gay person (even though that person is his brother, not his lover).

Another kind of compartmentalization—class conflict—is evidenced in Charlie's sometimes-violent interactions with boys of privilege at his school. This begins to change, though, when Charlie befriends Brandon, one of the privileged (or, as Hinton would call them, "Socs"). However, their growing friendship is shattered when Charlie tells Brandon that Trent is gay. Brandon, who may be conflicted about his own sexuality, violently overreacts, ends his friendship with Charlie and, worse, outs Trent to Luke, the unpleasant de facto leader of the privileged boys. Luke taunts Charlie, lisping cruel jokes about Trent and suggesting Charlie may also be gay like his brother ("I hear it's genetic" [162].).

Charlie—thinking "God. I can take almost anything but I can't take it when people who don't know Trent see him as less than he is. And *laugh*" (178)—physically attacks Luke. Events thereafter conspire plausibly to bring Charlie and Brandon back together and to restore their friendship.

Charlie's acceptance of and devotion to his older brother is touching. More importantly, A.M. (Amanda) Jenkins displays an extraordinary ability to create multidimensional male characters, both straight *and* gay, and to capture the authentic sounds of their conversation. As in *Witch Baby*, the revelation of a member's homosexuality ultimately strengthens the emotional viability of the family.

Unfortunately, the opposite situation—homosexuality driving families apart (at least initially)—is a more common outcome in YA novels of the nineties, such as Marilyn Levy's *Rumors and Whispers* (1990); Christina Salat's *Living in Secret* (1993); Nancy Springer's *Looking for Jamie Bridger* (1995); Margaret Bechard's *If It Doesn't Kill You* (1999); and Han Nolan's *A Face in Every Window* (1999). All of these books feature punishing fathers who seek to expel a gay/lesbian character from the nuclear family.

It is interesting to note, however, that among the books published in the nineties, the large majority of adult secondary characters who come out are family members. The exceptions are the novels that include AIDS, in which the PWA might be a father, uncle, or older brother, but is equally likely to be a teacher. The other non-family adult to come out in these books is also a teacher, the protagonist's social studies teacher Mr. Padovano in Ellen Jaffe McClain's ironically titled *No Big Deal* (Lodestar, 1994).

Of far more compelling interest to this study are the sixteen 1990s novels of homosexual visibility in which the gay/lesbian character who is outed or who voluntarily comes out is the protagonist. As was the case with the novels already discussed, these range from the very good (e.g., *Baby Bebop* by Francesca Lia Block, *Deliver Us from Evie* by M.E. Kerr, *Peter* by Kate Walker, *What I Know Now* by Rodger Larson, and *Dare Truth or Promise* by Paula Boock) to the frankly unfortunate (Bette Greene's *The Drowning of Stephan Jones*).

Three of the best titles—*Peter* by Kate Walker, *The Blue Lawn* by William Taylor, and *Dare Truth or Promise* by Paula Boock—are not about American teens but are set in Australia (Walker) and New Zealand (Taylor and Boock). Together, they demonstrate that the often exciting but sometimes painful experience of becoming aware of one's homosexuality, coming to terms with the discovery, and telling others is shared by teens in other Western societies.

Peter (Houghton Mifflin, 1993) is the story of a fifteen-year-old Australian boy, whose ambitions are simple: finish school, get a road license for his dirt bike, and find a job with cameras. But things begin to change when he meets David, his college student brother's best friend. David is openly gay, and Peter begins to worry that the strong attraction he feels to the older boy may mean that he, too, is gay. For Peter, whose knowledge of homosexuality is rooted in societal stereotypes, the prospect is not pleasing. Despairingly, the boy at one point thinks, "I didn't want to be a poofter joke, a social outcast, a candidate for AIDS" (144).

Yet, as author Walker dramatically demonstrates, identifying as a straight male can mean subscribing to ignorant and often mean-spirited sexual stereotypes: it can mean repeatedly having to prove your manhood by performing empty-headed and dangerous feats of derring-do on your dirt bike and by having urgent, impersonal, exploitative sex with girls you hardly know. As he contemplates these problematic macho expectations, Peter worries, "You could die of this" (144).

Fortunately, he finds in David a gay young adult who is a warm, intelligent, caring human being. "David wasn't a creep," Peter muses. "He was nice, ordinary" (42). When David gently rebuffs Peter's awkward advances, the younger boy learns that sexual identity is not simply the act of sex, but rather one of the most complexly ambiguous aspects of being human. Indeed, when the book ends, Peter is still uncertain about his own sexual identity. At David's suggestion, however, he decides to give himself time to see how his life unfolds. Readers will understand that whatever Peter ultimately discovers, he will turn out to be—like David— nice and ordinary on his own terms. And most importantly, he will be loved and cared about like everyone else.

Another international novel that explores young teenagers' uncertainties about their sexuality is William Taylor's *The Blue Lawn* (Alyson, 1999). Set in New Zealand, where it was first published in 1994, this is the story of fifteen-year-old David, a star rugby player who is strongly attracted to Theo, a new boy in school. The slightly older Theo is living with his wealthy grandmother while his mother is abroad for a year. David soon learns that Theo is similarly drawn to him. Ironically, it is a car crash (yes, another one) that provides the evidence. Theo wrecks his car while the two are on a drive in the country. Neither boy is hurt and, giddy with relief, Theo covers David's hand with his. It's an awkward moment; neither boy says anything but both seem to realize that their friendship might be more complex than they had thought.

While David is comfortable with this, Theo is deeply conflicted about his feelings. "'See,' he later tells David, 'I don't want to live with the idea that I'm a queer and that I'll always feel like this.'

'Bloody hell, Theo,' David hotly replies. 'If you're made this way, you go on being made this way.'

But Theo is unconvinced. 'You could go through your life as a queer? As a poof? As a pansy? And there's worse words than them for what it is'" (71–72). David responds by chiding Theo: "Just let things be as they are for as long as it seems right." Though not completely convinced, Theo is willing to continue the friendship, which gradually deepens. However, the two rarely give physical expression to their feelings except for occasionally holding each other and sleeping entwined in each other's arms.

It is on one of those occasions that Theo's grandmother discovers the boys asleep together. David is unaware of her discovery until his next visit, three days later, when he discovers that Theo, without even a word of farewell, has gone home to Auckland. Devastated, David understands immediately that the grandmother has sent Theo away.

"We never did no harm," David tells her in a deeply moving scene of confrontation. "'We never did anything wrong and it's not wrong. It isn't. You know about him'n'me, eh? And you got rid of him.'

'My dear, my dear,' she replies, 'it is better . . . better . . .'

'Better?' David asks bitterly. 'Better for who?'" (104).

After a month without hearing from Theo, David finally goes to visit his older sister, who conveniently lives in Auckland, and to find Theo, who remains conflicted about his own feelings toward David. "I don't know how I see you. I don't know whether I see you as a friend. As a brother. As a lover. God knows, maybe we do need a bit of time apart so's we can see what our feelings really are and what it is we really are" (112). David can do little but accept this; the two boys embrace and Theo promises he will visit again, but it seems unlikely that he will sort out his feelings any time soon.

Later David poignantly asks his sister if she has ever been in love. When she acknowledges that she has, he asks, "Can you tell me, does it always hurt? Does it always hurt so really, really bad?" (116). She can offer no answers to her brother's questions, but she proves to be an accepting and sympathetic listener. For readers who prefer unambiguously happy endings, this may seem like cold comfort but love can be both painful and mysterious. Is the wisdom of the heart deeper than that of the mind? Perhaps David and Theo will find out . . . in their own time. From a different perspective, this narrative could also be viewed as a more recent version of the story told over and over again in the lesbian pulp romances of the 1950s: two same-sex, star-crossed lovers meet only to be driven apart by social taboos. One partner heads toward a limited but socially acceptable heterosexual future, while the other, remaining homosexual, is left with painful memories and a broken heart.

Another nineties novel from New Zealand (whose plot also includes a car crash) is Paula Boock's *Dare Truth or Promise* (1999), which recounts the story of two girls, Louie (short for Luisa) and Willa, who meet and fall in love. For Louie, this is a first experience of romantic love. Willa, however, is slowly mending from the emotionally traumatic break-up of an earlier relationship with a girl named Cathy, whose family— religious fundamentalists—have been instrumental in separating the two girls. Once burned, twice shy, Willa is initially reluctant to open her heart to Louie but in fairly short order the two fall mutually and deeply in love. But even then the relationship is a difficult one. Cathy, now deeply disturbed emotionally, re-appears. Though the young women are "out" selectively (Willa's loving mother knows and is supportive; Louie comes out to her best friend, Mo, who is also supportive), they are well aware that there is no place in their small, conservative community where they can go to be open about their love. Religion becomes a problem again, since Louie's Roman Catholic family regards homosexuality as sinful.

When Louie's mother discovers the two girls together in bed, she orders Willa out of the house and thereafter makes every effort to keep the two apart. Finally, Louie gives in and asks Willa for a "time out" from their relationship, and Willa is heartbroken. Louie's mother pressures her to accept a date with a boy to the school dance. But when Willa, too, appears at the dance with a boy, Louie is devastated and finally drives off. It is not hard to guess what happens next.

Concerned, Willa follows and finds Louie in the wreck of her car, which she has crashed in a suicide attempt. Fortunately, Willa is able to perform impromptu first-aid, saving Louie's life, and the two are reconciled in the hospital. Although this melodramatic finale is by now a cliché in GLBTQ YA fiction, it is the only off-key note in an otherwise satisfying and realistic romance. And the car crash as catalyst for salvaging a relationship is a neat twist that turns this convention of early GLBTQ fiction on its head. (Unfortunately the equation of homosexuality and death by automobile still occasionally continues to appear, most recently in Sharon Dennis Wyeth's 2004 novel *Orphea Proud*.

A few of the plot elements in Boock's otherwise successful novel do seem a bit too pat; i.e., the author is overly fond of parallels that seem— *a la* a school examination—to compare and contrast: Willa's mother is the direct opposite of Louie's, for example; warm and understanding where the other is cold and rigid. Too, as the relationship between Willa and Louie starts to unravel, it begins to seem eerily like Willa's failed relationship with Cathy. Even Willa has a sense of *déjà vu*.

Religion is negatively involved in both relationships. Yet the author offers a contrast here as well when Louie has a heart-to-heart talk with her extraordinarily understanding parish priest: "How lucky you are to love and be loved in return," he says. According to him, love is a gift from God; thus, to reject love—any kind of love—is to reject God. He also manages to avoid didacticism as he simply states his beliefs, which Louie is free to take or leave. Any failures of plotting are redeemed, however, by the characterizations that are strong throughout, even those of the minor characters. Another plus factor is that the point of view of the story shifts back and forth between Willa and Louie, a device that helps readers track the characters' respective emotional developments. With its focus on homosexuality as an aspect of love, this novel may be regarded by many readers as an *Annie on My Mind* for the 1990s.

Speaking of *Annie* invites the observation that its author Nancy Garden remains one of a small group of published American writers for teens who have produced a number of insightful and emotionally satisfying novels about young people discovering and coming to terms with their sexual identities. Other prolific authors in this group are M.E. Kerr, Jacqueline Woodson, and Francesca Lia Block

In 1995, for example, Block wrote the fifth—and final—novel in her Weetzie Bat cycle. Titled *Baby Bebop*, it is a prequel to *Weetzie Bat* and tells the story of Weetzie's friend, Dirk McDonald, and his life before he met either Weetzie or the love of his life, Duck Drake. Like *Witch Baby*, Dirk is in search of his place in the world. Raised by his Grandmother Fifi, Dirk has known "since he could remember" (3) that he likes boys. Though he dreams of being on trains with "naked fathers . . . taking showers together," Fifi says it's just a phase. "Just a phase. Dirk thought about those words over and over again. Just a phase. Until the train inside of him would crash. Until the thing inside of him that was wrong and bad would change" (6).

When it doesn't, Dirk decides "the main thing was to keep to himself and never to seem afraid."[5] He doesn't want to be like his Grandmother's friends, Martin and Merlin, a longtime gay couple who "had been hurt because of who they were. Dirk didn't want to be hurt that way. He wanted to be strong and to love someone who was strong." Unfortunately he falls in love with someone who isn't—his best friend, Pup Lambert. "Dirk's heart sent sparks and flares through his veins like a fast wheel on cement when he was with Pup." But when he attempts to tell Pup about his feelings, the other boy responds, "'I love you, Dirk. But I can't handle it.' And then before Dirk knew it, Pup was gone."

This rejection leaves Dirk fearful and riddled with self-hatred. In an act of borderline self-mutilation he shaves his hair into a Mohawk and begins to dress in black. Concerned, his grandmother gives him a family heirloom, a lamp (perhaps the same magic lamp that Weetzie Bat is given in the first of Block's series of novels) and tells him that when he is ready, he can tell his story into the lamp.

This time, however, it is the lamp that will tell *him* stories. Going to a club to hear a band (symbolically) named "Fear," Dirk is set upon by a gang of skinheads and beaten nearly to death. Somehow he manages to get home and collapses onto his bed with the lamp his grandmother has given him. "Help me," he thinks, "tell me a story. Tell me a story that will make me want to live because right now I don't want to live. Help me."

In fact, in an echo of Dickens' *Christmas Carol*, Dirk will receive stories of past, present, and future from the spirits of his dead great-grandmother, his parents, and the genie of the lamp. From them he learns the importance of being true to oneself, of being different, of rejecting fear, of telling one's own story unashamedly. In a beautiful moment he comes out to his father who has told him, "'I want you to fight, I want you not to be afraid.'

'But I'm gay,' Dirk said. 'Dad, I'm gay.'

'I know you are, buddy,' Dirby said. And his lullaby eyes sang with love."

Perhaps best of all, Dirk receives from the genie a vision of his future love, Duck Drake, thus reassuring him that love is waiting, that love will come.

Block writes so luminously and open-heartedly about the viability of love in whatever form it may come to us that it seems almost a disservice to attempt to synopsize her texts. In a way, all of her work is itself a dream, a vision of the transformative power of love. Indeed, a number of teens and adults have found reading Block's powerfully lyrical texts to be a transformative experience in itself. Certainly the Weetzie Bat Dangerous Angel series is essential reading for all gay and lesbian teens, but it is also—in its urgent celebration of love *and* of human difference—essential, life-affirming reading for heterosexual teens, as well. In recognition of this, Block was named the recipient of the 2005 Margaret A. Edwards Award for lifetime achievement in young adult literature.

Published a year earlier than *Baby Bebop*, M.E. Kerr's *Deliver Us from Evie* (1994) is the strongest of her novels with GLBTQ content. In it a sixteen-year-old Missouri farm boy, Parr Burrman, tells the reader about his attractive, eighteen-year-old sister, Evie, who—with her short, slicked-back hair—looks like Elvis Presley, is good with machinery, and is jeeringly called Parr's "brother" by the other boys at school.

Evie, though not officially out to anybody, is nevertheless a walking, talking stereotype of the "butch" lesbian. However, she is unapologetically so. As she tells her anxious father, "I don't give a ding-dong-damn what people say about me! Okay?" (57–58). And later, after she comes out to her mother, she says about her appearance, "Some of us *look* it, Mom! I know you so-called normal people would like it better if we looked as much like all of you as possible, but some of us don't, can't, and never will! And some others of us go for the ones who don't, can't, and never will" (86).

This echoes author Kerr's own feelings as expressed in her foreword to Roger Sutton's 1994 book *Hearing Us Out: Voices from the Gay and Lesbian Community* (Little, Brown). Recalling how "very early into our own self-acceptance, we [Kerr and other gay and lesbian people] could not yet tolerate those among us who 'looked it.' It took a while," she concludes, "to grasp the meaning of gay pride, and that it did not mean looking and acting as straight as possible" (5).

The occasion for Evie's coming out is her having met and fallen in love with beautiful Patsy Duff, daughter of the local banker. Her mother's first reaction is to question the validity of her daughter's conclusion ("You don't know that for sure, honey" [85].) and then to blame Patsy ("*She* did this to you" [85].). Both parents are grieved by their daughter's revelation but do not reject her.

As for Parr—he is less concerned that his sister is a lesbian than he is about her affairs taking her away from the farm and leaving it to him to stay to work the land, something neither he nor their older brother wants to do. After getting drunk with Cord, an older boy who is still smarting from his rejection by Evie, Parr goes along with Cord's plan to publicly post a sign outing Evie and Patsy. Cord justifies this by telling Parr it's for Evie's own good—that it will force Patsy's father to send his daughter away and Evie will, presumably, come to her senses.

As it happens, it is Evie who goes away—to St. Louis—in the wake of the resulting parental firestorm. Ultimately, Patsy follows and the two go to Paris and then move, together, to New York. The book concludes with their reconciling visit home. As Evie says her good-byes to her family and begins to drive away, her mother calls after her, "Don't you two be strangers" (177). And the reader realizes that mutual acceptance of personal differences is a viable and attainable goal, despite the emotional obstacles one must overcome to reach it.

Unlike Evie and Patsy, the two girls who are the co-protagonists of Nancy Garden's second lesbian love story *Good Moon Rising* (996), initially deny the rumors that they are lovers but, following a campaign of increasingly vicious innuendo that begins to destroy their relationship, courageously choose to come out.

In contrast to her earlier *Annie on My Mind*, which is set in New York City, Garden sets this story in a small town in New Hampshire. Jan and Kerry—a new girl in town!—meet when they both audition for their high school's production of Arthur Miller's play *The Crucible*. Their drama teacher, Mrs. Nicholson, explains the theme of the play (and also, the reader realizes, the novel), thus: "It is a play about misguided power and the cruelty of falsehood and about the sin of blindly following the common herd" (36). The equation between the alleged witches in Salem and contemporary gays is underscored when the teacher later gives her cast a pep talk, "I want to weep over this play, over the injustice that is done to these innocent people. I want to be at the edge of my chair by the end of the first act, and in tears by the final curtain" (93).

The element of suspense in Garden's novel is not whether the two girls will realize and acknowledge their attraction to each other; they have already done that by page seventy-five of this 230-page novel. Nor is it whether guilt or homophobia will poison their new relationship. They know their feelings are rooted in love. And as Kerry says, "I don't see how loving someone can be wrong, like some people say. What could be immoral or sick about love?" (117).

No, the element of suspense comes over whether "the injustice that is done to these innocent people" will ultimately destroy their relationship. The injustice is an increasingly strident smear campaign launched by Kent, a homophobic senior who plays the lead in the play. The climate of fear this creates evokes that of witch-hunting Salem and provides a dramatic and plausible motivation for the two young women's fear of coming out.

Unfortunately, public denial of their feelings begins to compromise their capacity for being true to themselves. Jan even allows herself to participate in a singularly hare-brained scheme proposed by her older friend, Raphael, whom she had met in summer-stock theater. An openly gay man, he is as stereotypical a character as Charlie Gilhooley in *Night Kites*. Improbably he suggests taking Jan to the cast party where they will pretend to be boyfriend and girlfriend. Jan goes along with this until Kerry arrives at the party, when the charade becomes unbearable to both of them and they publicly declare their love.

The reaction of the other students is generally positive, though both girls recognize, as Jan says, "It's not going to be easy, Kerry, for either of us" (229). Kerry replies, "Nothing worthwhile is easy." And adds, in an echo of the ending of *Annie on My Mind*, "What do we care what people think of us? Some of them will probably never understand. But maybe we can try to show them the truth. Maybe we've already started." Jan has the last word: "Right. Maybe we have" (230).

Like *Annie*, this is another important book about the equation of homosexuality and love and of being open, honest, and truthful about one's feelings. It is not without its flaws, however. Kent seems to lack motivation powerful enough to fuel his almost psychotic behavior, though there are suggestions that he is jealous of Jan's acting abilities and may be afraid that he, himself, is a latent homosexual. For an out gay man, Raphael's suggestion that Jan pretend to be straight seems improbable, though, again, there is some motivation in the story he tells her of his having been the victim of gay-bashing when he was in high school. His story evokes a similar scene from Scoppettone's *Trying Hard to Hear You*. Finally the scenes in which the girls express their feelings for each other seem a bit awkward and their dialogue sometimes stilted. However, the sincerity of the author's feelings, the power of her convictions, and the intelligence she brings to her writing make this a book that remains worthy of readers' attention.

Garden published two other books with GLBTQ content in the 1990s: *Lark in the Morning* and *The Year They Burned the Books*. The former will be treated in our discussion of the literature of gay assimilation and the latter in our discussion of books featuring queer consciousness and community.

Before we get to those, however, a few words about two of the least successful of the GLBTQ books of the '90s: Bette Greene's *The Drowning of Stephan Jones* (1991) and Jack Gantos' *Desire Lines* (1997). Both involve the death of a gay character as the result of the same kind of rabid homophobia, rooted in bigotry and religious fundamentalism, that motivated the problem novels of the 1970s.

The Greene novel charts the course of the persecution of two gay men, Frank and Stephan, lovers who improbably move from Boston to a small town in rural Arkansas to open—of all stereotypical things—"The

Forgotten Treasures Antique Shop." Why on earth two gay men would move to a town that the local real estate agent, pointing a "pudgy finger toward the crest of the mountain where a seven-hundred foot high concrete Jesus was visible for miles in any direction," proudly describes as "the crown jewel on the glittering buckle known as the Bible Belt" is beyond understanding. And, once there, why on earth do they stay? They've scarcely arrived in town before locals are calling them "sodomites, faggots, fruit flies" and worse, and an outraged local merchant has ordered them out of his store, observing, "Somebody with a little guts would do the whole world a favor if they'd blow both of those fags' brains to smithereens" (13).

His melodramatic declaration is followed by this clumsy bit of foreshadowing: "From the far side of the store, his son thoughtfully took in his dad's words. Removing his hand from the pocket of his chinos, he fashioned a pretend gun with his right hand . . . and announced with an air of finality, 'Bang! You're dead. And bang! You're dead, too'" (13).

Predictably the boy, Andy, becomes the leader of a pack of other teenagers who will hound Stephan, a lapsed Roman Catholic seminarian and the more "sensitive" of the two (it's hard to tell who is more ill-served by stereotypical characterization, the two gay men or the small town residents), to his death by drowning. Though the teens—now called "The Rachetville Five"—are brought to trial, they will receive a suspended sentence contingent on their doing one hundred hours of community service. The reader is to believe that justice is served, however, when the author has the surviving partner, Frank, approach Andy after the trial and loudly assure him, in the presence of his parents and "more than a dozen members of the press," that he needn't fear "exposure" from him, since the proof of his (i.e., Andy's) affair with Stephan "is no more." Of course, Andy had no such affair but his punishment is to be perceived by his family, friends, and neighbors as being gay himself. Clearly, this is intended by the author to be a fate worse than death, and though she surely didn't intend it, this is tantamount to gay bashing every bit as savage as anything the Rachetville Five did.

Any defects in the Gantos book pale by comparison. Also set in the small town south—in Florida this time—*Desire Lines* is the story of a sixteen-year-old boy named Walker who discovers that two of his class-

mates, Karen and Jennifer, are lovers. This remains his secret until an itin-
erant preacher and his son arrive in town, and the son, setting up shop
on the high school's playing field, begins a campaign of gay-baiting, with
Walker as his principal target. Though Walker is straight, he panics and
offers up his secret knowledge about Karen and Jennifer. Unable to cope
with being publicly outed, the two attempt suicide. Jennifer succeeds, but
Karen survives to confront Walker, accusing him of being the "real" killer
of her dead friend.

Although parts of Gantos' book are quite good—especially the
richly realized setting, a consistently bleak tone, and a kind of darkly
gothic religiosity that evokes moments of Flannery O'Connor—the plot
seems contrived, and the girls' instant leap from being outed to attempting a double suicide turns a contemporary, realistic story into a version
of Lillian Hellman's 1930s melodrama *The Children's Hour.*

Overall, homosexual visibility books tell stories of truth, of the positive and negative results when GLBTQ characters (and people) are honest about their sexual orientation. They are important stories, but fortunately they are no longer the only ones that can be told.

GAY ASSIMILATION

The second category of GLBTQ literature, gay assimilation, began to appear more frequently in the nineties. Its hallmark, remember, is the inclusion of characters whose homosexuality is not an issue; it's simply a
given and assumes a melting pot of sexual and gender identity. Not surprisingly, though, such stories remained rare even in the '90s. Of the seventy GLBTQ novels published during that decade, only a handful could
be described as true examples of assimilation. More often, the characters
who "happen" to be gay are openly gay for a reason that is central to the
purpose of the plot; e.g., the character has AIDS (Morris Gleitzman's *Two
Weeks with the Queen*, Deborah Davis' *My Brother Has AIDS*, and Theresa
Nelson's *Earthshine*) or is a parent whose open homosexuality poses a
problem for the protagonist. Examples of the latter include A. M. Jenkins' *Breaking Boxes* (where the parent figure is an older brother); Chris
Crutcher's short story "A Brief Moment in the Life of Angus Bethune,"
in which a boy has not one but two sets of gay parents; and Carol Dines'

story "Lezboy" about a boy who has two mothers. A third type is the case of the openly gay secondary character who is necessary to a protagonist's struggle for sexual or personal identity, e.g., David in *Peter* or Dirk and Duck in *Witch Baby*.

Purer examples of gay assimilation novels with minor secondary characters whose homosexuality is simply an integral part of who they are include Jacqueline Woodson's *The Dear One* (1991), in which a lesbian couple are close friends of the protagonist's mother. (This was only the second novel in the genre to include characters of color who are homosexual, Rosa Guy's *Ruby* being the first.) Other books with unproblematic gay minor characters are Francesca Lia Block's *Missing Angel Juan* (1993) in which an elderly gay couple, Mallard and Meadows, become friends with Witch Baby, and Adele Griffin's *Split Just Right* (1997), which includes a gay neighbor of the protagonist Danny and her mother.

Major secondary characters who just "happen" to be gay are rarer still but include Waylon, the protagonist's older friend and mentor in Gary Paulsen's novel *The Car* (1994); Barbie's friend Griffin in Block's *I Was a Teenage Fairy* (1998); Pook, one of the three friends featured in Jess Mowry's *Babylon Boyz* (1997); and—most prominently—Gio's friend and unrequited love, Marisol in Ellen Wittlinger's Printz Honor Award title *Hard Love* (1999). This last novel is also an example of our third category, Queer Consciousness/Community and is discussed further in that context below.

In only one novel of gay assimilation from the nineties, Nancy Garden's *Lark in the Morning* (1991), is the protagonist a person whose homosexuality is a given. In this case it is Gillian, seventeen, who is in a loving relationship with her best friend Suzanne. The issue that drives the novel, however, is Gillian's attempts to help a younger girl, Lark, and her little brother, who are abused runaways. However, the plot's logistics dictate that Gillian must continually choose between assisting the children (sneaking food to them, for example) and spending time with Suzanne, whom she initially elects not to tell about her "rescue" work because of the potential legal consequences of harboring runaway children. This leaves Suzanne little to do besides trusting her girlfriend and not minding getting left out of the action. *Lark in the Morning* is one of the first YA novels to include GLBTQ people whose sexual orientation is not The Problem, but readers will probably wish they'd gotten a chance to see more of Gillian and Suzanne together (perhaps in a mutual effort to helping the runaways?).

QUEER CONSCIOUSNESS/COMMUNITY

During the 1990s, the idea of queer community also began to appear more frequently in young adult novels, though the community itself was not necessarily any more visible or immediate than before. In fact, the model that had begun to appear in the 1970s, that of the queer community being somewhere off-stage, often in the past, sometimes in the future, usually urban, and definitely far from the teen protagonist's home, persisted through the '80s and well into the '90s. This was particularly true for novels that included AIDS as a plot element and that typically involved a gay character and his family dealing with the disease.

One common scenario—always told from the perspective of a young person—involved an older brother or an uncle who had made his home in a city with a sizeable gay/lesbian community. Before the book opens, however, the character has contracted AIDS and in the course of the story he returns to his family of origin to die. This plot first appears in M.E. Kerr's *Night Kites* (1985) and is repeated in other books published throughout the 1990s. In Penny Raife Durant's *When Heroes Die* (1992), for example, the protagonist is a boy whose uncle has AIDS. In Deborah's Davis' *My Brother Has AIDS* (1994), a teenage girl's older brother returns to the family home. In both Melrose Cooper's *Life Magic* (1996) and Gregory Maguire's *Oasis* (1996), an uncle is taken in by the protagonist's parent(s).

These books provide few details about the gay community except to locate it Somewhere Else. Since the lives of these gay men—even those whose families fully accept and embrace them—have been led off-stage, the gay community exists only in the past and is, thus, entirely invisible.

In other books of the 1990s, the GLBTQ community, though still off-stage, is—more optimistically—placed in the future. This time the temporal distance is not insurmountable—it's just a matter of getting there. Chris Lynch's *Dog Eat Dog* (1996), the final book in the author's Blue-Eyed Son trilogy, is an example. Over the course of the three books, Toy has been the straight protagonist Mick's friend, a good-looking motorcycle-riding loner whose cool and quiet presence has been a rare constant in Mick's chaotic life. Toy is also gay, and his departure is not unexpected news to Mick:

> "Toy began dropping hints that he might not be around anymore once the summer came.
>   'What, you mean like a trip, only longer?' I asked hopefully.
>   'Ya, like longer,' he said. . . .
>   'I know I'm not supposed to ask this, but where are you gonna go?'
>   Under the straw hat, a big grin pushed his ears up, pushed the hat up.
>   'Home,' he said, almost sadly. 'I'm thinking I'm going to go home.'
>   This seemed like a lot of information from Toy. I tried not to sound surprised. 'Where's home?'
>   'I don't know yet,' he said." (135–36)

In a few cases—even when the queer community is located off-stage—the reader gets to see the gay characters after they've finally found their kindred spirits. In M.E. Kerr's *Deliver Us from Evie*, for example, the prodigal daughters return to Missouri for a reconciling visit. Still as butch and femme as ever, Evie and Patty are obviously prospering in the gay-friendly environment of New York City. As Evie's father wryly observes, "You're like the railroad worker's daughter. You made tracks for a better station in life" (175).

In some books, the gay community is actually close enough to visit. In Paul Robert Walker's *The Method* (1990), for example, the reader can observe a community of gay people in their native habitat—in this case a gay restaurant—and even stay to have a root beer float. "There was an old-fashioned ice-cream parlor in the middle of the next block. It was decorated like something out of the 1890s, with wicker ceiling fans slowly circulating the air. On the walls there were posters of Marilyn Monroe, Bette Davis, and Joan Crawford" (135). As the two friends sit at the counter, Mitch tells Albie that he is gay. As Albie reflects on this news, he watches as "the gay waiters run up and down the counter, dishing out sundaes and sodas and shakes and banana splits. He watched the gay customers, eating and laughing at the tables" (138). Thus, along with Albie, the reader is given the opportunity to see a community socializing in the mellow euphoria of a celebratory day as it slowly winds down.

In another restaurant scene, the young male protagonist of Rodger Larson's *What I Know Now* (1997) visits a pizza parlor with a mixed gay and straight clientele. "These men and women looked comfortable, happy. I believed the men and women in the Gay Nineties Pizza Parlor had interesting thoughts, told funny stories, enjoyed being together. I had a wish then. The wish was to be a part of this group of people, to belong among them, to fit in" (180).

The queer community may also be found at parties, picnics, and get-togethers with friends. In Cristina Salat's *Living in Secret*, for example, Amelia attends a New Year's Eve party with her mother and her mother's partner Jane: "Denise shares a large house near Golden Gate Park with her brother, Michael, and his boyfriend, Andy. The white-rugged living room is full of people dancing. I notice men are dancing with men, and women are dancing with women. I've never seen so many gay people in one place before. Then I notice that some women are also dancing with men. Nobody seems to mind anyone else. I am amazed. I didn't know gay people and straight people ever hung out together" (94).

Jacqueline Woodson's *From the Notebooks of Melanin Sun* (1995) features Mel, an African American teen, and his mother EC, who are a tight-knit family of two. When Kristin, who is white, comes into EC's life, Mel is upset by Kristin's racial and cultural difference and what he perceives as her intrusion into his home. After Mel's initial rejection of his mother and Kristin as a couple, EC convinces him to join her and Kristin for a picnic at Jones Beach—and to see what he is gaining rather than what he is losing through his mother's lesbian relationship: "Kristin led us to the area that was mostly gay. It was strange seeing so many of them all coupled up in one place, but it made it feel less weird to be there with Ma and Kristin. We passed a group of people that Kristin knew and she stopped and introduced us." Mel and Kristin walk on the beach, and she tells him how much the two of them have come to mean to her. "'I've always wanted a family,' Kristin was saying. 'I lost mine [when] they found out I'm queer.'" Now she has a different family: "'Not the family I was born into,' she said, 'the family I made for myself. Close friends.'" This need for family and community is underlined in a later conversation. "'Yesterday,' Kristin said. 'I was thinking about buffalo. Can you imagine being the last to die off?' I shook my head. 'I'd want to go in the crowd.' 'Me too,' Kristin said softly, 'Me too'" (132–37).

In all of these books, however, the GLBTQ community is a community of adults being observed by a straight teen protagonist. What does such a community look like when it's comprised of GLBTQ teens themselves? Young adult fiction's first gay/lesbian peer support group appears in Jesse Maguire's 1991 novel, *Getting It Right*. In it, Eric, a closeted high school student, mistakenly believes that Josh, one of his classmates, is gay. When Eric queries Josh about his own coming-out story, Josh explodes, "'I'm not gay!' After an anguished Eric attempts suicide, a more enlightened Josh and his friends nudge the boy into attending a program sponsored by the high school Gay and Lesbian Alliance, a sketchily rendered group that includes a music geek, a self-described "gay radical," and a lesbian planning to go into the ministry.

Four years later, a more fully realized gay/lesbian support group is depicted in R.J. Hamilton's two-volume Pride Pack series, *Who Framed Lorenzo Garcia?* (1995) and *The Case of the Missing Mother* (1995). As typical series books, their plots are predictable, their characters are unidimensional, and much of their dialog reads like the transcript of a television police drama, but these titles provide an attractive, if perhaps unrealistic, picture of a community that embraces many differences.

In the first title, sixteen-year-old Ramon has been rejected by his family of origin for being gay. After living on the street and in foster homes for two years, he finds an adoptive gay father in police officer Lorenzo Garcia. He also finds a family of friends who hang out together at the Gay and Lesbian Center: Cady, an Asian-American lesbian; Aron, whose older brother is gay; Maddie, a Jamaican-born computer genius; Sammi, a lesbian punk rocker, and George, a handsome white athlete. Some of the teens are gay or lesbian, while others have gay/lesbian family members, but all welcome Ramon into their group, which later becomes the Pride Pack as they begin to investigate drug charges trumped up against Officer Garcia. In the book that follows, *The Case of the Missing Mother*, the Pride Pack investigates the disappearance of a lesbian political activist and discovers that she has been kidnapped by members of a radical right group. The Pride Pack utilizes its members' various skills—from computer wizardry to physical tracking—to locate and release the activist and bring her kidnappers to justice.

Formal groups are certainly useful but teens may also find their GLBTQ peers and a sense of community in informal friendship networks. However, where one gay/lesbian person or a single gay/lesbian couple may go unnoticed in the mainstream world of YA fiction, three or more gays or lesbians can be frightening, discomfiting, or, yes, liberating representations of gay/lesbian people as a community. To closeted teens who are uncomfortable with their own same-sex attractions, such a group of "people like me" is understandably threatening. For example, Cary, the narrator of *Tomorrow Wendy: A Love Story*, by Shelley Stoehr (1998), is struggling with her attraction to her boyfriend's sister. Hence her dismay when the clique she calls "the lesbian collective" sit down at her table in the high school cafeteria. Her discomfort increases when she sees them at the dance club she and her boyfriend frequent:

> "I watched the lesbian girls hanging out by the bathroom. A couple of the girls were too heavy for me. One had beautiful hair and a mysterious parched face, but her legs were too spindly-long, and I didn't like the way she dressed. . . . I wouldn't want to be in a clique like that. I mean, in school those girls were never separated. It was like they couldn't stand on their own. I guessed it must be hard, but I still didn't like the almost political force they tried to be, and meanwhile people still laughed at them from across the room. Besides being pathetic, it pissed me off that their public hand-holding and kissing had nothing to do with love. It was more like they were spitting in unison at the rest of us." (32)

For gay/lesbian teens on the lookout for kindred spirits, however, meeting not just one, but a whole group of gay/lesbian people can offer the thrill of self-affirmation and at least the promise of community. John, the narrator of *Hard Love*, by Ellen Wittlinger, falls in love with Marisol, a self-identified "Cuban American Yankee lesbian" and creator of the *Escape Velocity*. Marisol values John's friendship but (gently and firmly) rejects his longing for something more. When the two go to a writers' conference together, they meet a group of lesbians from New York whom John observes warily. "There were four women sitting at the table, three of whom stared intently at Marisol, trying to decide if what they suspected was true. For her part, Marisol locked onto each of them as Bill said their names (Sarah, BJ, June) and she couldn't seem to move past them as the other names were announced"(207). They invite Marisol to return with them to New York City and she joyfully accepts—she's finally reached escape velocity and is traveling on her own toward her future life as part of the community she's been heading for all her life.

Hard Love, a Printz Honor Award-winner, was a ground-breaking book not only for its portrayal of a single GLBTQ teen seeking out a queer community but also—after a number of stories about straight girls who fall for gay boys—as the first portrayal in young adult fiction of a straight young man falling for a lesbian. Perhaps most importantly, it was the first YA novel with significant GLBTQ content to win a major literary honor. Thus, it set the stage for the next decade's gradual movement of the genre from the literary margins to the mainstream of literary acceptance and recognition.

We conclude this chapter with a description of a final nineties text, Marion Dane Bauer's *Am I Blue?: Coming Out from the Silence* (1994). As a collection of short stories, *Am I Blue?* is technically beyond the scope of our text; nevertheless, this remarkable book anticipates many of the publishing and narrative trends in GLBTQ that began in the nineties and have continued into the twenty-first century. *Am I Blue?* is an anthology of sixteen original short stories with GLBTQ content, all by established YA authors. The sixteen stories demonstrate a gender equity and narrative diversity not generally found in this body of literature: half of the stories include gay males, half lesbians, and the GLBTQ content is a mix of protagonists and secondary characters (nine protagonists, seven secondary characters). By way of comparison, six YA novels with GLBTQ content were also published in 1994. Of these six novels, one had a GLBTQ protagonist, while five had GLBTQ secondary characters. Two of these novels included lesbian characters, while four included gay male characters. All of these characters were Caucasian Americans. In contrast, the sixteen short stories represent a remarkable diversity of characters and genre. The first (and titular) story is a humorous fantasy; the final story is a memoir of a girl who realized she was "different from other little girls" when she was four years old. Settings include Viet Nam, San Francisco, rural Wyoming, a beach on Lake Erie, a summer community on Nantucket Island. The GLBTQ characters themselves are likewise diverse, of varying race, class, and cultural backgrounds, and stand in varying relationships with the protagonist. One protagonist is a boy returning from the funeral of his father's lover; one is a girl whose older sister brings home a friend for the summer, a lesbian who has been disowned by her parents. A boy surreptitiously watches a male sunbather on a deserted beach; a girl comes out to her grandmother; a group of gay teens—male and female—staff a literature table for their school's gay-straight alliance at Parents Night; another group of friends that includes a gay couple make a movie depicting an unorthodox and touching version of the Nativity; a young lesbian agonizes over her future career options; a boy who has just been gay-bashed is visited by Melvin, a wish-granting fairy godfather. Taken together, these stories anticipate future trends toward a (slowly) increasing diversity of GLBTQ YA fiction in a number of directions: narrative distance, writing style and techniques, genre and language, and setting, as well as expanding the gender, race, class, and culture variables of YA fiction that has so often defined "gay" as white, middle class, suburban, and male.

GAY AND LESBIAN NOVELS OF THE 1990s

1990

Levy, Marilyn. *Rumors and Whispers.* Ballantine. 156 pages.

> HV. Gay. After Sarah's father kicks her older brother Doug out of the house, she learns that her favorite teacher is HIV positive—and her father is leading the charge to have him fired. But when she visits the AIDS ward of a local hospital, she finds Doug working there as a volunteer care-giver and finally learns—to no one's surprise but her own—that her brother is gay.

Sweeney, Joyce. *Face the Dragon.* Delacorte. 231 pages.

> HV. Gay. Each of the new students in a class for gifted teens must face a dragon. Eric's friend Paul's "dragon" is his sexual orientation. Though at first Eric responds unsympathetically, the two finally resume their friendship.

Walker, Robert Paul. *The Method.* Harcourt Brace Jovanovich. 181 pages.

> HV. QC. Gay. Albie, fifteen, joins an acting workshop and discovers both his new friend, Mitch, and their drama teacher, Mr. Pierce, are gay. First inclusion in a YA novel of a gay pride parade.

Westall, Robert. *The Kingdom by the Sea.* Farrar Straus Giroux. 176 pages.

> HV. Gay. Twelve-year-old Harry, orphaned in a German bombing raid, sets off to find a home for himself. He meets a number of adults, including the predatory Corporal Merman, whose attempt to molest the boy is thwarted by an adult friend. Set in England during World War II.

1991

Block, Francesca Lia. *Witch Baby.* Zolotow/HarperCollins. 103 pages.

> HV. GA. Gay. Setting out to find her own place in the world, the alienated Witch Baby outs Dirk and Duck, to the shock of Duck's mother. This is the second *Weetzie Bat* novel.

Crutcher, Chris. *Athletic Shorts.* Greenwillow. 154 pages

> HV. GA. Crutcher's collection includes two gay stories: "A Brief Moment in the Life of Angus Bethune," which includes not one but two sets of gay parents, and "In the Time I Get" in which the protagonist meets a gay man with AIDS.

Garden, Nancy. *Lark in the Morning.* Farrar Straus Giroux. 240 pages.

> GA. Lesbian. When Gillian attempts to help two abused runaways, her romantic relationship with Suzanne takes a back seat. The saintly Suzanne is remarkably understanding.

Gleitzman, Morris. *Two Weeks with the Queen.* Putnam. 144 pages.

> GA. Gay. Originally published in Australia for mid-range readers, this is the story of a boy who finds the hospital where his cancer-stricken brother is being treated and meets a gay young man whose lover is dying of AIDS.

Greene, Bette. *The Drowning of Stephan Jones.* Bantam. 240 pages.

> HV. Gay. Gay partners Stephan and Frank move to a small southern town to open an antique store. The protagonist, Carla, is one of the few people in town who is friendly to them, but then she witnesses her boyfriend Andy and his homophobic friends brutalize Stephan and toss him into the river, where he drowns. The subsequent trial results in near-acquittal, but Frank gets the last laugh by convincing others that Stephan and Andy were actually lovers.

Maguire, Jesse. *Getting It Right.* Ivy/Ballantine. 185 pages.

> HV. QC. Gay. One of several books about a group of friends at Norwell High, this story focuses in part on a secondary character, Eric, who comes out, and attempts suicide, but the gang is there to support him and convince him to attend the school dance. The first YA novel to include a gay/lesbian peer support group, a Gay and Lesbian Alliance.

Woodson, Jacqueline. *The Dear One.* Delacorte. 160 pages.

> GA. Lesbian. Catherine, Marion, and Clair became close friends as students at Spelman College. Now, Catherine's twelve-year-old daughter Afeni (Swahili for "dear one") tells the story of the changes

that Clair's daughter, fifteen-year-old Rebecca, sets in motion when she comes to stay during the final months of her pregnancy. Marion and her partner Bernadette are an integral part of Afeni's network of family and friends. The first novel to include adult homosexuals of color.

1992

Durant, Penny Raife. *When Heroes Die.* Atheneum. 144 pages.

HV. Gay. Twelve-year-old Gary lives with his mother, whose gay brother has been a father figure and hero to the boy through much of his life. Sadly, the uncle has full-blown AIDS and must rely on his sister to care for him during his final months.

Isensee, Rik. *We're Not Alone.* Lavender Press. 126 pages.

HV. Gay and Lesbian. Sixteen-year-old Mike is in the process of coming out, and so is his girlfriend Susie! Their now-platonic friendship deepens as they face harrassment from some high school peers. Others are supportive and help Mike and Susie establish a gay/lesbian/bisexual student association at their school.

Wieler, Diana. *Bad Boy.* Delacorte. 185 pages.

HV. QC. Gay. From Canada, this is the story of hockey-playing, sixteen-year-old A.J. who responds to the news that his best friend and fellow hockey player, Tully, is gay by becoming their team's violently out-of-control "bad boy" who routinely injures members of the opposing team.

1993

Bess, Clayton. *The Mayday Rampage.* Lookout Press. 208 pages.

HV. Gay. A novel written in the form of conversations and interviews. Molly and Jess, high school journalists and a couple decide to investigate the impact of the AIDS epidemic on their community. As they proceed with their project, they learn that Jess's English teacher and his partner—characters who first appeared in Bess' *Big Man and the Burn-out* (1985)—are among the many whose lives have been changed forever by AIDS.

Block, Francesca Lia. *Missing Angel Juan.* HarperCollins. 138 pages.

GA. Gay and Transsexual. Witch Baby goes to New York, meets Mallard and Meadows, an elderly gay couple, and also encounters two beautiful women who are clearly intended as transgender or transsexual; they re-appear in Block's later short story "Dragons in Manhattan" (the first appearance of a transsexual character in YA literature).

Dhondy, Farrukh. *Black Swan*. Houghton Mifflin. 217 pages.

HV GA Gay. Rose is a British teen who becomes research assistant to the mysterious "Mr. Bernier," an irascible and scholarly West Indian political refugee living in a secluded London "safe house." This multilayered historical mystery focuses on an Elizabethan manuscript account of Lazarus, a former slave who becomes Christopher Marlowe's lover and co-author of the plays ascribed to that no-account drunk, William Shakespeare.

Kaye, Marilyn. *Real Heroes*. Harcourt Brace Jovanovich. 144 pages.

HV. Gay. Mr. Logan, Kevin's favorite teacher, is HIV-positive. When conservative members of the school community learn this, they organize a school boycott. Although his father is one of the boycott leaders, Kevin is dismayed to learn that Mr. Logan will resign. "If I stayed, you kids would suffer. So I chose to leave" (132).

Murrow, Liza Ketchum. *Twelve Days in August*. Holiday House. 160 pages.

HV. Gay. Todd, sixteen, is a member of a soccer team headed for the league playoffs, but the team's cohesiveness is disrupted by a team member's harassment of newcomer Alex, who is rumored to be gay. At first Todd joins in, but when he learns that his beloved Uncle Gordo is gay, Todd knows that he must do all he can to resist peer pressure and support Alex.

Salat, Cristina. *Living in Secret*. Bantam. 192 pages.

HV. QC. Lesbian. The story begins with a riveting opening line: "In the middle of the night my mother comes to steal me away." Amelia, eleven, wants to live with her mother and mother's partner Janey, but her father demands full custody to keep her away from her mother's "lesbian lifestyle." When his demands escalate, mom, Janey, and Amelia make a clandestine escape and start their new "living in secret" lives as fugitives.

Walker, Kate. *Peter*. Houghton Mifflin. 176 pages.

HV. GA. Gay. Peter, a fifteen-year-old Australian boy, spends his days with his dirt-biking peers who continually challenge each other to perform macho—and often physically dangerous—feats of derring-do. But Peter begins questioning his own sexual identity when he develops a crush on David, his older brother's gay best friend.

1994

Bauer, Marion Dane. *Am I Blue?: Coming Out from the Silence.* Harper-Collins. 224 pages.

A landmark collection of sixteen original short stories that include GLBTQ content. All are by noted YA authors and are accompanied by autobiographical sketches.

Davis, Deborah. *My Brother Has AIDS.* Atheneum. 186 pages.

GA. Gay. Thirteen-year-old Lacy's adult brother Jack is a gay lawyer who has been living in Colorado with his partner. When the AIDS epidemic hits, however, Jack's partner dies, and Jack himself grows increasingly disabled, and finally must return to his family in Maine to be cared for until his own inevitable death.

Donovan, Stacey. *Dive.* Dutton. 175 pages.

HV. Lesbian. V (short for Virginia) and her family are suddenly in crisis mode when her father is diagnosed with a disabling and fatal disease (acute milofibrosis). As her father grows weaker and his hospital stays longer, V grows increasingly close to a striking new classmate, Jane. The two are drawn together in a romantic relationship as Jane helps V cope with the inevitable loss of her father.

Kerr, M.E. *Deliver Us from Evie.* HarperCollins. 179 pages.

GA. QC. Lesbian. A story about Evie, who looks "a little like Elvis Presley," and her romance with the daughter of the local banker who holds the mortgage on the family farm. Set in rural Missouri against a backdrop of the Midwestern floods of 1993.

McClain, Ellen Jaffe. *No Big Deal.* Lodestar. 187 pages.

HV. Gay. Janice's junior high social studies teacher, Mr. Padovano, is gay, a fact incidental to his gift for teaching. However, when Mr. Padovano's car is vandalized and Janice's mother leads the parental charge to get him fired, Janice must speak up.

Nelson, Theresa. *Earthshine.* Orchard Books. 192 pages.

GA. Gay. Slim, twelve, has been raised primarily by her actor father Mack and his partner Larry. But now Mack is dying of AIDS. They long for a miracle cure while coping with the difficulties of caring for Mack in his rapidly deteriorating condition. In the end, Slim and Larry comfort each other: As Slim says of Larry, "He's my family, that's all I know."

Paulsen, Gary. *The Car.* Harcourt Brace. 180 pages.

GA. Gay. An on-the-road story of a teen and his car. Terry is deserted by both his parents and seizes this unsupervised opportunity to put together the automobile kit his father kept in the garage. Once the car is built, he heads west and eventually joins forces with Waylon, a warm-hearted drifter and genius auto mechanic. Terry is momentarily alarmed when he is told that Waylon is gay, but quickly realizes that this fact is irrelevant to their friendship.

1995

Bantle, Lee F. *Diving for the Moon*. Macmillan. 163 pages

GA. Gay. Bird is spending a leisurely pre-seventh grade summer at her family's lake cottage when she finds out that her friend Josh, who has hemophilia, is HIV positive. Bird's long-time lake neighbors and family friends—including a gay male couple—help her learn what Josh's diagnosis does and does not mean for their friendship.

Block, Francesca Lia. *Baby Bebop*. HarperCollins. 106 pages.

HV. Gay. This moving prequel to *Weetzie Bat* tells the story of Dirk's life growing up in the loving home of his gentle Grandma Fifi. Dirk is well aware of his same-sex attractions ("Dirk has known it since he could remember"), but when he attempts to come out, he is re-jected by his best friend and beaten by skinheads. Finally family spirits—his great-grandmother, father, and mother—visit him and tell him the stories that will make him want to live.

Brown, Todd. *Entries from a Hot Pink Notebook*. Washington Square. 320 pages.

HV. Gay. A novel in journal format told by thirteen-year-old Ben, an angst-filled high school freshman whose family is coming apart and who finds himself falling in love with his classmate Aaron. When word of their romance gets around, however, his life starts falling apart.

Crutcher, Chris. *Ironman*. Greenwillow. 181 pages.

HV. Gay. When athletic but ornery Bo Brewster smarts off to his sadistic former football coach, he avoids suspension by joining his school's anger-management group. The group members and their leader not only help Bo find his way back to himself but also to suc-cessfully challenge his homophobia when he learns that Mr. Ser-bousek, his swim coach and mentor, is gay.

Fox, Paula. *The Eagle Kite*. Orchard Books. 127 pages.

HV. Gay. Liam's parents are divorced, and now his father is diag-nosed with AIDS. Liam's mother blames a tainted blood transfusion, but it becomes increasingly clear that her husband actually contracted the disease from his now-dead male lover. A beautifully written but ultimately negative portrait of a gay man who chooses a beautiful youth over his wife and child and is punished by death.

Hamilton, R.J. *Who Framed Lorenzo Garcia?* and *The Case of the Missing Mother.* (Pride Pack series). Alyson. 128 pages each.

QC. GA. Gay. Lesbian. The first two novels in what was initially projected as a longer series featuring a racially, culturally, and sexually diverse group of teens who meet at the Gay and Lesbian Community Center and play a major role in solving the knotty and mysterious problems of gay/lesbian adults and their friends. *Who Framed Lorenzo Garcia?* is one of the first two YA GLBTQ novels to include a Latina/o protagonist (as well as secondary characters). (See also Velasquez below.)

Springer, Nancy. *Looking for Jamie Bridger.* Dial. 159 pages.

HV. Gay. Fourteen-year-old Jamie discovers that the harshly strict grandparents who raised her are actually her parents and that she has an older brother who was kicked out and disowned for being gay.

Van Dijk, Lutz. *Damned Strong Love.* Henry Holt. 138 pages.

GA. Gay. Polish teenager Stefan falls in love with a German soldier during World War II. Based on a true story, this is the first historical novel for YAs to deal with GLBTQ issues.

Velasquez, Gloria. *Tommy Stands Alone.* Arte Publico. 135 pages (paperback original).

HV. Gay. The story of a gay Mexican American teen, Tomas, who is rejected by his family and attempts suicide. He is rescued by a caring adult therapist.

Woodson, Jacqueline. *From the Notebooks of Melanin Sun.* Scholastic. 141 pages.

HV. Lesbian. Melanin Sun, a black teen with a talent for writing, and his mother EC have been a tight two-person family for as long as he can remember. But when EC and Kristen, a white woman, fall in love, Mel's world is irrevocably altered as he battles his own homophobia to reconcile with EC and accept Kristin.

1996

Block, Francesca Lia. *Girl Goddess #9.* HarperCollins. 181 pages.

HV. Gay. Lesbian. Transsexual. Two of the nine stories in this collection deal with GLBTQ issues: "Winnie and Cubby" is about a girl whose boyfriend comes out to her. "Dragons in Manhattan" is about a girl who discovers that her mother's lesbian lover is a transsexual and also her biological father. (We first met these characters in *Missing Angel Juan*.)

Cart, Michael. *My Father's Scar*. Simon & Schuster. 204 pages.

> HV. Gay. During his first year of college, Andy Logan comes to accept his same-sex attractions as he reflects upon the friends and family members who hindered or helped his younger self's struggle toward a positive gay identity. His controlling father looms large, as does his gentle, book-loving great-uncle.

Cooper, Melrose. *Life Magic*. Holt. 116 pages.

> HV. Gay. AIDS. Gr. 4-6. Crystal, an African American sixth grader, has always had a special relationship with her artist uncle. When he develops full-blown AIDS, he is gladly taken in by her family, and the pain of losing him is ameliorated—at least in part—by the valuable time that Crystal gets to spend with him.

Garden, Nancy. *Good Moon Rising*. Farrar Straus Giroux. 230 pages.

> HV. Lesbian. The high school drama club is holding tryouts for *The Crucible* and Kerry, a talented newcomer, gets the starring role that Janna wanted. Despite this inauspicious beginning, Jan and Kerry fall in love. They are circumspect about their relationship but are still harassed by homophobic classmates—most notably the actor playing opposite Kerry. The pressure on the two increases until the girls finally come out to their peers.

Lynch, Chris. *Dog Eat Dog*. (Blue Eyed Son Trilogy). HarperTrophy. 144 pages.

> HV. Gay. When fifteen-year-old Mick succeeds in breaking free from the influence of his evil older brother, his Latino friend Toy comes out to him, and their friendship remains strong as the two ride off together on Toy's motorcycle.

Maguire, Gregory. *Oasis*. Clarion. 176 pages.

> HV. Gay. Hand and his divorced father run a motel, but when his father dies suddenly, Hand's long-estranged mother steps in and takes on the running of Oasis. Hand's Uncle Wolfgang has not been close to his family, but when he and his lover contract AIDS and his lover dies, he comes to spend the final months of his life at Oasis.

Zalben, Jane Breskin. *Unfinished Dreams*. Simon & Schuster. 169 pages.

> HV. Gay. Jason, an eleven-year-old sixth-grade violin prodigy, is encouraged by his kind and caring principal, Mr. Carr, who is gay and

contracts AIDS. After Mr. Carr dies, his grieving partner gives Jason the principal's final gift to him, his beautiful and valuable violin.

1997

Coville, Bruce. *The Skull of Truth.* ("A Magic Shop Book"). Harcourt, Brace. 195 pages.

> HV. Gay. A humorous fantasy in which Charlie visits a magic shop and ends up with Yorick, a wise-cracking human skull with the power to force people to tell the truth. Charlie's Uncle Bennie comes under its influence at the dinner table and comes out to his entire extended family.

Dines, Carol. *Talk To Me.* Delacorte. 225 pages.

> HV. GA. Lesbian. A collection of six original short stories and a novella. One story, "Lezboy," is about a boy who travels to France with his two moms.

Donoghue, Emma. *Kissing the Witch: Old Tales in New Skins.* Cotler/HarperCollins. 240 pages.

> GA. Lesbian. A haunting and brilliantly conceived collection of thirteen interconnected fairy tales re-told from a lesbian/feminist perspective.

Gantos, Jack. *Desire Lines.* Farrar Straus Giroux. 137 pages.

> HV. Lesbian. One night high school sophomore Walker sees two of his female classmates making love in a deserted corner of the golf course near his home. In a moment of stoned camaraderie, Walker brings several friends with him to spy on the girls, who are then outed to the community. The next night he sees the girls enact a murder-suicide pact that leaves one dead. A genuinely creepy tale of betrayal, despair, and religion gone wrong.

Griffin, Adele. *Split Just Right.* Hyperion. 176 pages.

> GA. Gay. For most of Danny's fourteen years she has been raised by three adults: her mother and Gary and Elliott, a gay male couple. She has no memory of or contact with her biological father, but her curiosity finally leads her to write him a letter, which brings him momentarily into her life.

Jenkins, A. M. *Breaking Boxes.* Delacorte. 182 pages.

> HV. GA. Gay. Charlie's older brother Trent works a full time job while going to college in order to support the parentless duo. That Trent is also gay is a fact that Charlie has known forever, but that Charlie's new friend Brandon finds so appalling he tells everyone he

knows. The resulting conflict eventually resolves positively as Charlie and Brandon renew their friendship.

Kerr, M.E. *"Hello," I Lied.* HarperCollins. 192 pages.

HV. Gay. Bisexual. Lang, seventeen, is gay and in a relationship with Alex, who is several years older and is pressing Lang to come out. But when Lang meets a young French girl, Huguette, he finds himself attracted to her. The first YA novel to explore bisexuality.

Ketchum, Liza. *Blue Coyote.* Simon & Schuster. 198 pages.

HV. Gay. A sequel to the author's *Twelve Days in August*, this one features soccer star Alex, who is indeed gay. Alex and his father spend the summer in Los Angeles where Alex searches for his lost love Tito. When he finally succeeds, he learns that Tito has been recovering from the brutal beating he received when his father learned his son was gay.

Larson, Rodger. *What I Know Now.* Henry Holt. 262 pages.

HV. QC. Gay. Set in 1957, this memoir-like novel tells the story of Dave's fourteenth summer and the emotional coming-of-age that results. When his parents separate, he meets master gardener Gene Tole, a gay man who shows him a different way to be a man than the brutal machismo of his despicable father.

Mowry, Jess. *Babylon Boyz.* Simon & Schuster. 188 pages.

GA. Gay. A story of Wyatt, Dante, and Pook, three African American inner-city teens in Oakland who find a suitcase full of cocaine. Pook's gay identify is presented as a fact, not an issue.

Wersba, Barbara. *Whistle Me Home.* Henry Holt. 108 pages.

HV. Gay. Noli meets and falls in love with TJ, a beautiful boy with a fondness for poetry. She is heartbroken when she learns that he is gay.

Woodson, Jacqueline. *The House You Pass on the Way.* Delacorte. 100 pages.

HV. Lesbian. Quiet loner Staggerlee, fourteen, falls in love one memorable summer with her cousin, a girl named Trout. The resulting relationship remains ambiguous. As they write in the riverbank mud, "Staggerlee and Trout were here today. Maybe they will and maybe they won't be gay."

1998

Block, Francesca Lia. *I Was a Teenage Fairy.* HarperCollins. 186 pages.

GA. Gay. Barbie, sixteen, is a successful model with a celebrity boyfriend, Todd, who has a gay roommate, Griffin. Both Barbie and

Griffin have been molested by the same photographer and, perhaps as a result, both can see Mab, the teenage fairy of the title.

Stoehr, Shelley. *Tomorrow Wendy: A Love Story.* Delacorte. 166 pages.

HV. Lesbian. High school senior Cary is confused by her feelings for her boyfriend's twin sister, Wendy. Meanwhile a group of girls called "the lesbian collective" hang around her like a Greek chorus.

1999

Atkins, Catherine. *When Jeff Comes Home.* Puffin. 231 pages.

HV. Gay. After several years of captivity and sexual abuse, fifteen-year-old Jeff is returned to his family by his kidnapper. The first YA novel to deal with pedophilia. Unfortunately the author never clearly differentiates between pedophilia and homosexuality.

Bechard, Margaret. *If It Doesn't Kill You.* Viking. 156 pages.

HV. Gay. High school freshman Ben's father, a former football hero, has recently left Ben and his mom for another man. At first Ben shuns his father and rejects meeting his father's partner, but his growing friendship with the new girl living across the street gives him a fresh perspective and a reason to reach out.

Boock, Paula. *Dare Truth or Promise.* Houghton Mifflin. 176 pages.

HV. Lesbian. From New Zealand the story of two girls, Louie and Willa, who meet and fall in love. Despite the barriers of family and religious disapproval, the rightness of the girls' relationship finally overcomes opposition. Another story with a car crash, but this one brings the girls together at last.

Chbosky, Stephen. *The Perks of Being a Wallflower.* MTV/Pocket. 213 pages.

HV. GA. Gay. Fifteen-year-old Charlie enters high school and meets two siblings, Samantha and Patrick, who quickly become his closest friends. When he discovers Patrick kissing another boy at a party, Charlie (accurately) concludes that Patrick is gay and assures him of his continuing friendship and support.

Durbin, Peggy. *And Featuring Bailey Wellcom as the Biscuit.* Little Blue Works.

GA. Lesbian. Bailey and her mother move to a small Southwestern town where her mother will work as a teacher. Her mother falls in love with a woman rancher and they move to the ranch. A story for upper elementary/middle school age readers.

Garden, Nancy. *The Year They Burned the Books.* Farrar Straus Giroux. 256 pages.

HV. QC. Gay. Lesbian. Sexual orientation, homophobia, and censorship are the themes of this novel about high school journalists. One of the first novels to feature a friendship between a lesbian and a gay.

Naylor, Phyllis Reynolds. *Alice on the Outside.* Atheneum. 176 pages.

HV. Lesbian. The eleventh title in this excellent series finds Alice in the second half of eighth grade, curious about sex and taking part in Consciousness Raising Week at school. Alice's own consciousness is raised when a new friend, Lori, turns out to be both gay and interested in her.

Nolan, Han. *A Face in Every Window.* Harcourt Brace. 272 pages.

HV. Gay. Teenager JP, his mentally slow Pap, and his mentally young Mam move into a new house and see their family begin to expand as they take in human strays and runaways. One of these, Larry, is a teen neighbor whose father has kicked him out for being gay.

Taylor, William. *The Blue Lawn.* Alyson. 122 pages.

HV. Gay. Another novel from New Zealand, this is the story of the growing relationship between two boys, David and Theo. In a twist on an old stereotype, a car crash is a catalyst to the relationship.

Taylor, William. *Jerome.* Alyson. 120 pages.

HV. Gay. Lesbian. Another—but less successful—novel from New Zealand's Taylor. Jerome, a gay teen, has committed suicide, an act that is the catalyst for a long-distance conversation between his friend Marco and Jerome's best friend, Kate, who is a lesbian.

Torres, Laura. *November Ever After.* Holiday House. 171 pages.

HV. Lesbian. Amy's mother has died in a car crash (!), leaving her and her pastor father bereft. Amy tries to find comfort in her friendship with Sara until she learns that Sara is a lesbian. And that's the end of *that.*

Wittlinger, Ellen. *Hard Love.* Simon & Schuster. 224 pages.

GA. QC. Lesbian. A Printz Honor Award book, this celebrated novel tells the story of John, who falls in love with Marisol, a self-proclaimed lesbian. The only YA novel to explore this territory.

Yamanaka, Lois-Ann. *Name Me Nobody.* Hyperion. 230 pages.

HV. Lesbian. Set in Hawaii, this is a story of Emi-Lou Kaya, fourteen, whose best friend, Yvonne, discovers girls.

NOTES

1. Cart, Michael. *From Romance to Realism: Fifty Years of Growth and Change in Young Adult Literature.* NY: HarperCollins, 1996.

2. Advocates for Youth. http://www.advocatesforyouth.org

3. Cart, Michael. "A Place for Energy, Activity, and Art." *English Journal.* 93:1 (September 2003).

4. Jenkins, Christine. "From Queer to Gay and Back Again." *Library Quarterly.* 68:3 (1998).

5. Kerr, M.E. In *Hearing Us Out. Voices from the Gay and Lesbian Community* by Roger Sutton. Boston: Little, Brown. 1994.

A New Literature for a New Century?

$\mathcal{T}$he rapid growth of every aspect of young adult publishing that began in the 1990s has continued apace in the early years of the twenty-first century. One indication of this is the appearance of new publisher imprints created specifically to publish non-series young adult books. This trend began in the nineties with HarperTempest and MTV Books; more recent imprints include Scholastic's PUSH, Penguin Putnam's Razorbill, Abrams' Amulet, Houghton Mifflin's Graphia, and Simon & Schuster's Simon Spotlight Entertainment.

With the expansion of the genre overall, the number of YA titles with GLBTQ content has also grown. In the five publishing years from 2000 to 2004, a total of sixty-six YA titles with GLBTQ content appeared, as compared to the total of seventy titles that appeared during the entire decade of the 1990s. The annual rate of publication of novels with GLBTQ content has grown steadily from one per year in the 1970s to four in the 1980s to seven in the 1990s to the current rate of thirteen per year.

Just as the GLBTQ titles reflected the growth in sheer numbers of all YA books being published, so they have also mirrored the larger YA world in terms of their newly expansive inclusion of new forms, faces, genres, themes, voices, narrative strategies, and more. In a sense, it seems, YA literature with GLBTQ content itself has begun to move—as have many of the individual titles that comprise it—toward assimilation; moving, that is, from being an isolated or "ghettoized" subgenre to becoming a more integrated part of the total body of young adult literature. To demonstrate this, let us briefly consider eight important trends that have informed the growth and enriched the content of YA literature in the first five years of this new decade—and new century—and how each trend is represented by GLBTQ titles.[1]

Crossover Titles

Whether a book will be published as an adult title or a young adult title is more often a marketing decision than an editorial one. Though such YA classics as Robert Cormier's *The Chocolate War* (1972) and Bruce Brooks' *The Moves Make the Man* (1984) were originally written as adult titles, their publishers felt they would find a greater readership as YA books and that is how they were published and marketed. A similar but slightly different case is Block's *Weetzie Bat*, which was also written as an adult title but published as a YA book. *Weetzie* successfully blurred the line between YA and adult by attracting legions of readers who were not only in their teens but also in their twenties and thirties. A.M. Homes' *Jack* also falls into this category. Called "crossover" books because they crossed over the traditional boundary that had separated YA and adult readerships, these novels heralded the advent of a newly expansive definition of the term "young adult." This trend was spurred by publishers' growing attempts through the nineties and continuing to the present to expand the retail market for YA books by publishing titles that appeal to readers as old as twenty-four and twenty-five. Recent examples of GLBTQ YA titles that illustrate this trend include Julia Watts' *Finding H.F.* (2001), Benjamin Alire Sáenz's *Sammy & Juliana in Hollywood* (2004), and Linda Newbery's *The Shell House* (2002).

But the crossover phenomenon goes both ways, and an increasing number of titles published as adult fiction incorporate the same teen perspective, protagonist, and issues found in YA fiction.[2] One of the first of these was Chbosky's already-discussed *Perks of Being a Wallflower*. More recent examples of adult titles with GLBTQ content and a YA sensibility include Michael Lowenthal's *Avoidance* (Graywolf, 2002), a novel about a twenty-something camp counselor who falls in love with a teenage boy; Brian Malloy's *The Year of Ice* (St. Martin's, 2002), a novel about a teenage boy's gradual recognition—in the wake of his mother's accidental death—that he is gay; and Bart Yates' *Leave Myself Behind* (Kensington, 2003), a novel about a teenage boy who moves to a small New England town with his single-parent mother and falls in love with the boy next door. Underscoring their crossover appeal was the selection of the latter two as ALEX Award titles.[3]

Literary Fiction

In a departure from traditional problem- and plot-driven YA fiction, a number of publishers have begun issuing literary novels that are character-driven and are enriched by considerations of ambiguity, complex structures, and nuanced treatment of situation and theme. Such novels respect the sophistication of many contemporary young adult readers and encourage their emotional and intellectual development. As noted earlier, this excellence was noted by the establishment of the Michael Printz Award by ALA's Young Adult Library Services Division in the late 1990s. The first Printz Award was given in 2000, and one of the three Printz Honors went to a book with GLBTQ content, Ellen Wittlinger's *Hard Love*. In 2003 two YA novels with GLBTQ content, Aidan Chambers' *Postcards from No-Man's Land* and Garret Freymann-Weyr's *My Heartbeat*, were named the Printz Award winner and a Printz Honor title, respectively.

New Narrative Techniques

Closely related to the trend in more literary fiction is the increasing number of novels that employ nontraditional narrative techniques. Aidan Chambers pioneered this strategy within the body of GLBTQ YA fiction in *Dance on My Grave* (1982), an assemblage of narrative, news articles, and other formats. More recently Ellen Wittlinger has experimented with a variety of techniques in her 1999 Printz Honor novel *Hard Love* which is told in a textual collage comprised of John's first-person narrative, excerpts from his zine *Bananafish,* Marisol's zine *Escape Velocity*, John and Marisol's letters to their parents and to each other, and the lyrics of the titular song. Wittlinger's more recent *Heart on My Sleeve* (2004), whose characters include the lesbian older sister of the protagonist, is told via e-mails, instant messages, hand-written letters, notes, and postcards.

Short Story Renaissance

The renaissance of the American short story that began in the 1980s has now become a major trend in young adult publishing, manifesting itself

in both theme-driven collections of original short stories by multiple authors, and as collections of stories—sometimes linked—by a single author. In GLBTQ fiction this trend began in 1994 with *Am I Blue? Coming Out from the Silence,* Marion Dane Bauer's groundbreaking anthology
of sixteen original short stories. Other short story anthologies with
GLBTQ content include *Love and Sex: Ten Stories of Truth* (2001) and *Necessary Noise: Stories about Our Families As They Really Are* (2003), both edited by Michael Cart. Anthologies of GLBTQ short stories for teen readers have also appeared in Australia and Great Britain, respectively, with
Hide and Seek: Stories about Being Young and Gay/Lesbian, edited by Jenny
Pausacker (1996) and *The Gay Times Book of Short Stories: The Next Wave,*
edited by P.-P. Hartnett (2001). Examples of single-author collections include Chris Crutcher's *Athletic Shorts* (1993), Carol Dines' *Talk to Me*
(1997), Emma Donoghue's *Kissing the Witch* (1997), Kathi Appelt's *Kissing Tennessee* (2000), Ellen Wittlinger's *What's in a Name?* (2000), and
Rich Wallace's *Losing Is Not an Option* (2003).

Poetry Renaissance

Poetry has become an enormously popular literary form with young
adult readers, especially the novel in free verse. Virginia Euwer Wolff's
True Believer (2001), Sonya Sones' *One of Those Hideous Books Where the
Mother Dies* (2004), and David Levithan's *The Realm of Possibility* (2004)
are three recent examples of verse novels with GLBTQ content; a related
title is poet Billy Merrell's memoir in verse, *Talking in the Dark* (2004).

Internationalization of Young Adult Literature

Though originally an American contribution to world culture—like the
Broadway musical and jazz—young adult literature is now a staple of
publishing in virtually every English-language speaking country in the
world.

Editor Marc Aronson pioneered the American publication of YA ti-
tles from abroad in the Edge imprint he created when he was at Henry
Holt. He has subsequently spoken and written widely on this topic.[4]
However, these are not the first imported titles in this body of literature.
As noted in Chapter Two, British authors Aidan Chambers, David Rees,
and Jean Ure were published in the U.S. in the 1980s. There were also a

small handful of imports published in the U.S. in the 1990s: Lutz Van Dijk's *Damned Strong Love* (1995), translated from German and published in Aronson's Edge series; Diana Wieler's *Bad Boy* first published in Canada; and Kate Walker's *Peter* from Australia. More imported titles have begun to appear in the 2000s. Recent GLBTQ titles illustrating this trend include Tamara Williams' *Truth and Lies* (2002) from Canada, William Taylor's *Pebble in a Pool* (2003) from New Zealand, Eddie De Oliveira's *Lucky* (2004) from England, and Nick Earls' *48 Shades of Brown* (2004) from Australia. During the first five years of the twenty-first century, fourteen YA imports with GLBTQ content appeared—a number well ahead of the total of ten YA imports with GLBTQ content that appeared during the entire decade of the 1990s.

Graphic Novels and Comic Books

The novel of sequential art or "graphic novel" might be regarded as the traditional comic book of earlier generations now come of age for a new generation of visually sophisticated young readers. Underground gay-themed comics began appearing in the 1970s, and many included coming-out and first-love stories featuring a teen protagonist (*Gay Comix, Come Out Comics*). And as early as 1993 the daily syndicated comic strip "For Better or for Worse" by Canadian artist Lynn Johnston created a furor when teenage Lawrence, the neighbor boy who grew up with Michael Patterson, one of the strip's central characters, came out first to Michael, and then to his family.[5] Because this strip is presented in "real time," Lawrence is now an adult with his own plant nursery business and a life partner, Nicholas.[6] More thematically complex and artistically richer than traditional comic books, the graphic novel is finding enormous popularity with today's young adults. Recent examples with GLBTQ content include Howard Cruse's *Stuck Rubber Baby*; Eric Shanower's ongoing graphic re-telling of the Trojan War, *The Age of Bronze*; and Judd Winnick's graphic biography of the late AIDS activist Pedro Zamora, *Pedro and Me. Green Lantern,* Winnick's superhero series for DC Comics, also features GLBTQ content. The growing GLBTQ presence in comics was further evidenced by the 2003 creation of Prism Comics, a not-for-profit group dedicated to promoting the work of GLBT creators and encouraging exploration of LGBT themes in comics.[7] *Manga*, the increasingly popular print comics from Japan, are published in a wide range of genres,

including *shonen-ai.yaoi* ("boy's love" or "BL" comics) that feature romantic relationships between teenage boys. For example, *Only the Ring Finger
Knows,* by Satoru Kannagi and Hotaru Odagiri (Digital Manga, 2004) is a
BL comic that features Wataru Fujii, a high school junior boy who contemplates the various rings that his classmates wear and their relationship
symbolism. He sees a much-admired senior boy and the two realize they
are wearing identical rings. The relationship that follows is filled with mutual sarcasm and angst, but love prevails, even between two sensitive and
easily offended teenage boys.[8]

Historical Fiction

Comparatively little historical fiction was published specifically for a
young adult audience until recently when, seemingly overnight, novels
set in the past became one of the most popular genres in the field. While
it's difficult to pinpoint the causes for the upsurge in interest in historical settings, evidence of this trend may be seen in both children's and
young adult books, from the runaway popularity of the *American Girls* series and of Scholastic's two historical fiction imprints, *Dear America* and
My Name Is America, to the fact that all four of the 2005 Newbery Award
winners (one medalist and three honor books) are set in the American
past. Recent examples of young adult historical fiction include Jennifer
Donnelly's Printz Honor-winning *A Northern Light,* K.M. Grant's *Blood
Red Horse,* Iain Lawrence's *The Convicts,* Julius Lester's *Day of Tears,* and
Ann Rinaldi's *Nine Days a Queen.*

Recent examples of historical YA novels with GLBTQ content include Catherine Jinks' *Pagan in Exile* (set in twelfth century France),
George Ella Lyons' *Sonny's House of Spies* (set in the American South in
the 1950s), and Kim Taylor's *Cissy Funk* (set in the American West in the
1930s).

HOMOSEXUAL VISIBILITY

Despite the many innovations and changes that continued to make YA
literature one of the most dynamic areas of publishing in the first decade
of the twenty-first century, one feature in YA novels with GLBTQ content remained constant: homosexual visibility continued to be the largest

category. Even though there is clearly more visible support for GLBTQ teens in the twenty-first century than previously, discovering one's sexual identity, agonizing over whether or not to come out and suffering the slings and arrows of outrageous homophobia remain as central to current YA fiction as they have been from the earliest days of the genre.

An additional aspect of this traditional theme, however, began to emerge in the late 1990s: the consideration of bisexuality. The first YA novel to specifically address this theme—bisexuality as an identity, not a phase—was M. E. Kerr's *"Hello," I Lied* (HarperCollins, 1997). Set on Long Island during the summer, the story is told by Lang, a seventeen-year-old, self-identified gay teen who is in a relationship with twenty-one-year-old Alex. But Alex is away doing summer stock theater, and Lang is disconcerted to find himself drawn to a visiting French girl named Huguette. She returns his interest and the two give physical expression to their mutual attraction. Their relationship predictably ends with the summer and Lang and Alex happily reunite, even as Lang unregretfully acknowledges, "I knew that I'd always think of it as the summer that I loved a girl" (171).

While there are no statistics on the actual number of bisexual persons, Freud called bisexuality a "universal disposition" and, indeed, by the mid-1990s mainstream media like "Newsweek" magazine were reporting that "an independent bisexual movement is starting to claim its own identity."[9]

In the current decade three novels have dealt with this aspect of sexuality: Sara Ryan's *Empress of the World* (2001), Eddie De Oliveira's *Lucky* (2004), and Maureen Johnson's *The Bermudez Triangle* (2004). Ryan's novel explores the complex relationship between two fifteen-year-old girls, Nic and Battle, who meet at a summer program for gifted youth and fall in love. The two break up when Battle begins dating a boy, but Nic acknowledges that she, too, has feelings for boys and may be bisexual herself. Or maybe not. As she argues to her friend Katrina, "Why are you so obsessed with the whole lesbian thing? I've liked boys before. I probably will again, so I believe that the appropriate word is *bisexual*, since you're so desperate to give me a label." To which Katrina responds "Why are *you* so obsessed with *not* being one? I believe that the appropriate word is *denial*." And Nic sighs and admits to herself, "I don't know what I am" (139). The point? Although labels may seem simpler, a teen's self-definition may well resist an either/or sexual identity and instead insist upon claiming *both*.

Nineteen-year-old Sam, the narrator and protagonist of De Oliveira's British import *Lucky*, is equally conflicted. At the novel's outset he meets an avowedly bisexual boy named Toby and is smitten. Then the two boys meet a girl named Lucy and are equally smitten with *her*. Then Sam sees a young man whom he will always think of as HIM at a football game and is smitten by, well, HIM. After endless agonizing, Sam finally decides he's drawn to both boys and girls. In the end Toby asks Sam, "'So what are we calling ourselves? Not straight?' . . . 'Who cares?' I replied. And I truly meant it" (238). He declares this to his friends and then to his football teammates, all of whom prove to be accepting and supportive.

The title of Maureen Johnson's *The Bermudez Triangle* refers to Nina, Mel (Melanie), and Avery, three girls who are long-time best friends. When Mel and Avery fall into bed together one night, their changed relationship has different meanings for each: Mel sees it as confirmation of her own lesbian identity, while Avery views it as a companionable continuation of their friendship. The two break up when Avery hooks up briefly with a boy in her rock band, but neither relationship is as important to her as her application to the Julliard Conservatory of Music (she's a gifted pianist). At this point in her life, Avery's primary identity appears to be that of musician.

Considerations of sexual identity and occasional ambiguity figure large in several other important novels from the first half of the new decade. In Garret Freymann-Weyr's *My Heartbeat* the fourteen-year-old protagonist, Ellen, is in love with James, her older brother Link's best friend. When Ellen discovers that some of her classmates assume Link and James are a couple, she asks them directly if they are. Link hotly denies that he is gay, and James, while acknowledging that he has slept with several men, insists that he's not sure. Ultimately he and the just-turned-fifteen Ellen will have sex—she for the first time and he for the first time with a female. Will there be more? Neither the reader nor Ellen knows. Some readers might feel the author is a bit too coy in her insistence on the sexual ambiguity of the two boys, especially since they are seniors in high school. But critics greeted the book enthusiastically and it was awarded a Printz Honor in 2003.

Interestingly, that same year the Printz Award itself went to a novel that offers an even more complex investigation of love and human sexuality: Aidan Chambers' *Postcards from No Man's Land*, originally published in England, where it received the Carnegie Medal, Britain's equivalent to America's Newbery Medal. The novel is the story of a seventeen-year-old British boy, Jacob, who goes to Holland to represent his family at a ceremony honoring British soldiers like his late grandfather, who died in a nearby village during World War II.

As Jacob's story unfolds, a second story, that of a Dutch woman named Geertrui, also unfolds. As a teenager, she met Jacob's grandfather (also named Jacob), in 1944 and the two become lovers. Recalling this, the now elderly Geertrui muses, "It seemed obvious to me, though I do not know how or when I had learned it, that love that is real is always dangerous. And more dangerous to the one who gives it than to the one who receives it" (200).

Jacob's own ideas about love will be challenged and expanded by this visit to Holland as the story moves from homosexual visibility to gay assimilation. First he meets a girl at a café, feels strongly attracted to her, and is then bewildered to discover that the girl is actually an androgynous boy named Ton. It turns out that Ton is the occasional lover of Jacob's Dutch cousin Daan, who also loves a girl named Simone. "There are no rules about love," Daan tells the startled Jacob. "Who you love. How many people you can love . . . All the stuff about gender. Male, female, queer, bi, feminist, new man, whatever—it's meaningless. We're beyond that now" (277–278). The more conventional Jacob is dubious, replying, "You are maybe." And yet—though he has by now met a Dutch girl named Hille for whom he has developed strong feelings—there is a suggestion that he continues to be attracted to Ton as well. This sexual duality is further underscored—or perhaps symbolized—by the Amsterdam setting with its *avant garde* culture amidst the old buildings and canals, a place where, Jacob reflects, "It was as if two surfaces of life, two ways of living, rubbed together" (244). *Postcards from No Man's Land* is one of the most complex treatments to date of the intricacies of both the human heart and of human sexuality, as well as being one of the most sophisticated literary depictions of these subjects in the field of young adult literature.

The year 2003 turned out to be a signal one for GLBTQ literature, not only in Chambers and Freymann-Weyr's receiving Printz recognition, but also in Nancy Garden's receiving the prestigious Margaret A. Edwards Award presented for lifetime achievement in young adult literature. Garden was recognized specifically for *Annie on My Mind*, which

the award committee praised as "the first lesbian love story with a positive ending." Thus, the award was an acknowledgment of the importance
of GLBTQ literature as well as Garden's specific contribution to it.[10]

And happily, Garden is neither the first nor the last prolific author
of GLBTQ YA fiction to receive the Edwards Award. A decade earlier,
M.E. Kerr received the 1993 Edwards Award; the award citation singles
out *Night Kites,* but does not mention its gay content. And most recently,
the 2005 Edwards Award went to Francesca Lia Block.

The years 2002–2003 saw several other attempts to enlarge upon
the category of homosexual visibility. Some were more successful than
others. Andrew Matthews' 2003 title *The Flip Side,* for example, is a light-
weight British import about a fifteen-year-old boy, Rob, who while playing the part of Rosalind in Shakespeare's "As You Like It," discovers that
he enjoys wearing women's clothing, which puts him in touch with a female side of himself he has never before encountered. Several other
rather heavy-handed plot points underscore the theme of gender issues,
notably that his father works at home and takes care of the house while
his mother is a high-powered business executive. There is also a subplot
involving Rob's best friend Kev who comes out to him, attempts suicide
(unsuccessfully), and finally begins to find self-acceptance along with a
renewed friendship with Rob.

Also in 2003 Canadian author Glen Huser told the gender-bending
story in *Stitches* of Travis, a junior high school boy with a penchant for
sewing who aspires to a career as a professional puppeteer. Predictably,
this exposes him to charges of being gay, homophobic name-calling, and
attempts at gay-bashing. This novel is reminiscent of Mary Sullivan's
1976 novel *What's This About Pete?* but is more open-ended with regard
to the protagonist's future life and relationships. *What's This About Pete?*
ends by reassuring the reader that the protagonist really is straight after
all. In contrast, *Stitches* ends with Travis happily enrolled in a fine arts
high school where "no one seems to mind how different you are" (196),
making new friends (one who wants to be a fashion designer, another a
musical actress, a third a screen writer), and continuing to pursue his puppeteer dreams.

Gender issues and sexual stereotyping were also the focus of Carol
Plum-Ucci's *What Happened to Lani Garver* (2002). Lani (pronounced
"Lonnie") is the new boy in town, a small fishing village on Hackett Is-
land. But Lani is so conspicuously androgynous that popular Claire, the

protagonist, and her friends wonder if he might actually be a she. Claire befriends Lani, but her friends decide he/she must be gay, and the gay-
bashing that follows results in Lani's death. Lani is so tantalizingly circum-
spect about him/herself that the reader—and Claire—are invited to believe
in the possibility that Lani might actually be an angel. But his/her refusal
to be pinned down to identity specifics also underscores the author's too
didactic message when Lani tells Claire "I don't like being put in boxes.
Boy, girl, dork, popular—those are boxes" (46). Lani also regards age as a
box and refuses to tell Claire how old he is. Still later Lani will also an-
nounce that "gay is a box" and "bisexual is a pretty sizable box" (95).

It is not sexual stereotyping but sexual identity that is the subject of
Julie Anne Peters' *Luna* (2004), the first YA novel to address transsex-
ual/transgender issues. The term "transgender" refers to people who are
uncomfortable in the gender of their birth, while "transsexual" refers to
those who are in the process of or have completed a physical transfor-
mation from one gender to another through hormone treatments and/
or surgery. As is the case with homosexuals, no one knows how many
people are transgender, but the issue is now sufficiently public to be included in *Time* magazine, which noted that transpeople began forming
political and support groups in the early 1990s.[11] Since then, their situation has gradually received more public attention and, according to the
New York Times, some colleges and universities are now beginning to provide separate living and bathroom facilities for students who identify as
transgender/transsexual.[12]

One of the first appearances of this subject in YA fiction was a short
story with a transgender character, Emma Donoghue's "The Welcome,"
which appeared in Michael Cart's 2001 anthology *Love and Sex: Ten Stories of Truth*, but *Luna* is the first full-length novel for young adults to deal
with the issue. In *Luna* the transgender character is the older brother of
the narrator, Regan, who introduces the issue in the first chapter. Thereafter, fairly long sections of the novel, set in italics, are flashback sequences
in which Regan recalls germinal events in Liam/Luna's evolving sexuality, while the sections set in the present detail how her brother—who is
called, variously, Liam, Lia Marie and Luna—deals with "transitioning"
(i.e., transforming himself into a female). Regan is the only one in the
family who is aware of her brother's secret and tries to help him, even
going shopping with him when he's dressed as Luna. Nevertheless, she
sees her brother's situation as robbing her (at least potentially) of her own

identity with her peers, especially when he shows up at school dressed as Luna. "Liam and I would never be disassociated now," she thinks in horror. "They'd always see me as Regan—the one with the transgender brother. I'd never be able to separate from him. Never have my own identity" (209).

It's significant that her feelings are similar to those expressed by other straight teens when a gay/lesbian family member comes out. The book's ultimate point is also similar: "Why couldn't people just be accepted for who they were?" (52). Happily Liam/Luna does not die; instead, he/she opts to leave home for Seattle and future gender reassignment surgery.

Though Peters and her publisher are to be applauded for their courage in addressing this previously "untouchable" subject, the novel suffers from a tendency common to ground-breaking fictional treatments of previously unacknowledged issues: it's driven by the "problem" rather than by the characters themselves. But it is always heartfelt, and many readers will be both moved and informed about a life circumstance that needs broader exposure and understanding. And it should be noted that *Luna* was shortlisted for a 2004 National Book Award.

Another kind of gay visibility in GLBTQ YA literature that began in the 1990s with books like Morris Gleitzman's *Two Weeks with the Queen* (1991) and Bruce Coville's *The Skull of Truth* (1997)—i.e., the apparent phenomenon that people are coming to terms with their own or others' sexual identity at younger ages than before—continued in the twenty-first century. Thus we have seen books like Nancy Garden's *Holly's Secret*, a novel about an eleven-year-old girl's efforts to hide from her friends the fact that she has lesbian parents. In George Ella Lyon's *Sonny's House of Spies* it's a thirteen-year-old boy who learns that both his father and his surrogate uncle are gay. And in Marlene Fanta Shyer's *The Rainbow Kite* a twelve-year-old boy learns his fifteen-year-old brother is gay. In one of the stories in Kathi Appelt's *Kissing Tennessee* it's an eighth-grade boy who is wrestling with his feelings for another boy. In *City Girl Country Girl* by Lisa Jahn-Clough, it's thirteen-year-old Phoebe who falls in love with another girl. And in Alex Sanchez's *So Hard to Say*, it's thirteen-year-old Frederick who questions his feelings for another boy.

Guilt, self-hatred, social opprobrium, and homophobia with their corollary threats of violence—either self-imposed or imposed by others— remained fixtures of many homosexual visibility novels throughout this period. One aspect of violence, though, which had previously received little or no attention—sexual abuse—also began to surface during this period, a reflection of the higher visibility being accorded this issue by both the media and society in general. Five novels dealt with same-sex abuse: Catherine Atkins' *When Jeff Comes Home* (Putnam, 1999); Kathleen Jeffrie Johnson's *Target* (Roaring Brook, 2003); Adam Rapp's *33 Snowfish* (Candlewick, 2003); Brian Doyle's *Boy O'Boy* (Groundwood, 2003); and Rebecca Fjelland Davis's *Jake Riley: Irreparably Damaged* (HarperTempest, 2003).

The first of these is the story of fifteen-year-old Jeff, who has returned to his home after being kidnapped two and a half years earlier by a man who calls himself "Ray." During his period of captivity Jeff was routinely forced to have sex with his captor, who also photographed the boy naked. Even after Ray is finally apprehended, Jeff refuses to talk about what has happened until his former captor, who is about to be released on bail, insists that Jeff was a willing and complicit sexual partner.

Although it's clear to the reader that Jeff hates himself for submitting to sex with Ray, most other people—including virtually every student at Jeff's school—believe he must be gay and subject him to horrible—even gothic—verbal and emotional abuse. Only one of his former friends, Vin, comes to his defense, but then admits that he himself may be gay and in love with Jeff. The matter is never pursued further and many readers will, accordingly, view Vin as potentially suspect and wonder if his offer of friendship is actually a bid for sexual gratification.

Similarly, we never see enough of Ray to understand his motivations beyond his sexual appetite for young boys, which will be enough to convince many readers that the man is gay. But is he? This blurring of the line between homosexuality and pedophilia is dangerous, especially when it moves one of the characters (Vin's mother!) to say, "These faggots that prey on our kids, they should be strung up, electrocuted, tortured . . ." (102). In the book—as is often the case in real life—this portrayal of adult gay men as depraved pedophiles goes unchallenged. And the fact that most pedophiles are heterosexuals is never mentioned.

This gay-man-as-child-molester stereotype is seen again in Johnson's *Target*, a novel about the consequences of the rape of sixteen-year-old Grady by two men. This time, however, the motivation for a male's sexual abuse of another male is at least mentioned when the point is made that such attacks are seldom sexually motivated but are, rather, exercises in power and domination. That said, *Target* is a disturbing book that leaves unresolved the relationship between the boy's assault and homosexuality, an issue that is further confused by Grady's terror that his having been singled out for an attack—and his failure to resist that attack—must mean that he, himself, is gay. Which, once again, is presented as a fate worse than death.

There is no question that the adult pedophile, a heavily stereotyped, effeminate church organist, in Doyle's *Boy O'Boy* is gay. It is also clear that his interest in the angelically beautiful Martin O'Boy is part of a pattern that the working-class community is aware of but tolerates (the book is set in Canada at the end of World War II)—until Martin's hero, his older neighbor Buz Sawyer, returns from the war, learns about the organist, and resolves the problem by threatening the man with violence: "If I ever hear about you again, I've got your address here and we'll come after you, my friends and I, and you'll wind up the sorriest organ player that ever had a fondness for fiddling with choir boys . . ." (157). Here a gay man is typecast as a pedophile who must be stopped at all costs, a situation nearly identical to Robert Westall's *Kingdom by the Sea* (1990), in which the repulsive pedophile Corporal Merman is beaten to a pulp by the young protagonist's Buz Sawyer-like soldier rescuer. Once again, the only effective solution offered for stopping him is threats and physical violence, while the viability of "curing" violence with more violence is neither addressed nor questioned.

In Rebecca Fjelland Davis' *Jake Riley* it is the title character who has apparently been sexually abused while in reform school and thus considered by school counselors to be "irreparably damaged." The irony, however, is Jake's admission that he has lied when he said the "bigger boys" made him "do it." "Nobody ever forced me," he admits, "I liked it" (251). The situation is darker and more intense in Adam Rapp's haunting *33 Snowfish*. Here the sexual violence is suffered by a young teen named Custis who has been abused and sexually exploited by the man who, he says, "owns" him. Custis ultimately escapes and finds the promise of a hopeful future when an elderly black man named Seldom gives him sanctuary.

More than any other issue we have addressed, the sexual abuse of young people is one that requires extraordinarily skillful and balanced treatment. Books about it can inform thoughtful discussion and provide teens with knowledge and strategies for recognizing abusive situations they or their friends may encounter.

A number of other novels dealing with homosexual visibility were published during this period—Monte Killingsworth's *Equinox* (2001), Tina Benduhn's *Gravel Queen* (2003), etc.—but few of them offered much in the way of innovation, either in terms of content or style and structure. Exceptions to this include Sonya Sones' *One of Those Hideous Books Where the Mother Dies* (2004) and Virginia Euwer Wolff's *True Believer* (2001), both of which deal with a traditional issue—a girl's discovery that her father and boyfriend, respectively, are gay—in the nontraditional form of the novel in verse. Similarly in Ellen Wittlinger's *Heart on My Sleeve* (2004) a girl learns that her older sister is a lesbian, but in a novel told in the form of e-mails, instant messages, and letters. In another book, *What's in a Name* (2000), Wittlinger presents a novel in the form of linked short stories, in one of which a boy comes out and in another of which the reader sees the impact of the action on his older brother, a football star.

One of the most interesting of the recent novels of homosexual visibility is Maureen Johnson's *The Bermudez Triangle* (2004), a novel that begins with homosexual visibility but ends with queer community. As previously noted, the triangle of the title refers to the lifelong friendship of three girls, two of whom discover that their friendship involves deeper feelings and begin a sexually active relationship. One of these two ultimately—and plausibly—decides that she is probably not a lesbian and ends the relationship. In the meantime, however, the two are outed and forced to deal with the mixed reactions of the third friend and their respective families—not to mention the difficulty of re-adjusting their relationship from romantic involvement to being "just good friends."

What is notable about this novel is that it comes from a packager, 17th Street Productions, which is also responsible for Anne Brasheres' wildly popular *Sisterhood of the Traveling Pants* series, and is published by Razorbill, a new Penguin Putnam YA imprint specializing in commercial fiction. In other words this may be the first GLBTQ novel that is aimed squarely at the mainstream reader and at the retail market, a major development in the publishing of GLBTQ fiction, and one that needs to be followed closely.

GAY ASSIMILATION

Just as the heightened visibility of teens and their increased purchasing power led to the dramatic expansion of young adult publishing in the 1990s, so, too, gay assimilation in the new century is due—at least in part—to heightened gay visibility and market forces accruing from the discovery of homosexuals as consumers. The expanding presence of gays in commercial advertising (both print and electronic) and as characters in motion pictures—and especially in television programs—has led to their more general assimilation into mainstream culture.

Such popular television programs as *Will and Grace, Queer Eye for the Straight Guy, Queer as Folk, The L Word,* and others do suggest that gays and lesbians are, indeed, everywhere. More important, so far as gay and lesbian teens are concerned, is the now routine presence of their peers on teen-targeted dramas like *The O.C., Dawson's Creek,* and *Felicity* as well as on MTV's reality series *The Real World.* Meanwhile the gay playwright and actor Harvey Fierstein appeared in Macy's nationally televised 2003 Thanksgiving Parade dressed as Mrs. Santa Claus (a year earlier his picture book *The Sissy Duckling* was published by Simon & Schuster). In 2002 the Supreme Court, in *Lawrence and Garner v. Texas,* overruled a longstanding Texas sodomy law, thus legalizing gay sexual conduct and, as the New York *Times* put it, "underlined . . . that the nation's attitudes toward gays and lesbians are radically changing."[13] If history is any indicator, it will be a while before those radical changes become routine staples of young adult literature. Nevertheless, gay assimilation is starting to make its presence felt not only in popular culture but also in American society as well. In August 2003 the Episcopal Church approved the election of its first openly gay bishop. Three months later, in November 2003, the Massachusetts Supreme Judicial Court ruled that denying same-sex couples marriage licenses was a violation of the state constitution. In the wake of this decision, mayors in a number of American cities and towns began allowing same-sex marriages, an extremely controversial act that led to eleven states passing initiatives during the November 2004 election that defined marriage exclusively as the union of a man and a woman.

One manifestation of such heightened homosexual visibility is the growing number of secondary characters in YA fiction who "just happen" to be gay in novels like *Split Just Right* (1997) by Adele Griffin, *Gingerbread* (2002) by Rachel Cohn, *The Slightly True Story of Cedar B. Hartley* (2003) by Martine Murray, and *The King of Slippery Falls* (2004) by Sid Hite.

Two recent, purpose-driven novels, Catherine Atkins' *Alt Ed* (2003) and James Howe's *The Misfits* (2001), include gay characters who are already out but are paying a price for it in peer opprobrium. In both of these novels the gay character is one of a group of various types of outsiders who are brought together by their authors for frankly didactic purposes; i.e., to educate readers in respecting the differences of others and to discourage any kind of verbal or physical abuse targeted at them. This type of book recalls the "rainbow" books of the eighties and nineties that brought together groups of multicultural characters like those in the "Pride Pack" books from Alyson.

While Alex Sanchez's two novels, *Rainbow Boys* (2001) and *Rainbow High* (2003), about Jason, Kyle, and Nelson—three gay high school friends who are in various stages of coming out—are definitely examples of queer community books, they fit into this category, as well. Though sometimes didactic—they seem almost encyclopedic in their inclusion of GLBTQ issues ranging from stereotyping to gay-bashing, from body image to support groups—both novels are redeemed by the author's ability to create realistic, sympathetic characters who are on a quest to prove the truth of what another character says early in *Rainbow Boys*: "Coming out means you're no longer ashamed to tell people. It's a question of liking yourself and feeling good about being gay" (7).

Sanchez also has a good ear for the way teens really talk and, at a time when AIDS seems largely forgotten in GLBTQ literature, he pays serious attention to the disease and the corollary need for practicing safe sex. Though his characters are sexually active, as are many teens, the author never fails to focus on love as the heart of homosexuality. He also demonstrates that coming out is actually coming in to a circle of support and self-acceptance that may, ultimately, lead to a more universal community of acceptance and tolerance.

In only one title of this half-decade are gay characters truly—even blithely—accepted and assimilated: David Levithan's splendid novel *Boy Meets Boy* (2003). This is an authentic breakthrough book in the sense that it is the first feel-good gay novel for teens. Think of it as being the spiritual younger brother of Armistad Maupin's *Tales of the City* or of Stephen McCauley's equally engaging and endearing novels for adult readers like *The Object of My Affection, The Man of the House,* and *The Easy Way Out.*

This is surely the first time a gay teenage character has ever said—without being ironic—"I'm not used to being hated." (18) or that a gay-themed novel could end with the words "And I think to myself, 'What a wonderful world.'" (185).

Like Block's *Weetzie Bat,* Levithan's novel contains elements of magical realism (or wish-fulfilling idealization). Thus, it's set in a town and high school where gays are totally accepted and are free to be exactly who and what they are. The protagonist Paul and his new boyfriend Noah, for example, walk through town holding hands and, as Paul notes, "If anybody notices, nobody cares" (65–66).

For another example, the football team's quarterback is also the cross-dressing homecoming queen, Infinite Darlene. The school has a Harley-riding biker cheerleading squad, a quiz bowling team whose members score strikes while listing the complete works of the Bronte sisters, there's a school "cover" band, etc. The humor agilely skirts the cliff's-edge of whimsy without ever toppling over into preciousness.

The real world does intrude in subplots, one of which involves Paul's best friend Tony, the gay son of ultra-religious parents, who manages to be true to himself. A second sees Paul's friend Joni fall in love with a straight (and rather obnoxious) football player; as a result, the two old friends have a falling-out that is never completely repaired. And in a third, Paul's ex-boyfriend Kyle tries to reconcile with him. Paul, believably, makes a bit of a mess of his attempt to deal with this. The heart of the story, though, is Paul's meeting—and falling head over heels in love with—a new boy, Noah, who is an artist and a free spirit. The two proceed to fall out of love (to the reader's distress) but then, sweetly, to fall back in love. There is no sex involved but there is lots of hugging and kissing and even more heart-warming, deeply satisfying expressions and manifestations of loving and caring. In its acceptance and celebration of human differences, this is one of the most important gay novels since *Annie on My Mind* and it represents a near-revolution in social attitudes and the publishing of GLBTQ books.

That Levithan is quickly emerging as a major new writer for young adults is further evidenced by his second novel, *The Realm of Possibility* (2004), which also includes elements of gay assimilation. Though not a GLBTQ novel, per se, this much-praised story in verse form about the disparate (and sometimes desperate) lives of high school kids does include three beautifully realized stories of lesbian and gay characters who are classmates, who open their hearts to the reader, and who give voice—in verse—to their deepest feelings.

QUEER CONSCIOUSNESS/COMMUNITY

If the first years of the new century saw significant progress toward a literature of gay assimilation and acceptance, similar progress was made in terms of queer community. Consider that in the earlier decades of young adult novels with GLBTQ content, the reader would nearly always find only one or—at most—two gay/lesbian characters. If there were one, the story would be a coming-of-age narrative. If there were two, the story would be either a young adult romance or a story that included a lesbian or gay adult couple. There were exceptions to this pattern, such as Nancy Garden's *Annie on My Mind,* which includes four lesbian characters: one teen couple and one adult couple. But such exceptions were rare. This meant that readers would almost never see queer community as an ongoing, present-tense entity that was part of the characters' day-to-day lives. Given this history, a novel with three gay/lesbian characters is not just unusual, but ground-breaking.

Such a novel is *Rainbow Boys*, by Alex Sanchez, which features Jason, Kyle, and Nelson, three gay high school students whose lives include Rainbow Youth meetings at a community center and a campaign for a Gay-Straight Alliance in their high school. The presence of community in the book is further emphasized by the supportive friendship and occasional camaraderie that the three provide for each other as they negotiate the treacherous world of high school and their own mercurial relationships with other family members. The story is told from the alternating perspectives of the three classmates, each of whom is wrestling with issues of sexual orientation and personal survival. Jason, a high school jock with a longtime girlfriend, struggles to come out to himself as he acknowledges his strong attraction to men. Kyle, an intelligent but shy ugly duckling with glasses, braces, and a baseball cap, accepts his own gay identity but struggles to quell his seemingly hopeless, long-time crush on Jason. Nelson, Kyle's flamboyant best friend, is an out, "queer and proud" teen whose multicolored hair, multi-pierced ears, and camp sensibility reflect his long-time acceptance of his own gay identity. Nelson, however, faces perhaps the most overt struggle of the three in his tenacious resistance to the ongoing verbal and physical harassment from his homophobic classmates. Nelson is smart-mouthed and irritating and he knows it. As he himself says, "It's not easy being me. Imagine what I have to put up with twenty-four/seven. At least you can get away from me occasionally" (21).

These, then, are the Rainbow Boys. The story is their story, the narrative is told from behind their eyes, and the fact that there are three gay kids at the novel's core who are friends is revolutionary. *Rainbow Boys* and its sequel *Rainbow High* (2003), which follows the boys through their senior year in high school, gives readers the opportunity to see the world from the boys' perspectives as they move in and out of a queer community, attending Rainbow Youth meetings, campaigning for a Gay-Straight Alliance in their school, and simply hanging out after school, eating brownies, doing math homework, and looking forward to the large and interesting world that awaits them after high school.

Maureen Johnson's *The Bermudez Triangle* (2004) is another example of a queer community novel. As noted earlier, the title refers to three girls—Avery, Mel (Melanie), and Nina—who have been best friends since grade school. Think *Sisterhood of the Traveling Pants* if one of the sisterhood was a lesbian. It's the summer before their final year of high school in Saratoga Springs and while Nina heads out to a high school leadership summer school, Avery and Mel are waiting tables at P.J. Mortimer's Pub, a strip mall faux-Irish pub, home of Irish nachos, Irish birthday jigs, and servers' name tags that double as beer ads (i.e., "Molly Guinness," "Shane O'Douls"). By the end of the summer, Mel and Avery have slipped into a romantic relationship. Not surprisingly, when Nina returns, the dynamics among the three have shifted. For Mel the relationship confirms the lesbian identity she has long known but not acted upon; for Avery, dating a longtime friend is warm and comfortable but not exactly electrifying, and for Nina, her new position as a "three's a crowd" outsider makes her the reluctant confidante of both her best friends as they struggle toward what appears to be the inevitable breakup of their romance. And sure enough, Avery breaks up with Mel. And once the dust settles, Nina embarks on Operation Drag Mel Out of the House. When she sees a notice for a gay and lesbian post-Valentine dance at a nearby high school, she insists that Mel attend it with her. Dancing is an effective ice-breaker, and Mel ends up meeting other gay people.

One common coming out story of an earlier generation is "the first time I went to a gay bar," which begins with nervous trepidation and ends at the bar surrounded by "people just like me." Mel has the same experience at the dance. After her initial shyness, she looks around her and sees girls with short hair, long hair, and everything in between dancing, talking, and simply standing around. As she says to Nina, "All those people there—they were just being *normal* about it. It made me feel normal" (309). Later, when Mel comes out to her clueless mother, Avery comes to her rescue, and it's clear that their friendship is reparable. Mel begins to find a new community of GLBTQ teens, and learns that she need not give up her existing community of Avery and Nina in order to come out. In the world of the Triangle, a GLBTQ identity and an ordinary life are not mutually exclusive, and Mel needn't sacrifice every element of her current life in order to have a future as a lesbian woman.

Although actual GLBTQ teens often have friends of both sexes, this reality is rarely found in young adult novels. Brent Hartinger's *The Geography Club* (2003) breaks free from this confining stereotype, using images of place throughout to describe the variable terrain of risk and safety that the gay narrator and protagonist Russel must negotiate in his search for community. "I desperately wanted to be somewhere where I could be honest about who I was and what I wanted" (11). He begins in an Internet chat room, where he meets another gay teen—Kevin, the handsome jock in his P.E. class. This discovery gives him the courage to come out to his best friend Min, who reveals that she is involved in a romantic relationship with Terese. These four, plus another gay friend, create a small safe space for themselves by meeting as the after-school Geography Club, a name they hope is sufficiently dull to discourage anyone else from joining. This is an amusing notion but what is significant is that instead of looking elsewhere for a gay community, the young people set about creating their own. "We were telling each other things we'd never told our best friends before, things we'd never even said out loud. The five of us may have been alone in the pizza place, but we weren't really alone. Not anymore" (42).

At Kevin's urging, Russel joins the school baseball team and finds himself eating lunch at the baseball jocks' lunchroom table "in the Land of the Popular"(159). During the weeks that follow, Russel's odyssey takes him across "the whole terrain of a typical high school," from the Land of the Popular to the Borderlands of Respectability and even to Outcast Island. Some of the club members—including Kevin, alas—are finally too fearful to come out in their high school. But by the end of the story, a few—including Russel—have formed the nucleus for a new club, the Gay-Straight-Bisexual Alliance, and in so doing have settled in for the long journey toward making a place for themselves in the world of their high school.

> "Would we be banished to Outcast Island? Or would we maybe, just maybe, be allowed to stay in the Borderlands of Respectability? (Let's face it: the Land of the Popular was no longer an option.) . . . I didn't care. None of us did. Because wherever we ended up, we'd be there together. And now I knew that even the ugliest place in the world can be wonderful if you're there with good friends" (225).

Like the members of the Geography Club, the GLBTQ teen class-mates in David Levithan's *Boy Meets Boy* focus on finding each other, but there is no Outcast Island in Levithan's high school setting, as the reader steps into the utopian hometown of the protagonist and narrator, fifteen-year-old Paul:

> "There isn't really a gay scene or a straight scene in our town. They got all mixed up a while back, which I think is for the best. Back when I was in second grade, the older gay kids who didn't flee to the city for entertainment would have to make their own fun. Now it's all good. Most of the straight guys try to sneak into the Queer Beer bar. Boys who love boys flirt with girls who love girls. And whether your heart is strictly ballroom or bluegrass punk, the dance floors are open to whatever you have to offer. This is my town. I've lived here all my life." (1–2)

Within this world, however, are high school students involved in the usual forms of teen angst-ridden romances and friendships.

As the story opens, Paul and his friends are heading for a dance at a nearby bookstore. "I move through the crowd with ease, sharing nods and smiling hellos. I love this scene, this floating reality. I am a solo flyer, looking out over the land of Boyfriends and Girlfriends. I am three notes in the middle of a song" (2). In some ways, this community might be likened to Weetzie Bat's Los Angeles. Although this is definitely a town, not a city, its denizens are awash in Weetzie-like sensory detail as they stroll through the park, cruise out to the mall with friends, or move through the halls of their high school on the lookout for who is passing notes to whom, who is at whose locker, and who is looking to catch whose eye.

Noah is the new student who has caught Paul's eye, and Paul leaps at the opportunity to show him around town ("the I Scream Parlor, which shows horror movies as you wait for your double dip . . . the Pink Floyd shrine in our local barber's backyard"). Noah loves what he sees and Paul muses, "I know people always talk about living in the middle of nowhere—there's always another place (some city, some foreign country) they'd rather be. But it's moments like this that I feel like I live in the middle of somewhere. My somewhere" (70).

Will Paul get together with Noah? Will Joni ditch Chuck? Will Tony's parents let him go to the dance? *Boy Meets Boy* is a realistic story of the ins and outs of high school life and relationships, yet it is set in a utopian world in which the difference between heterosexual and homosexual attractions and love are about as significant as the difference between blondes and redheads.

Strictly speaking, *Boy Meets Boy* might be considered a story of "gay assimilation," since the difference of sexual orientation truly makes no difference here, but we would argue that it is also a story of a queer community as envisioned by GLBTQ teens who would just like to hold hands or attend a school dance without getting gay-bashed or facing the peer rejection of Outcast Island.

Finally, Julia Watts' *Finding H.F* (2001) is a particularly authentic portrayal of the multiple strands of connection and community in gay/lesbian "families of choice." Abandoned as an infant by her fifteen-year-old mother, H.F. (Heavenly Faith) has been raised in Morgan, Kentucky, by her loving and very religious grandmother, Memaw. As an illegitimate tomboy with a growing attraction to women, H.F.'s sense of difference has been lifelong. Her best friend Bo, a self-described "sissy-boy," understandably shares her sense of alienation; both teens dream of the larger landscape that they believe lies outside their small town.

The voice of H.F. is fresh, intelligent, and wryly self-aware, as when she pokes fun at her name:

> "I never believed those Bible stories were real any more than I believed *The Poky Little Puppy* was real when Memaw read it to me. I

didn't believe in those Bible things any more than I believed in talking dogs that ate strawberry shortcake. That's what makes my name so funny. Heavenly Faith, my foot! If I can't see it, hear it, smell it, touch it, or taste it, I don't believe in it"

(4). The voice of Bo is likewise humorous, though with a more overtly camp sensibility. In one characteristic exchange, H.F. and Bo explore an unfamiliar path through the woods, H.F. forging ahead while Bo fusses about getting his shoes muddy. H.F. tells the reader in mock exasperation: "I swear, it's like his number one concern in life is being well groomed. The boy irons his jeans, for crying out loud. 'What's the matter, Beauregard? Afraid of messin' up your snazzy new shoes?'" To which he retorts, "Excuse me, sugar, but some people take pride in their personal appearance" (15).

Both of these gender nonconformists are well-aware of their deviance from the norms of their small town high school. As H.F. explains, "The cheerleaders and the jocks and popular kids know I'm different. Different on the inside. Like lions on nature shows that sniff out which giraffe is ripest for the picking, those people can sniff out difference and it's a smell they hate" (80). Yet both are managing to struggle through their adolescence toward a nebulous vision of the terrain outside Morgan, Kentucky.

Just when H.F. is rejected by the girl of her dreams, she finds the address of the mother she's never known and persuades Bo to drive with her to Tippalula, Florida, in search of her. As the two friends make their way from Kentucky to Florida by way of Atlanta, Georgia, they meet three homeless lesbian teens, visit a gay bookstore, attend a gay-friendly church service, and experience the thrill of seeing two men casually walking hand in hand through a public park.

They discover, in short, a community with its own heroes and traditions, gathering places, and lore made up of those elusive people "like us" that they've wondered about but never quite believed in. An older gay couple (Bo marvels "they've been together for longer than we've been alive!" [79]) provides a safe haven for the night and some plain-spoken reassurance: "Adolescence sucks, Beauregard. Just wait . . . life'll get easier" (80).

H.F. and Bo return home to the same lives but with a vision of the world that awaits them outside of Morgan: not a utopia by any means, but one that has ample room for H.F., Bo, and all those other "people like us."

"We learned that the world isn't just flooded with meanness—that there are people like us loving each other, living happy lives out in the open.... And to me, the rainbow sign God put up in the sky for Noah said pretty much the same thing as the sign I saw at the gay bookstore, at the church, and in the faces and hearts of the rainbow of people who are my gay family: 'Here you were, thinking it was the end of the world, when it turned out it was only the beginning.'" (165)

GLBTQ NOVELS PUBLISHED FROM 2000–2004

2000

Appelt, Kathi. *Kissing Tennessee.* Harcourt. 128 pages.

> HV. Gay. "Starbears," one of the eight stories in this collection about an eighth grade school dance, recounts the experience of fifteen-year-old Cub, as he becomes aware of his own same-sex attractions.

Ferris, Jean. *Eight Seconds.* Harcourt. 192 pages.

> HV. Gay. John, eighteen, goes to rodeo camp where he meets an older boy named Kit, whom he admires and respects. The two become friends but when John learns that Kit is gay, he responds with homophobic violence. By summer's end, John has come to the realization that he, too, is gay, but Kit is understandably reluctant to resume their friendship.

Garden, Nancy. *Holly's Secret.* Farrar Straus Giroux. 132 pages.

> HV. Lesbian. Holly, eleven, is the adopted daughter of a lesbian couple. When the family moves from New York to Massachusetts, she urgently tries to hide that fact from her new classmates and friends.

Hines, Sue. *Out of the Shadows.* HarperTempest. 213 pages

> HV. QC. Lesbian. Rowanna, who is straight, lives with Deb, her late mother's lover. Ro's best friend, Mark, has fallen in love with new girl in town, Jodie, only to discover that she is a lesbian and actually has a crush on Rowanna. The story is told in the alternating voices of Rowanna and Jodie. Originally published in Australia.

Wittlinger, Ellen. *What's in a Name?* Simon & Schuster. 160 pages.

> HV. QC. Gay. A collection of short stories told by ten high school students and linked by a common theme of personal identity. Three

of the stories focus on fifteen-year-old O'Neill, who comes out to his classmates via a poem published in the school's literary magazine, much to the consternation of his older brother, Quincy, a football star.

2001

Cart, Michael. *Love and Sex.* Simon & Schuster. 225 pages.

HV. Gay. Lesbian. Transgender. Two of the stories in the collection have GLBTQ content. Michael Lowenthal's "The Acuteness of Desire" is about a boy's falling in love with a classmate; they "do it" but the next day the classmate acts as if nothing had happened. Emma Donoghue's story "The Welcome" is a story about a girl who falls in love another girl, who she later learns is actually a male to female transsexual.

Hartnett, P.-P., ed. *The Gay Times Book of Short Stories: The Next Wave.* Gay Times Books. 323 pages.

HV. GA. QC. GLBTQ. All 28 of the short stories in this British collection are by young gay/lesbian writers. Seven of the stories are from U.S. writers, the rest from Great Britain, Ireland, Australia, and New Zealand.

Howe, James. *The Misfits.* Simon & Schuster. 274 pages.

HV. GA. QC. Gay. Four twelve-year-old misfits (Bobby the fat boy, Skeezie the hood, Joe the queer boy, and geek girl Addie) campaign against name-calling by running a slate of candidates for student council on the No-Name Party ticket. It turns out that Colin, a popular, nice, and sensible boy in their class is also gay, and he and Joe become boyfriends. This book has inspired actual "no name-calling" campaigns in schools throughout the United States.

Killingsworth, Monte. *Equinox.* Holt. 188 pages.

HV. Lesbian. Fourteen-year-old Autumn lives on an island off the coast of Washington with her artist father and executive commuter mother. Upset and mystified as to why her parents decide to move to the urban mainland, she eventually learns that her mother has become involved with another woman.

Reynolds, Marilyn. *Love Rules.* (True to Life series of Hamilton High) Morning Glory Press. 269 pages.

HV. Lesbian. When seventeen-year-old Lynn learns that her best friend, Kit, is a lesbian, she wants to be supportive, particularly when

Kit's determination to be as out as possible makes her a target for homophobic harassment. At last count, *Love Rules* is one of six titles in the True-to-Life Series of Hamilton High by this author.

Ryan, Sara. *Empress of the World*. Viking. 192 pages.

> HV. GA. QC. Lesbian. Bisexual Nic (short for Nicola) is fifteen and a student at the Siegel Institute Summer Program for Gifted Youth, where she meets beautiful Battle and the two fall in love. Battle becomes uncomfortable with their relationship and turns her attention to a boy; Nic is understandably devastated. This is one of the few YA titles about bisexuality.

Sanchez, Alex. *Rainbow Boys*. Simon & Schuster. 256 pages.

> HV. GA. QC. Gay. Three high school boys—Jason, Kyle, and Nelson—narrate this account of their individual struggles to accept a gay identity and also become part of a gay/lesbian community by attending Rainbow Youth meetings.

Taylor, Kim. *Cissy Funk*. HarperCollins. 211 pages.

> HV. Lesbian. During the Great Depression, Cissy's life in rural Colorado with her abusive mother is a bleak one, so she is overjoyed when her Aunt Vera takes her with her to Denver. What Cissy doesn't know is that Vera and her friend Maxine are lovers, and Vera may well be her mother.

Vande Velde, Vivian. *Alison, Who Went Away*. Houghton Mifflin. 211 pages.

> HV. Gay. Fourteen-year-old Sibyl learns that her father, who deserted the family when she was five, is gay.

Watts, Julia. *Finding H.F.* Alyson. 165 pages.

> QC. Gay. Lesbian. Two sixteen-year-old teens—lesbian H. F. (short for Heavenly Faith) and her gay friend Bo (short for Beauregard)—take a road trip from their tiny hometown of Morgan, Kentucky, to Florida in search of H. F.'s mom. Along the way, they discover a new family of choice as they meet other gay/lesbian people.

Withrow, Sarah. *Box Girl*. Groundwood. 181 pages.

> HV. Gay. From Canada. Thirteen-year-old Gwen's best friend rejects her when she discovers that Gwen's father is gay, but Gwen heals from this hurt through Clara, a new and accepting friend.

Wittlinger, Ellen. *Razzle*. Simon & Schuster. 247 pages.

> GA. Gay. An incidental character—an adult plumber—is gay in this novel about a fifteen-year-old boy who falls in love with Razzle, the teenage girl who is the caretaker of the town dump.

Wolff, Virginia Euwer. *True Believer.* Atheneum. 264 pages.

HV. Gay. This is a sequel to *Make Lemonade*, Wolff's first book told by LaVaughn, a working-class high school girl who is fiercely determined to earn the good grades she needs to get into college. But her academic ambitions take a back seat to her emotions when she discovers that the boy she has a crush on is gay, and she starts skipping school.

2002

Alphin, Elaine Marie. *Simon Says.* Harcourt. 258 pages.

HV. Gay. Artist Charles enters a boarding school for the arts in large part to meet teen novelist Graeme, and the two form a tentative friendship with a strong homoerotic undercurrent. Graeme—for unrelated reasons—commits suicide. The homosexual subplot is reinforced by the fact that Charles's roommate, Adrian, is openly gay.

Chambers, Aidan. *Postcards from No Man's Land.* Dutton. 312 pages.

HV. GA. QC. Gay. In Holland to represent his family at a memorial ceremony, Jacob finds himself attracted both to a boy, Ton, and a girl, Simone. Winner of the Carnegie Medal and the Printz Award, this is a richly textured literary novel about the complex nature of love and human sexuality.

Cohn, Rachel. *Gingerbread.* Simon & Schuster. 172 pages.

GA. Gay. Cyd Charisse, girl with an attitude, is sent to New York City to spend the summer with her father's family and away from her surfer boyfriend, Shrimp. Her gay half-brother, Danny, and his partner, Aaron, own a West Village café, where Cyd goes to work as a *barista*.

Desai Hidier, Tanuja. *Born Confused.* Scholastic. 512 pages.

GA. Lesbian. Dimple Lala, the cherished only child of Indian immigrant parents, describes herself as "born confused." On the one hand, she lives in suburban New Jersey and shops the malls for the latest teen fashions. On the other hand, her traditional parents are on the lookout for a nice Indian boy for their daughter. Yet these same parents are entirely comfortable having Dimple's lesbian cousin Kavita and her girlfriend Sabina over for dinner.

Freymann-Weyr, Garret. *My Heartbeat.* Houghton Mufflin. 154 pages.

HV. Gay. Fourteen-year-old Ellen is in love with her older brother's best friend. But are the two boys more than "just friends"? A Printz

Honor Award-winning examination of the complexities of the human heart and sexual identity.

Newbery, Linda. *The Shell House.* Fickling/Random House. 256 pages.

HV. Gay. First published in England, this novel offers parallel stories—one set in the present, one set during World War I—about two young men who are similarly conflicted about their sexual identity.

Plum-Ucci, Carol. *What Happened to Lani Garver.* Harcourt. 307 pages.

HV. Gay. Transgender. Popular Claire befriends Lani, the new boy—or is he a girl? or an angel?—in town. Androgynous Lani refuses to conform to gender expectations and is killed by local homophobes. This is *The Drowning of Stephan Jones* meets *Boys Don't Cry.*

Shimko, Bonnie. *Letters in the Attic.* Academy Chicago Press. 194 pages.

HV. Lesbian. This coming-of-age novel set in the 1960s is the story of a twelve-year-old girl whose mother moves her from Phoenix to upstate New York, where the girl falls in love with a (female) classmate.

Shyer, Marlene Fanta. *Rainbow Kite.* Marshall Cavendish. 205 pages.

HV. Gay. Fifteen-year-old Bennett is dealing with both coming out and being outed to his family and middle school peers. After Bennett tries to kill himself, he becomes the school's "emblem of tolerance" and, in a remarkably sudden show of support, the other kids at his eighth grade graduation ceremony remove their caps to reveal they've dyed their hair rainbow colors.

Wallens, Scott. *Exposed (Sevens, Week 2).* Puffin. 182 pages.

HV. Gay. This is one of seven books that focus on a group of seven teens over the course of seven weeks. In this one, seventeen-year-old Jeremy is seen at a party kissing a boy and—despite a girlfriend and a spot on the high school football team—admits to himself that he is gay. And coming out to his friends is an easy task indeed compared to coming out to his parents.

Williams, Tamara. *Truth and Lies.* Lorimer. 123 pages.

HV. Gay. Another novel from Canada. A girl's good friend, a gay teen named Marcel, is beaten nearly to death. His attackers accompany their beating with plenty of homophobic verbal abuse but the attack is actually the work of the girl's boyfriend, Jon, who has been selling Marcel marijuana, and set up Marcel with the gang that has been selling *him* drugs (Jon's behind in his payments).

Wilson, Barbara. *A Clear Spring.* Girls First/Feminist Press. 173 pages.

GA. Lesbian. A middle school-age girl spends the summer with her

Aunt Ceci and her aunt's partner Janie. The girl and her friend solve an ecological mystery.

2003

Atkins, Catherine. *Alt Ed*. Dutton. 224 pages.

HV. *The Misfits* meets *The Breakfast Club* as half a dozen in-trouble kids must take an alternative education course in lieu of being expelled. The protagonist, Susan, befriends the token gay character, Brendan, and together they learn courage and self-confidence.

Benduhn, Tea. *Gravel Queen*. Simon & Schuster. 152 pages.

HV. Lesbian. Gay. A lesbian romance set in Greensboro, NC, during the summer before would-be filmmaker Aurin's final year in high school. While hanging out with her long-time best friends (straight female) Kenney and (gay male) Fred, Aurin meets Neila, a beautiful ultimate frisbee player and out lesbian.

Brennan, Herbie. *Faerie Wars*. Bloomsbury. 368 pages.

HV. Lesbian. Henry's life changes dramatically when, in short order, he discovers that his mother is a lesbian and then saves a Faerie from the clutches of a cat.

Cart, Michael, ed. *Necessary Noise: Stories About Our Families As They Really Are*. Cotler/HarperCollins. 239 pages.

HV. Gay. A collection of ten stories, one of which, "Sailing Away," is about a boy who discovers he's gay and in love with his best friend, who has long been regarded as a de facto member of his family.

Davis, Rebecca Fjelland. *Jake Riley: Irreparably Damaged*. HarperTempest. 265 pages.

HV. Gay. Lainie is dismayed to find that Jake, her new neighbor who has come to live with his father, is abusive, physically aggressive, and potentially dangerous. The adults who have labeled him "irreparably damaged" attribute his problems to his having been molested by older boys at his correctional school, but he finally tells Lainie that the sexual activity was, in fact, consensual.

Doyle, Brian. *Boy O'Boy*. Groundwood. 161 pages.

HV. Gay. Martin O'Day tells this story set in Ottawa, Canada, in 1945. Martin learns first-hand that Mr. George, his church's kindly organist, is actually a pedophile and then finds out that George is also molesting his best friend Billy. The two boys exact a revenge of sorts and when they tell a returning war veteran neighbor what has happened, he protects them by threatening the organist with retaliatory violence.

Frost, Helen. *Keesha's House*. Farrar, Straus Giroux. 116 pages.

HV. Gay. When Joe was a teen, he was taken in by his aunt. As an adult he now owns the house of the title, which has become a haven for runaway teens. One of them, Harris, was disowned by his father when he came out. An award-winning novel written in verse.

Hartinger, Brent. *The Geography Club*. HarperCollins. 226 pages.

HV. QC. Gay. Lesbian. Russel is a closeted gay teen who learns that the totally cute guy in his gym class is also gay, that his best friend Min is bisexual, and that there is a real need for a GLBTQ support group at their high school. A lively, witty, and heartfelt first novel. (A sequel, *The Order of the Poison Oak*, was published early in 2005).

Huser, Glen. *Stitches*. Groundwood. 198 pages.

HV. Gay. From Canada. Travis, a junior high school student, is different from the other boys—he loves to sew and wants to become a professional puppeteer. Predictably, his gender nonconformity makes him the target of homophobic harassment that escalates to violence. The story is reminiscent of Mary Sullivan's much earlier *What's This About Pete?*

Johnson, Kathleen Jeffrie. *Target*. Roaring Brook. 175 pages.

HV. Gay. Since he was savagely assaulted and raped by two men, sixteen-year-old Grady West's life has become an exercise in "after the night of" and nothing means what it used to. One of the few novels to deal with male sexual abuse.

Levithan, David. *Boy Meets Boy*. Knopf. 187 pages.

GA. QC. Gay. The first authentically feel-good gay novel, this is a groundbreaking work in which a gay character can say, "I'm not used to being hated" without being ironic. Paul is smitten by new boy Noah but must first deal with Kyle, his ex-boyfriend who is disconcertingly eager to get back together. The story of Paul and his friends—including Infinite Darlene, the school's cross-dressing quarterback and homecoming queen—is a sweet-spirited and funny celebration of human differences.

Matthews, Andrew. *The Flip Side*. Delacorte. 147 pages.

HV. Gay. A slight story about a cross-dressing boy. When Rob, fifteen, plays the part of Rosalind in "As You Like It," he discovers that he likes being in women's clothing. Meanwhile his best friend, Kev, comes out to him and then makes a failed attempt at suicide, but all's well that ends well—Rob gets the girl and Kev gets . . . well, a friend like Rob. Originally published in England.

Murray, Martine. *The Slightly True Story of Cedar B. Hartley.* Levine/ Scholastic. 233 pages.

GA. Gay. Twelve-year-old Cedar lives with her mother in an eclectic neighborhood populated by immigrants and families, old and young, including the two men next door who adopt a baby. Originally published in Australia.

Myracle, Lauren. *Kissing Kate.* Dutton. 198 pages.

HV. Lesbian. Kate and Lissa have been best friends forever, but when Kate gets drunk and kisses her, Lissa realizes that she is in love with her friend. After a number of painful and futile efforts to talk about her feelings with Kate, Lissa finally understands that she must distance herself from this increasingly problematic friendship and have faith that she will meet other kindred spirits.

Oates, Joyce Carol. *Freaky Green Eyes.* HarperTempest. 341 pages.

HV. Gay. Franky (Francesca) Pierson, who lives with her younger sister, older half-brother, and controlling father, has two personas: a young "good girl" teenager and a more mature self she calls "Freaky Green Eyes." When Franky's mother finds refuge from her abusive marriage in her friendship with a gay man in a nearby town, it appears that she has abandoned her children. Or has something more dire happened?

Peters, Julia Anne. *Keeping You a Secret.* Little, Brown. 250 pages.

HV. QC. Lesbian. Holland is a high school senior with a boyfriend and an Ivy League future, but when she meets Cece, a transfer student who is an out lesbian, the two fall in love. As a result, Holland encounters homophobia in various guises and is finally kicked out of the house by her angry mother. Though the novel sometimes verges on melodrama, the relationship between Holland and Cece grows convincingly stronger, and true love prevails.

Rapp, Adam. *33 Snowfish.* Candlewick Press. 179 pages.

HV. Gay. Custis has been sexually abused and exploited by the man he says "owns him." He escapes and finds refuge and family with an elderly black man named "Seldom."

Ripslinger, Jon. *How I Fell in Love and Learned to Shoot Free Throws*. Roaring Brook. 170 pages.

> HV. Lesbian. Danny falls hard for Angel McPherson, the best female basketball player in Iowa. But Angel has secrets: her mom's a lesbian and the girl was conceived via alternative insemination.

Sanchez, Alex. *Rainbow High*. Simon & Schuster. 251 pages.

> HV. QC. Jason, Kyle, and Nelson, the three gay high school seniors who starred in Sanchez' first novel, *Rainbow Boys*, return in this sequel. All three are still seniors and still grappling with many of the same issues—AIDS, homophobia, gay stereotypes, and coming out—that drove the plot of the first story. Some unresolved loose ends leave the door open for a third story, *Rainbow Road* (Simon & Schuster 2005).

Taylor, William. *Pebble in a Pool*. Alyson. 124 pages.

> HV. Gay. Paul Carter, a teenage boy who is the son of a fundamentalist preacher, speaks out at a school assembly in defense of a gay teen who has been violently murdered. When word of this reaches his father, Paul is beaten up, disowned, and thrown out of the house. He is then taken in by a thirty-one-year-old man and the two fall in love. First published in New Zealand.

Wallace, Rich. *Losing Is Not an Option*. Knopf. 144 pages.

> HV. Gay. Nine intertwined short stories that star Ron, a cross-country and track runner, in his athletic journey from sixth grade to senior year. In one of the stories, "In Letters That Would Soar a Thousand Feet High," he spends an evening at a party where most of the athlete attendees are gay.

2004

De Oliveira, Eddie. *Lucky*. PUSH/Scholastic. 239 pages.

> HV. QC. Gay. Bisexual. The story of nineteen-year-old Sam, who is thoroughly confused about his sexual identity but finally decides he is attracted to both boys *and* girls. Originally published in England.

Earls, Nick. *48 Shades of Brown*. Graphia/Houghton Mifflin. 274 pages.

> HV. Lesbian The protagonist, Dan, is a senior in high school and is living for a year with his twenty-two-year-old Aunt Jacq. He falls in love with her roommate, Naomi, and quite late in the book learns that Jacq is a lesbian and is also in love with Naomi. Originally published in Australia.

Hite, Sid. *The King of Slippery Falls.* Scholastic. 217 pages.

HV. Gay. On his sixteenth birthday, adoptee Lewis Hinton receives a mysterious message hinting that he is actually a descendent of King Louis the XV of France. Among other surprises of the next several months is his learning that the boy he thought was his rival for a girl's affections is actually gay.

Jahn-Clough, Lisa. *Country Girl, City Girl.* Lorraine/Houghton Mifflin. 186 pages.

HV. Lesbian. Twelve-year-old country girl Phoebe lives a pleasantly low-key life with her father and brother on an isolated farm in Maine. She is dismayed to learn that city girl Melita, the daughter of a family friend, is coming to stay for the summer, but Melita proves to be lively and attractive, and Phoebe feels drawn to her as her first close friend. But do her feelings include something more than friendship?

Jinks, Catherine. *Pagan in Exile.* Candlewick. 326 pages.

HV. Gay. A novel (the second of Jinks' four-volume Pagan Chronicles series) set in twelfth-century Europe during the Crusades, narrated by Pagan, the seventeen-year-old squire to Lord Roland. Pagan accompanies his lord to his home in France and meets Lord Roland's unpleasant extended family, including his older brother, who is a "ganymede," i.e., homosexual. Other books in the Pagan Chronicles are *Pagan's Crusade* (#1), *Pagan's Vows* (#3), and *Pagan's Scribe* (#4). Originally published in Australia

Johnson, Maureen. *The Bermudez Triangle.* Razorbill/Penguin. 370 pages.

HV. QC. Lesbian. In one of the first examples of packaged commercial fiction to deal with homosexuality, three girls (Avery, Melanie [Mel], and Nina) face various stresses on their long-time friendship, including the tensions that arise when Mel and Avery begin—and end—a romantic relationship, in the course of which Mel comes out as a lesbian to her family.

Kemp, Kristen. *The Dating Diaries.* PUSH/Scholastic. 266 pages.

HV. GA. Lesbian. Katie's boyfriend of five years dumps her just weeks before the school prom. She decides to get back into circulation with a campaign of high-intensity dating to make up for lost time—and hopefully find a prom date. Along the way she meets Frankie, a lesbian who is initially interested in a date (Katie's not interested), but sticks around to become a friend. (P.S. Both girls end up with dates to the prom.)

Levithan, David. *The Realm of Possibility*. Knopf. 210 pages.

HV. GA. Gay. Lesbian. Three of the twenty stories in this beautifully written novel in verse feature gay/lesbian characters falling in love. Their insights express the humor ("My parents are okay with me being gay / but they would kill me if they saw me with / a cigarette . . .") and the longing of adolescents ("You think you know your possibilities./ Then other people come into your life / and suddenly there are so many more.").

Lyon, George Ella. *Sonny's House of Spies*. Jackson/Atheneum. 298 pages.

HV. Gay. A novel set in the South on the eve of the Civil Rights movement. It's been seven years since Sonny's father abandoned his family, and Marty, their bachelor neighbor, has become a surrogate uncle. Part of the rather convoluted plot involves Sonny's discovery that both his father and Marty are gay.

Martin, Ann M. *Here Today*. Scholastic. 320 pages.

GA. Lesbian. Eleven-year-old Ellie Dingman and her family experience sudden change when her would-be actress mother leaves her husband and children to pursue a stage career in New York City. Much of the care of younger siblings falls to Ellie, who is helped by the old and young neighbors who become her de facto extended family. Among them is a middle-aged lesbian couple, who play a central role in the lives of neighborhood children.

Peters, Julie Anne. *Luna*. Little, Brown. 248 pages.

HV. Transgender. The first YA novel to feature a major transgender character. Teenage Regan, the only one to know about her older brother Liam's long-held sense of being female, tells the story of his transition/transformation first to Lia Marie and finally to Luna. Shortlisted for the National Book Award.

Sáenz, Benjamin Alire. *Sammy & Juliana in Hollywood*. Cinco Puntos Press. 291 pages.

HV. Gay. A painful and beautifully written story set in 1969 in a New Mexico barrio. Sammy is trying to put his life back together after his girlfriend Juliana's violent death at the hands of her father. In the course of the novel, two of his friends, a gay male couple, are forced to leave their home in order to be together.

Sanchez, Alex. *So Hard to Say.* Simon & Schuster. 230 pages.

> HV. Gay. Frederick is starting eighth grade at his new school in California and meets Xio, a talkative Latina who quickly becomes his friend. It's clear that she sees him as boyfriend material, but when Frederick realizes that he feels toward another boy what Xio feels for him, he knows he must come out to her. After Xio's initial anguish subsides, the two find that the new honesty between them has actually strengthened their friendship. One of the few GLBTQ novels for middle school readers.

Sones, Sonya. *One of Those Hideous Books Where the Mother Dies.* Simon & Schuster. 268 pages.

> HV. Gay. When Ruby's mother dies, the fifteen-year-old must move to California to live with her movie star father, whom she has never met and whom she blames for the breakup of her parents' marriage. She will discover he is gay and that his absence from her life had been her mother's doing. A novel in verse.

Wittlinger, Ellen. *Heart on My Sleeve.* Simon & Schuster. 219 pages.

> HV. QC. Lesbian. Chloe has been accepted at Cartwright College, where she meets that cute, incoming student, Julian. The story begins with an email from Julian to Chloe, the first of many in a novel told entirely in the emails, instant messages, letters, postcards, and notes exchanged by Chloe, Julian, their friends, siblings, and parents. One of the events/developments that center the narrative is Chloe's older sister Genevieve's coming out as a lesbian.

Wyeth, Sharon Dennis. *Orphea Proud.* Delacorte. 208 pages.

> HV. Lesbian. Orphea and her long-time best friend Lissa become lovers, but when Orphea's older brother discovers them in bed, Lissa flees and is killed in a car crash. Sent to live with her elderly great-aunts in rural Virginia, Orphea discovers acceptance and a new extended family. One of the few YA novels to feature gay/lesbian characters of color.

NOTES

1. Cart, Michael. "Young Adult Literature Comes of Age." In *Children's Literature Remembered.* Edited by Linda Pavonetti. Westport, CT: Libraries Unlimited. 2004.

2. So numerous had such titles become by early 2005 that ALA's *Booklist* magazine began treating them as a separate category and assigned their reviewing to this book's co-author Michael Cart.

3. First presented in 1998, the ALEX Awards are the American Library Association's annual list of the ten best adult books for young adults. For more information, see the YALSA website: www.ala.org/yalsa/

4. Aronson, Marc. *Exploding Myths.* Lanham, MD: Scarecrow Press, 2001.

5. Johnston, Lynn. *It's the Thought That Counts.* Kansas City: Andrews McMeel Publishing, 1994.

6. Johnston, Lynn. *The Lives Behind the Lives.* Kansas City: Andrews McMeel Publishing, 1999.

7. Prism Comics. *Your LGBT Guide to Comics.* Atlanta: Prism Comics, 2004.

8. Brenner, Robin. Review of *Only the Ring Finger Knows.* "No Flying No Tights: A Website Reviewing Graphic Novels for Teens." http://noflyingnotights .com/all.html#onlytheringfingerknows (accessed 7/28/05).

9. Leland, John. "Bisexuality." *Newsweek.* CXXVI:3 (July 17, 1995).

10. Jenkins, Christine A. "Annie On Her Mind." School Library Journal 49 (June 2003): 48–50.

11. Cloud, John. "Trans Across America." *Time.* (July 20, 1998).

12. Bernstein, Fred A. "On Campus, Rethinking Biology 101." *The New York Times.* March 7, 2004.

13. Greenhouse, Linda. "Justices, 6-3, Legalize Sexual Conduct." *New York Times.* June 25, 2003.

· 6 ·

What a Wonderful World?
Some Final Thoughts

 $\mathcal{T}$ here's an old saying in Indiana, "Bit by bit our sweaters we knit," that says a lot about the evolution of GLBTQ literature. Like the knitting of a sweater, it has been a similarly slow, sometimes tedious and often incremental process plagued by more than a few dropped stitches along the way. But despite occasional setbacks, progress has been made, especially in the area of queer consciousness and community. Even geographically and socially isolated teens now have their listserv and chatroom opportunities for building community. Meanwhile, stories of homosexual visibility continue to be written but their treatment has become more expansive and, as a result, readers now get to observe the increasing opportunities for assimilation that occur after the dramatic moment of coming out. And thanks to the growing visibility of gays and lesbians in motion pictures and especially in series television, YA literature is now also including more and more secondary characters who "just happen to be" gay and whose sexuality is no longer presented as being a "problem."

What advances remain to be made? Well, for starters we clearly need more GLBTQ books featuring characters of color, more lesbian and bisexual characters, more transgender youth, and more characters with same-sex parents. The literature, in short, needs to be more all-inclusive to offer a better reflection of the complexities of the real world and to insure that all young readers might see their faces reflected in it. We need to acknowledge that young people are grappling with their sexual identity at younger ages than in the past. We also need to recognize that gays and lesbians do not live on separate planets but, instead, go to the same schools, hang out at the same gay and lesbian centers, belong to the same gay/straight alliances, and often form lasting friendships.

By definition young adult literature will always feature rite-of-passage and coming-of-age experiences, including the sometimes arduous task of discovering one's sexual identity. However, there is more to life than sex; more to human identity than one's preference in sexual partners. And so GLBTQ literature needs to be—and is slowly becoming—more than coming-out stories. It needs to include more stories about young people whose homosexuality is simply a given and who are dealing with other issues and challenges—emotional, intellectual, physical, social, developmental, etc. that are part of teens' lives.

Homophobia and gay-bashing are still with us (for up-to-date information about this sad reality in the lives of GLBTQ youth visit the websites of such organizations as GLSEN [www.glsen.org], PFLAG [www.pflag.org], and Advocates for Youth [www.advocatesforyouth .org]), but many teens now make the transition from the closet to an out life without peril, often with the help of caring adults or peers in gay/straight alliances. Surely it is time for GLBTQ literature to abandon the traditional and too-easy equation of homosexuality with violent death. Suicide has already more or less disappeared from the pages of GLBTQ novels as this fiction has made the transition from problem novel to contemporary realistic fiction. Now, like the rest of young adult literature, it must continue to come of age *as literature.*

Certainly, it still needs to be evaluated on the basis of the authenticity of its portrayal of GLBTQ adults and teens and the world they inhabit but it also needs to be evaluated as literature. Does it offer multidimensional characters? Does it have a setting rich in verisimilitude? Does it have not only an authentic but an original voice? Does it offer fresh insights into the lives of GLBTQ people? Does it offer other innovations in terms of narrative strategy, structure, theme? Or is it the same old story, told in the same old way that readers have encountered countless times in the past? In short, GLBTQ literature must be not only an inclusive and authentic literature, it must be an artful literature, as well.

We close with the following words from an article Michael Cart wrote for *Booklist* magazine in 1999. We believe they are as relevant today as they were then.

> "Nonfiction gives us information for our minds. But we need good (GLBTQ) fiction, too, because novels give us information for our hearts. It is not enough to comprehend the homosexual experience on a cognitive level; we must develop an empathetic understanding as

well. Don't forget: the heart has its reasons that the mind cannot know. And if we are to insure that love—not ignorance and its evil twin hatred—wins, then it is imperative that good books on the homosexual experience be read not only by gay and lesbian teens but also by their heterosexual peers. Ignorance demonizes those who are different. Good books bestow knowledge by showing us the commonalities of our human hearts.[1]

NOTE

1. Cart, Michael. "Saying No to Stereotypes." *Booklist*, 95:19 & 20 (June 1 & 15, 1999).

Appendix A

Model for GLBTQ Portrayals/Inclusion in YA Fiction

*L*ongitudinal analysis of young adult novels with GLBTQ content as a body of literature is hampered by their relatively small numbers and recent vintage. Fortunately, there exists a much longer tradition of publication and analysis available in the study of children's books that include other minority-status characters, most notably African American characters. Thus, in seeking models that can be used to analyze gay/lesbian content in young adult novels, one logical place to turn is to the critical literature focused on African American content in texts for young readers.

African American characters have appeared in children's books for well over a century, but most of the early (pre–Civil Rights Movement) portrayals were stock characters such as the superhumanly strong laborer, the broadly smiling entertainer, the long-suffering but faithful servant, the stern but nurturing mammy, and other predictable figures. These stereotypical—and invariably secondary—characters appeared most frequently in mass market series books and were seen solely in relation to the central white characters. Black characters might be instrumental to the plot development, but these stories were not *their* stories. There were, however, a small number of books of children's literature—often by African American authors—that featured non-stereotypic African American characters. Beginning in the late 1960s with the blossoming of the Civil Rights Movement and the increase of federal aid to education (including funding for school library books), the number of books with African American characters (both as protagonists and as secondary characters) gradually began to grow. The much-noted "all-white world of children's literature" was slowly (*very* slowly) becoming integrated in the decades that followed (Larrick 1965, 62; Baker 1975; Harris 1997).

Rudine Sims Bishop's *Shadow and Substance: Afro-American Experience in Contemporary Children's Fiction* (1982) is one of the foundational studies of children's and young adult literature with African American characters. In this study of books with African American characters published from 1965 to 1979, Sims Bishop proposed a three-part chronological model to describe fictional portrayals of African American characters. The first and earliest category, "social conscience" books, presented race as the problem and desegregation as the solution. The second category, "melting pot" books, depicted racial diversity as present but generally unacknowledged and integration a given. The third type of books were "culturally conscious" books in which African Americans are portrayed in a culturally authentic manner. This deceptively simple three-part model has proved surprisingly durable over time, and its analysis of patterns of minority group inclusion in children's literature stands up as a relevant framework for analyses of other groups' patterns of inclusion.

The plots of "social conscience" books with African American characters focused on relationships between blacks and whites (Sims Bishop 17–32). Often they involved struggles around the integration of schools or neighborhoods. There was usually an initial discomfort between strangers that was exacerbated by racial stereotypes and prejudice and remedied by education and "getting to know you" efforts. Once the mutual reeducation occurred, racial prejudice could be—and was—overcome and mutual trust established, and multicultural friendship could flourish to the mutual benefit of all groups. The "social conscience" approach in YA literature with gay/lesbian content is most evident in "coming out" stories, in which a character who has been assumed to be heterosexual "comes out" as gay/lesbian. The initial responses to this news are often uncomfortable, rejecting, or even overtly hostile, but by the end of most of these stories, the characters have adjusted to this new information and the relationship is resumed. Less commonly, coming out is met with long-term estrangement.

"Melting pot" books, Sims Bishop's second category, recognize the universality of the human experience to such an extent that they "ignore all differences *except* physical ones: skin color and other racially related physical features" (Sims Bishop, 33). In "melting pot" fiction, differences may be noted in passing, but are then ignored as the characters assume a homogeneity that is seen as the key to cooperation, which means that gay/lesbian characters must appear to be no different from the heterosexual norm *except* for the fact of their sexual orientation. As Erick, the narrator of *Night Kites* glibly responds when his older brother Pete comes out to him, "It's just another way of being" (91). A "melting pot" story with gay/lesbian characters would be one in which a character's same-sex orientation was simply a given. As in portraying an African American character as someone who "just happens to be" dark-skinned or have other characteristically black physical features, a gay/lesbian character in such a "melting pot" story would be portrayed as someone who "just happens to be" gay. However, given that any noticeable indication of gay/lesbian identity is often viewed as "flaunting it," the closet appears to be mandatory for peaceful coexistence. Indeed, it is hard to imagine a young adult novel labeled "contemporary realism" in which sexual orientation *could* realistically go unnoticed in the face of adolescents' hyper-awareness of sexuality of all stripes and persuasions. However matter-of-factly or neutrally it is presented, the revelation of a character's gay/lesbian identity is almost inevitably a notable event in YA fiction. In truth, the only milieu in which a character's gay/lesbian identity could be noted in passing would probably be the gay/lesbian community itself. Which brings us to "culturally conscious" stories, Sims Bishop's third and final category for fiction with African American characters.

Sims Bishop describes "culturally conscious" books as those that "seek to reflect, with varying degrees of success, the social and cultural traditions associated with growing up Black in the United States." In contrast to the social conscience books, they are not primarily addressed to non-blacks, nor are they focused on desegregating neighborhoods or schools. They differ from the melting pot books in that they recognize, sometimes even celebrate, the distinctiveness of the experience of growing up simultaneously black and American. Their primary intent is to speak to African-American children about themselves and their lives, though as has been pointed out, they are by no means closed to other children (Sims Bishop, 103).

Sims Bishop calls for "culturally conscious" fiction that represents the lives and experiences of African Americans as told from within that community. Culturally conscious fiction assumes that this culture and these people may very well be different from the mainstream culture and from people who live within the norm of white America. Until relatively recently, the overwhelming tendency in young adult literature with gay/lesbian content has been for writers to tell the story from a mainstream heterosexual perspective. The novels told readers how gay/lesbian people were viewed by others, but did not tell readers how gay/lesbian people viewed themselves. Judging from some recent titles, it is possible that this literature is finally beginning to be written.

NOTES

1. Ford, Michael Thomas. "Gay Books for Young Readers: When Caution Calls the Shots," *Publishers Weekly,* 241:24 (February 21, 1994).

2. "Gay Teens' Lives Called More Risky" by Martha Irvine, *The Sacramento Bee,* 5/5/98, p. A10.

3. Cockett, Lynn. "Entering the Mainstream: Fiction about Gay and Lesbian Teens," *School Library Journal,* 41:2 (February 1995), p. 32.

4. Watkins, M. "James Baldwin Writing and Talking," *New York Times Book Review* 23:3 (September 1979), pp. 36–37.

5. Sims Bishop, Rudine. *Shadow & Substance: Afro-American Experience in Contemporary Children's Fiction.* Urbana, IL: NCTE, 1982.

Appendix B

Bibliography of Secondary Sources

Allan, Christina. "Poets of Comrades: Addressing Sexual Orientation in the English Classroom." *English Journal*. 88:6 (July 1999).

Alvine, Lynne. "Understanding Adolescent Homophobia." *The ALAN Review*. 21:2 (Winter 1994).

Anderson, Douglas Eric. "Gay Information: Out of the Closet." *School Library Journal* (June 1992).

Bernstein, Robin. "A Literature of One's Own." *Harvard Gay and Lesbian Review*. 1:23 (Spring 1994).

Bronski, Michael. "Touched." *Lambda Book Report*. 5:1 (July 1996).

Campbell, Patty. "The Sand in the Oyster." *The Horn Book Magazine* (September-October 1993).

Cart, Michael. "Carte Blanche: Annie . . . Still On Our Minds." *Booklist* (September 15, 1994).

Cart, Michael. "Carte Blanche: The Bleak Goes On." *Booklist* (September 15, 1999).

Cart, Michael. *From Romance to Realism*. NY: HarperCollins, 1996.

Cart, Michael. "Honoring Their Stories, Too." *The ALAN Review*. 25:1 (Fall 1997).

Cart, Michael. "Lives Are at Stake." *Young Adult Library Services*. 1:1 (Fall 2002).

Cart, Michael. "Saying No to Stereotypes." *Booklist*. 95:19 & 20 (June 1 & 5 1999).

Cart, Michael. "What a Wonderful World: Notes on the Evolution of GLBTQ Literature for Young Adults." *The ALAN Review*. 31:2 (Winter 2004).

Caywood, Carolyn. "Reaching Out to Gay Teens." *School Library Journal*, April 1993.

Children's Literature Association Quarterly. Special Issue: Lesbian/Gay Literature for Children and Young Adults. 23:3 (Fall 1998).

Cockett, Lynn. "Entering the Mainstream: Fiction about Gay and Lesbian Teens." *School Library Journal* (February 1995).

Daniel, Patricia L. and Vicki J. McIntire. "Rights of Passage: Preparing Gay and Lesbian Youth for Their Journey into Adulthood." In *Using Literature to Help Troubled Teenagers Cope with Family Issues.* Edited by Joan F. Kaywell. Westport, CT: Greenwood Press, 1999.

Donahue, Deirdre. "Innocence and Ignorance." *USA Today* (June 28, 2001).

Dunlap, David W. "Eager for Gay History and Finding Library Allies." *The New York Times.* March 13, 1996.

English Journal. Special Issue. Genderizing the Curriculum. 88:3 (January 1999).

Gallo, Don. "Bold Books for Innovative Teaching." *English Journal.* 94:1 (September 2004).

Garden, Nancy. "Dick and Jane Grow Up Gay." *Lambda Book Report.* 3:7 (1992).

Garden, Nancy. "Free Your Mind." *Lambda Book Report.* 5:1 (July 1996).

Garden, Nancy. "Not So Terrible Teens." *Lambda Book Report.* 12:01–12:02 (Aug/Sept 2003).

Greene, Bette. "America's Designated Victims: Our Creative Young." *The ALAN Review.* 21:2 (Winter 1994).

Hanckel, Frances and John Cunningham. "Can Young Gays Find Happiness in YA Books?" *Wilson Library Bulletin.* 50:7 (March 1976).

Hoffman, Mary. "Growing Up: A Survey." *Children's Literature in Education.* 15:3 (1984).

Hughes-Hassel, Sandra and Alissa Hinckley. "Reaching Out to Lesbian, Gay, Bisexual, and Transgender Youth." *Journal of Youth Services in Libraries.* 15:1 (Fall 2001).

Hunter, Joyce. "A Place to Call Home." *Lambda Book Report.* 7:04 (November 1998).

Interracial Books for Children Bulletin. Special double issue on Homophobia. 14:3 and 4 (1983).

Jenkins, Christine. "Annie on Her Mind." *School Library Journal.* 49:6 (June 2003).

Jenkins, Christine. "Being Gay: Gay/Lesbian Characters and Concerns in Young Adult Books." *Booklist* (September 1, 1990).

Jenkins, Christine. "From Queer to Gay and Back Again: YA Novels with Gay/Lesbian/Queer Content, 1969–1997." *Library Quarterly.* 68:3 (1998).

Jenkins, Christine. "Heartthrobs & Heartbreaks. A Guide to Young Adult Books with Gay Themes." *Out/Look.* 1:3 (Fall 1988).

Jenkins, Christine. "YA Novels with Gay/Lesbian Characters and Themes 1969–1992: A Historical Reading of Content, Gender, and Narrative Distance." *Journal of Youth Services in Libraries.* 7:1 (Fall 1993).

Jones, Jami. "Beyond the Straight and Narrow: Librarians Can Give Gay Teens the Support They Need." *School Library Journal* (May 2004).

Joyce, Steven. "Lesbian, Gay, and Bisexual Library Service: A Review of the Literature." *Public Libraries*. 39:5 (Sept./Oct. 2000).

Kanner, Melinda. "Young Adult Literature." *GLBTQ: An Encyclopedia of Gay, Lesbian, Bisexual, Transgender, and Queer Culture*. http://www.glbtq.com/literature/young_adult_lit.html A(accessed April 19, 2003).

Kenney, Brian. "Do the Right Thing." *School Library Journal* 52:1 (January 2006).

Kinder, Deborah Jean. "To Follow Your Heart: Coming Out Through Literacy." *English Journal*. 88:2 (November 1998).

Kloberdanz, Kristin. "Out on the Shelf." *Book Magazine* (Sept./Oct. 2001).

Lane, David. "The Emergence of Gay Literature for Young People." *Young Adult Library Services*. 1:1 (Fall 2002).

Levithan, David. "Supporting Gay Teen Literature." *School Library Journal* (October 2004).

Linville, Darla. "Beyond Picket Fences. What Gay/Queer/LGBTQ Teens Want from the Library." *VOYA*. 27:3 (August 2004).

Madison, Katie O'Dell. "Our Daughters in Danger." *School Library Journal* (January 1998).

Mitchell, Judith. "Search and Find." *VOYA*. 8 (February 1983).

Murdock, James. "A Brave Post-Gay World." *VOYA*. 27:3 (August 2004).

Norton, Terry L. and Jonathan W. Vare. "Literature for Today's Gay and Lesbian Teens: Subverting the Culture of Silence." *English Journal*. 94:2 (November 2004).

Pavao, Kate. "Out of the Closet." *Publisher's Weekly* (December 1, 2003).

Pela, Robert L. "When Hearts Are Young and Gay." *The Advocate* (October 28, 1997).

Phifer, Nan. "Homophobia: The Theme of the Novel *Jack*." *The ALAN Review*. 21:2 (Winter 1994).

Reinhard, Carol. "Student Survey. It's a Question of Identity." *Signal Journal*. 23:2 (Summer 1999).

St. Clair, Nancy. "Outside Looking In: Representations of Gay and Lesbian Experiences in the Young Adult Novel." *The ALAN Review*. 23:1 (Fall 1995).

Sanchez, Alex. "Open Eyes and Change Lives." *English Journal*. 94:3 (January 2005).

Shannon, George. "Making a Home of One's Own: The Young in Cross-Cultural Fiction." *English Journal* (September 1988).

Spence, Alex. "Gay Young Adult Fiction in the Public Library: A Comparative Survey." *Public Libraries*. 38:4 (July/August 1999).

Sumari, Dennis. "Gay and Lesbian Voices in Literature." *English Quarterly*. 28:1 (1993).

Tillapaugh, Meg. "AIDS: A Problem for Today's YA Problem Novel." *School Library Journal* (May 1993).

Webunder, Dave and Sarah Woodard. "Homosexuality in YA Fiction and Non-fiction: An Annotated Bibliography." *The ALAN Review.* 23:2 (Winter 1996).

Whelan, Debra Lau. "Out and Ignored: Why Are So Many School Libraries Reluctant to Embrace Gay Teens?" *School Library Journal* 52:1 (January 2006).

Wilson, David E. "Advocating Young Adult Novels With Gay Themes." *English Journal* (April 1986).

Wilson, David E. "The Open Library: YA Books for Gay Teens." *English Journal.* 73:7 (November 1984).

Wolf, Virginia L. "The Gay Family in Literature for Young People." *Children's Literature in Education.* 20:1 (1989).

Appendix C

Young Adult Fiction with GLBTQ Content 1969–2004: Author/Title Bibliography with GLBTQ Portrayal, Inclusion, and Narrative Role

Author	Title	Year	Portrayal			GLBTQ Content				GLBTQ Narrative Role	
			HV	GA	QC	Gay	Lesbian	Bisexual	Transgender	Primary	Secondary
Alphin, Elaine Marie	Simon Says	2002	X			X					X
Appelt, Kathi	Kissing Tennessee	2000	X			X				X	X
Atkins, Catherine	Alt Ed.	2003	X			X					X
Atkins, Catherine	When Jeff Comes Home	1999	X			X					X
Bantle, Lee F.	Dividing for the Moon	1995		X		X					X
Barger, Gary W.	What Happened To Mr. Forster	1981	X			X					X
Bauer, Marion Dane, ed.	Am I Blue [short stories]	1994	X	X	X	X		X		X	X
Bechard, Margaret	If It Doesn't Kill You	1999	X			X	X				X
Benduhn, Tea	Gravel Queen	2003	X			X	X			X	
Bess, Clayton	Big Man and the Burn-Out	1985	X	X		X					X
Bess, Clayton	The Mayday Rampage	1993	X			X					X
Block, Francesca Lia	Baby Bebop	1995	X			X				X	
Block, Francesca Lia	Girl Goddess #9 [short stories]	1996	X			X	X		X	X	X
Block, Francesca Lia	I Was a Teenage Fairy	1998		X		X					X
Block, Francesca Lia	Missing Angel Juan	1993		X		X			X		X
Block, Francesca Lia	Weetzie Bat	1989	X			X					X
Block, Francesca Lia	Witch Baby	1991	X	X		X					X
Boock, Paula	Dare Truth Or Promise	1999	X				X			X	
Brennan, Herbie	Faerie Wars	2003	X				X				X
Brett, Catherine	S.P. Likes A.D.	1989	X				X			X	
Brown, Todd	Entries from a Hot Pink Notebook	1995	X			X				X	
Bunn, Scott	Just Hold On	1982	X			X				X	
Cart, Michael, ed.	Love and Sex [short stories]	2001	X			X	X		X	X	
Cart, Michael	My Father's Scar	1996	X			X				X	
Cart, Michael, ed.	Necessary Noise [short stories]	2003	X			X				X	
Chambers, Aidan	Dance on My Grave	1983	X		X	X				X	
Chambers, Aidan	Postcards from No Mans' Land	2002	X	X	X	X				X	
Chbosky, Stephen	The Perks of Being a Wallflower	1999	X			X					X
Childress, Alice	Those Other People	1989	X			X				X	

Author	Title	Year						
Cohn, Rachel	Gingerbread	2002		X			X	X
Colman, Hila	Happily Ever After	1986	X	X			X	X
Cooper, Melrose	Life Magic	1996	X	X			X	X
Coville, Bruce	The Skull of Truth	1997	X	X		X	X	X
Crutcher, Chris	Athletic Short [short stories]	1991	X	X		X	X	X
Crutcher, Chris	Ironman	1995	X	X			X	X
Davis, Deborah	My Brother Has AIDS	1994	X	X		X	X	X
Davis, Rebecca Fjelland	Jake Riley: Irreparably Damaged	2003	X	X				X
De Oliveira, Eddie	Lucky	2004	X	X		X		
Dhondy, Farrukh	Black Swan	1993	X	X		X	X	X
Dines, Carol	Talk to Me [short stories]	1997	X	X		X	X	X
Donoghue, Emma	Kissing the Witch: Old Stories in New Skins [short stories]	1997	X	X		X	X	X
Donovan, John	I'll Get There. It Better Be Worth the Trip	1969			X			X
Donovan, Stacey	Dive	1994	X	X		X	X	X
Doyle, Brian	Boy O'Boy	2003	X	X				X
Durant, Penny Raife	When Heroes Die	1992	X	X			X	X
Durbin, Peggy	And Featuring Bailey Wellcom as the Biscuit	1999	X	X		X	X	X
Earls, Nick	48 Shades of Brown	2004	X	X		X	X	
Ecker, B.A.	Independence Day	1983	X	X			X	
Ferris, Jean	Eight Seconds	2000	X	X			X	
Fox, Paula	The Eagle Kite	1995	X	X			X	X
Freymann-Weyr, Garret	My Heartbeat	2002	X	X			X	X
Frost, Helen	Keesha's House	2003	X	X		X	X	X
Futcher, Jane	Crush	1981	X	X		X		
Gantos, Jack	Desire Lines	1997	X	X		X	X	X
Garden, Nancy	Annie on My Mind	1982	X	X		X	X	
Garden, Nancy	Good Moon Rising	1996	X	X		X	X	X
Garden, Nancy	Holly's Secret	2000	X	X		X	X	
Garden, Nancy	Lark in the Morning	1991	X	X	X	X		X

(continued)

| | | | Portrayal | | | GLBTQ Content | | | | GLBTQ Narrative Role | |
Author	Title	Year	HV	GA	QC	Gay	Lesbian	Bisexual	Transgender	Primary	Secondary
Garden, Nancy	The Year They Burned the Books	1999	X		X	X	X			X	
Gleitzman, Morris	Two Weeks with the Queen	1991		X		X					X
Greene, Bette	The Drowning of Stephan Jones	1991	X			X					X
Griffin, Adele	Split Just Right	1997		X		X					X
Guy, Rosa	Ruby	1976	X			X	X			X	
Hall, Lynn	Sticks and Stones	1977	X			X					X
Hamilton, R.J.	The Case of the Missing Mother	1995		X		X	X				X
Hamilton, R.J.	Who Framed Lorenzo Garcia?	1995		X		X	X				X
Hanlon, Emily	The Wing and the Flame	1980	X			X				X	
Hartinger, Brent	The Geography Club	2003	X		X	X	X			X	
Hartnett, P-P, ed.	The Gay Times Book of Short Stories [short story collection]	2001	X		X	X	X	X	X	X	X
Hautzig, Deborah	Hey, Dollface	1978	X				X			X	
Hidier, Tanuja Desai	Born Confused	2003		X			X				X
Hines, Sue	Out of the Shadows	2000	X		X		X			X	X
Hite, Sid	The King of Slippery Falls	2004	X			X					X
Holland, Isabelle	The Man without a Face	1972	X	X		X					X
Homes, A.M.	Jack	1989	X			X					X
Howe, James	The Misfits	2001	X	X	X	X					X
Hulce, Larry	Just the Right Amount of Wrong	1982	X			X					X
Huser, Glen	Stitches	2003	X			X				X	
Isensee, Rik	We're Not Alone	1992	X	X		X	X			X	X
Jahn-Clough, Lisa	Country Girl, City Girl	2004	X			X	X			X	
Jenkins, A.M.	Breaking Boxes	1997	X	X		X					X
Jinks, Catherine	Pagan in Exile	2004	X			X					X
Johnson, Kathleen Jeffrie	Target	2003	X			X				X	
Johnson, Maureen	Bermudez Triangle	2004	X				X			X	
Kaye, Marilyn	Real Heroes	1993	X			X					X
Kemp, Kristen	The Dating Diaries	2004	X	X			X				X

Author	Title	Year								
Kerr, M.E.	Deliver Us from Evie	1994					X			X
Kerr, M.E.	"Hello," I Lied	1997	X	X	X		X		X	
Kerr, M.E.	I'll Love You when You're More Like Me	1977					X	X		X
Kerr, M.E.	Night Kites	1986		X	X		X			X
Kesselman, Wendy	Flick	1983		X			X		X	
Ketchum, Lisa	Blue Coyote	1997		X					X	
Killingsworth, Monte	Equinox	2001		X	X					X
Klein, Norma	Breaking Up	1980								X
Klein, Norma	My Life as a Body	1987		X	X		X			X
Klein, Norma	Now That I Know	1988		X	X		X			X
Koertge, Ron	The Arizona Kid	1988		X	X		X			X
Larson, Rodger	What I Know Now	1997		X		X				X
L'Engle, Madeleine	A House Like a Lotus	1984		X		X			X	
Levithan, David	Boy Meets Boy	2003		X	X		X		X	X
Levithan, David	The Realm of Possibility	2004		X	X		X		X	X
Levy, Elizabeth	Come Out Smiling	1981		X			X			X
Levy, Marilyn	Rumors and Whispers	1990		X			X			X
Lynch, Chris	Dog Eat Dog	1996		X			X			X
Lyon, George Ella	Sonny's House of Spies	2004		X			X			X
Maguire, Gregory	Oasis	1996		X			X			X
Maguire, Jesse	Getting It Right	1991		X		X				X
Martin, Ann M.	Here Today	2004		X			X			X
Matthews, Andrew	The Flip Side	2003		X			X		X	X
McClain, Ellen Jaffee	No Big Deal	1994		X			X			X
Meyer, Carolyn	Elliott and Win	1986		X			X			X
Mosca, Frank	All-American Boys	1983		X		X			X	X
Mowry, Jess	Babylon Boyz	1997		X			X			X
Murray, Martine	The Slightly True Story of Cedar B. Hartley	2003		X			X			X
Murrow, Lisa Ketchum	Twelve Days in August	1993					X		X	X
Myracle, Lauren	Kissing Kate	2003		X			X			X

(continued)

			Portrayal			GLBTQ Content				GLBTQ Narrative Role	
Author	Title	Year	HV	GA	QC	Gay	Lesbian	Bisexual	Transgender	Primary	Secondary
Naylor, Phyllis Reynolds	Alice on the Outside	1999	X				X				X
Nelson, Theresa	Earthshine	1994									X
Newbery, Linda	The Shell House	2002		X						X	
Nolan, Han	A Face in Every Window	1999	X			X					X
Oates, Joyce Carol	Freaky Green Eyes	2003	X			X					X
Paulsen, Gary	The Car	1994		X		X					X
Pausacker, Jenny, ed.	Hide and Seek [short story collection]	1996	X	X	X	X	X	X	X	X	X
Peters, Julia Anne	Keeping You a Secret	2003	X		X		X			X	X
Peters, Julia Anne	Luna	2004	X						X		X
Plum-Ucci, Carol	What Happened to Lani Garver	2002	X			X			X		X
Rapp, Adam	33 Snowfish	2003	X			X					X
Reading, J.P.	Bouquets for Brimbal	1980	X				X				
Rees, David	In the Tent	1979	X		X	X				X	
Reynolds, Marilyn	Love Rules	2001	X				X				X
Rinaldi, Ann	The Good Side of My Heart	1987	X			X					X
Ripslinger, Jon	How I Fell in Love and Learned to Shoot Free Throws	2003	X				X				X
Ryan, Sara	Empress of the World	2001	X	X	X		X	X		X	
Saenz, Benjamin Alire	Sammy and Juliana in Hollywood	2004	X			X					X
St. George, Judith	Call Me Margo	1981	X				X				X
Sakers, Don	Act Well Your Part	1986	X			X				X	
Salat, Cristina	Living in Secret	1993	X	X	X		X			X	
Sanchez, Alex	Rainbow Boys	2001	X		X	X				X	
Sanchez, Alex	Rainbow High	2003	X		X	X				X	
Sanchez, Alex	So Hard to Say	2004	X			X				X	
Scoppettone, Sandra	Happy Endings Are All Alike	1978	X				X			X	
Scoppettone, Sandra	Trying Hard To Hear You	1974	X			X					X
Shannon, George	Unlived Affections	1989	X			X					X

Author	Title	Year						
Shimko, Bonnie	Letters in the Attic	2002			X			
Shyer, Marlene Fanta	Rainbow Kite	2002					X	X
Singer, Marilyn	The Course of True Love Never Did Run Smooth	1983			X			X
Snyder, Anne and Louis Pelletier	Counterplay	1981				X		
Sones, Sonya	One of Those Hideous Books Where the Mother Dies	2004				X		X
Springer, Nancy	Looking for Jamie Bridger	1995				X		
Stoehr, Shelley	Tomorrow Wendy: a Love Story	1998					X	X
Sullivan, Mary W.	What's This about Pete?	1976	X			X		
Sweeney, Joyce	Face the Dragon	1990	X			X		
Taylor, Kim	Cissy Funk	2001					X	X
Taylor, William	Blue Lawn	1999	X			X		
Taylor, William	Jerome	1999	X				X	X
Taylor, William	Pebble in a Pool	2003	X			X		
Tolan, Stephanie	The Last of Eden	1980					X	X
Torres, Laura	November Ever After	1999	X			X		X
Ure, Jean	The Other Side of the Fence	1986	X			X		
Ure, Jean	You Win Some, You Lose Some	1984		X		X		X
Van Dijk, Lutz	Damned Strong Love	1995	X	X		X		
Vande Velde, Vivian	Alison, Who Went Away	2001				X		
Velasquez, Gloria	Tommy Stands Alone	1995	X			X		X
Walker, Kate	Peter	1993		X		X		X
Walker, Robert Paul	The Method	1990			X	X		X
Wallace, Rich	Losing Is Not an Option	2003				X		X
Wallens, Scott	Exposed	2002				X		
Watts, Julia	Finding H.F.	2001	X			X	X	X
Wersba, Barbara	Crazy Vanilla	1986	X			X		X
Wersba, Barbara	Just Be Gorgeous	1988				X		X
Wersba, Barbara	Whistle Me Home	1997				X		X
Westall, Robert	The Kingdom by the Sea	1990				X		X

(continued)

Author	Title	Year	Portrayal			GLBTQ Content				GLBTQ Narrative Role	
			HV	GA	QC	Gay	Lesbian	Bisexual	Transgender	Primary	Secondary
Wieler, Diana	Bad Boy	1992	X		X	X					X
Williams, Tamara	Truth and Lies	2002	X			X					X
Wilson, Barbara	A Clear Spring	2002		X			X				X
Withrow, Sarah	Box Girl	2001	X			X					X
Wittlinger, Ellen	Hard Love	1999		X	X		X			X	
Wittlinger, Ellen	Heart on My Sleeve	2004	X		X		X				X
Wittlinger, Ellen	Razzle	2001		X		X					X
Wittlinger, Ellen	What's in a Name?	2000	X		X	X				X	X
Wolff, Virginia Euwer	True Believer	2001	X	X							X
Woodson, Jacqueline	The Dear One	1991		X			X				X
Woodson, Jacqueline	From the Notebooks of Melanin Sun	1995	X				X				X
Woodson, Jacqueline	The House You Pass on the Way	1997	X				X			X	
Wyeth, Sharon Dennis	Orphea Proud	2004	X				X			X	
Yamanaka, Lois-Ann	Name Me Nobody	1999	X				X				X
Zalben, Jane Breskin	Unfinished Dreams	1996	X			X					X

Appendix D

Young Adult Fiction with
GLBTQ Content, 1969–2004:
A Chronological Bibliography

1969

Donovan, John. *I'll Get There. It Better Be Worth the Trip: A Novel*. New York: Harper & Row, 1969.

1972

Holland, Isabelle. *The Man Without a Face*. New York: Lippincott, 1972.

1974

Scoppettone, Sandra. *Trying Hard to Hear You*. New York: Harper & Row, 1974 [Alyson, 1991].

1976

Guy, Rosa. *Ruby*. New York: Viking, 1976.
Sullivan, Mary W. *What's This About Pete?* Nashville, TN: Thomas Nelson, 1976.

1977

Hall, Lynn. *Sticks and Stones*. Chicago: Follett, 1977.
Kerr, M.E. *I'll Love You When You're More Like Me*. New York: Harper & Row, 1977.

1978

Hautzig, Deborah. *Hey, Dollface*. New York: Greenwillow Books, 1978.
Scoppettone, Sandra. *Happy Endings Are All Alike*. New York: Harper & Row, 1978 [Alyson, 1991].

1979

Rees, David. *In the Tent*. London: Dobson Books, 1979 [Alyson, 1985].

1980

Hanlon, Emily. *The Wing and the Flame*. New York: Bradbury, 1980.

Klein, Norma. *Breaking Up*. New York: Random House, 1980.

Reading, J.P. *Bouquets for Brimbal*. New York: Harper & Row, 1980.

Tolan, Stephanie *The Last of Eden*. New York: Bantam, 1980.

1981

Bargar, Gary. *What Happened to Mr. Forster?* New York: Clarion–Houghton Mifflin, 1981.

Futcher, Jane. *Crush*. Boston: Little, Brown, 1981 [Alyson, 1988].

Levy, Elizabeth. *Come Out Smiling*. New York: Delacorte, 1981.

Snyder, Anne and Louis Pelletier. *Counter Play* (reissued in 1987 as *The Truth about Alex*). NY: New American Library, 1981.

St. George, Judith. *Call Me Margo*. New York: G.P. Putnam's Sons, 1981.

1982

Bunn, Scott. *Just Hold On*. New York: Delacorte, 1982.

Garden, Nancy. *Annie on My Mind*. New York: Farrar, Straus & Giroux, 1982.

Hulse, Larry. *Just the Right Amount of Wrong*. New York: Harper & Row, 1982.

Rees, David. *The Milkman's on His Way*. London: Gay Men's Press, 1982.

1983

Chambers, Aidan. *Dance on My Grave*. New York: Harper & Row, 1983.

Ecker, B.A. *Independence Day*. New York: Avon/Flare, 1983.

Kesselman, Wendy Ann. *Flick*. New York: Harper & Row, 1983.

Mosca, Frank. *All-American Boys*. Boston: Alyson, 1983.

Singer, Marilyn. *The Course of True Love Never Did Run Smooth*. New York: Harper & Row, 1983.

1984

Ireland, Timothy. *Who Lies Inside*. London: Gay Men's Press, 1984.

L'Engle, Madeleine. *A House Like a Lotus*. New York: Farrar, Straus & Giroux, 1984.

Rees, David. *Out of the Winter Gardens*. London: Olive Press, 1984.

Ure, Jean. *You Win Some, You Lose Some*. New York: Delacorte, 1984.

1985

Bess, Clayton. *Big Man and the Burn-Out*. Boston: Houghton Mifflin, 1985.

1986

Colman, Hila. *Happily Ever After*. New York: Scholastic Point, 1986.

Kerr, M.E. *Night Kites*. New York: Harper & Row, 1986.

Meyer, Carolyn. *Elliott and Win*. New York: McElderry, 1986.

Sakers, Don. *Act Well Your Part*. Boston; Alyson, 1986.

Ure, Jean. *The Other Side of the Fence*. New York: Delacorte, 1986.

Wersba, Barbara. *Crazy Vanilla*. New York: Harper & Row, 1986.

1987

Klein, Norma. *My Life as a Body*. New York: Knopf, 1987.

Rinaldi, Ann. *The Good Side of My Heart*. New York: Holiday House, 1987.

1988

Klein, Norma. *Now That I Know*. New York: Bantam, 1988.

Koertge, Ron. *The Arizona Kid*. Boston: Joy Street/Little, Brown, 1988.

Wersba, Barbara. *Just Be Gorgeous*. New York: Zolotow/Harper & Row, 1988.

1989

Block, Francesca Lia. *Weetzie Bat*. New York: Zolotow/Harper & Row, 1989.

Brett, Catherine. *S.P. Likes A.D.* Toronto: The Women's Press, 1989.

Childress, Alice. *Those Other People*. New York: Putnam, 1989.

Homes, A.M. *Jack*. New York: Macmillan, 1989.

Rees, David. *The Colour of His Hair*. Exeter, England: Third House, 1989.

Shannon, George. *Unlived Affections*. New York: Zolotow/Harper & Row, 1989.

1990

Levy, Marilyn. *Rumors and Whispers*. New York: Ballantine, 1990.

Sweeney, Joyce. *Face the Dragon*. New York: Delacorte, 1990.

Walker, Paul Robert. *The Method*. New York: Harcourt Brace Jovanovich, 1990.

Westall, Robert. *The Kingdom by the Sea*. New York: Farrar Straus Giroux, 1990.

1991

Block, Francesca Lia. *Witch Baby*. New York: Zolotow/HarperCollins, 1991.

Crutcher, Chris. *Athletic Shorts*. New York: Greenwillow, 1991.

Garden, Nancy. *Lark in the Morning*. New York: Farrar Straus Giroux, 1991.

Gleitzman, Morris. *Two Weeks with the Queen*. New York: Putnam & Grosset, 1991.

Greene, Bette. *The Drowning of Stephan Jones*. New York: Bantam, 1991.

Maguire, Jesse. *Getting It Right*. New York: Ivy/Ballantine, 1991.

Woodson, Jacqueline. *The Dear One*. New York: Delacorte, 1991.

1992

Durant, Penny Raife. *When Heroes Die*. New York: Atheneum, 1992.

Isensee, Rik. *We're Not Alone*. Fairfield, CT: Lavender Press, 1992.

Wieler, Diana. *Bad Boy*. New York: Delacorte, 1992.

1993

Bess, Clayton. *The Mayday Rampage*. Sacramento, CA: Lookout Press, 1993.

Block, Francesca Lia. *Missing Angel Juan*. New York: Harper, 1993.

Dhondy, Farrukh. *Black Swan*. Boston: Houghton Mifflin, 1993.

Kaye, Marilyn. *Real Heroes*. New York: Harcourt Brace Jovanovich, 1993.

Mullins, Hilary. *The Cat Came Back*. Tallahassee: Naiad Press, 1993.

Murrow, Liza Ketchum. *Twelve Days in August*. New York: Holiday House, 1993.

Salat, Cristina. *Living in Secret*. New York: Bantam, 1993.

Walker, Kate. *Peter*. Boston: Houghton Mifflin, 1993.

1994

Bauer, Marion Dane, ed. *Am I Blue? Coming Out from the Silence*. New York: HarperCollins, 1994.

Davis, Deborah. *My Brother Has AIDS*. New York: Atheneum, 1994.

Donovan, Stacey. *Dive*. New York: Dutton, 1994.

Kerr, M.E. *Deliver Us from Evie*. New York: HarperCollins, 1994.

McClain, Ellen Jaffe. *No Big Deal*. New York: Lodestar, 1994.

Nelson, Theresa. *Earthshine*. New York: Orchard Books, 1994.

Paulsen, Gary. *The Car*. San Diego: Harcourt Brace, 1994.

1995

Bantle, Lee F. *Diving for the Moon*. New York: Macmillan, 1995.

Block, Francesca Lia. *Baby Bebop*. New York: HarperCollins, 1995.

Brown, Todd D. *Entries from a Hot Pink Notebook*. New York: Washington Square Press, 1995.

Crutcher, Chris. *Ironman*. New York: Greenwillow, 1995.

Fox, Paula. *The Eagle Kite*. New York: Orchard Books, 1995.

Hamilton, R.J. *Who Framed Lorenzo Garcia?* [Pride Pack #1] Boston: Alyson, 1995.

Hamilton, R.J. *The Case of the Missing Mother*. [Pride Pack #2] Boston: Alyson, 1995.

Springer, Nancy. *Looking for Jamie Bridger*. New York: Dial, 1995.

Van Dijk, Lutz. *Damned Strong Love: The True Story of Willi G. and Stephan K.* translated by Elizabeth D. Crawford. NY: Henry Holt, 1995.

Velasquez, Gloria. *Tommy Stands Alone*. Houston: Arte Publico/Piñata Books, 1995.

Woodson, Jacqueline. *From the Notebooks of Melanin Sun*. New York: Scholastic, 1995.

1996

Block, Francesca Lia. *Girl Goddess #9*. New York: HarperCollins, 1996.

Cart, Michael. *My Father's Scar*. New York: Simon & Schuster, 1996.

Cooper, Melrose. *Life Magic*. New York: Holt, 1996.

Garden, Nancy. *Good Moon Rising*. New York: Farrar Straus & Giroux, 1996.

Lynch, Chris. *Dog Eat Dog*. [Blue-Eyed Son series, book 3] New York: Harper Trophy, 1996.

Maguire, Gregory. *Oasis*. New York: Clarion, 1996.

Zalben, Jane Breskin. *Unfinished Dreams*. New York: Simon & Schuster, 1996.

1997

Coville, Bruce. *The Skull of Truth*. New York: Harcourt Brace, 1997.

Dines, Carol. *Talk to Me: Stories and a Novella*. New York: Delacorte, 1997.

Donoghue, Emma. *Kissing the Witch: Old Tales in New Skins*. New York: Cotler/HarperCollins, 1997.

Gantos, Jack. *Desire Lines*. New York: Farrar Straus & Giroux, 1997.

Griffin, Adele. *Split Just Right*. New York: Hyperion, 1997.

Jenkins, A.M. *Breaking Boxes*. New York: Delacorte, 1997.

Kerr, M.E. *"Hello," I Lied*. New York: HarperCollins, 1997.

Ketchum. Liza. *Blue Coyote*. New York: Simon & Schuster, 1997.

Larson, Rodger. *What I Know Now*. New York: Henry Holt, 1997.

Mowry, Jess. *Babylon Boyz*. New York: Simon & Schuster, 1997.

Wersba, Barbara. *Whistle Me Home*. New York: Henry Holt, 1997.

Woodson, Jacqueline. *The House You Pass on the Way*. New York: Delacorte, 1997.

1998

Block, Francesca Lia. *I Was a Teenage Fairy*. New York: HarperCollins, 1998.

Revoyr, Nina. *The Necessary Hunger*. New York: St. Martin's Press, 1998.

Stoehr, Shelley. *Tomorrow Wendy: A Love Story*. New York: Delacorte, 1998.

1999

Atkins, Catherine. *When Jeff Comes Home*. New York: Puffin, 1999.

Bechard, Margaret. *If It Doesn't Kill You*. New York: Viking, 1999.

Boock, Paula. *Dare Truth or Promise*. New York: Houghton Mifflin, 1999

Chbosky, Stephen. *The Perks of Being a Wallflower*. New York: MTV/Pocket Books, 1999.

Durbin, Peggy. *And Featuring Bailey Wellcom as the Biscuit*. Port Orchard, WA: Little Blue Works, 1999.

Garden, Nancy. *The Year They Burned the Books*. New York: Farrar Straus & Giroux, 1999.

Naylor, Phyllis Reynolds. *Alice on the Outside*. New York: Atheneum, 1999.

Nolan, Han. *A Face in Every Window*. New York: Harcourt, 1999.

Taylor, William. *The Blue Lawn*. Boston: Alyson, 1999.

Taylor, William. *Jerome*. Boston: Alyson, 1999.

Torres, Laura. *November Ever After*. New York: Holiday House, 1999.

Wittlinger, Ellen. *Hard Love*. New York: Simon & Schuster, 1999.

Yamanaka, Lois-Ann. *Name Me Nobody*. New York: Hyperion, 1999.

2000

Appelt, Kathi. *Kissing Tennessee, and Other Stories from the Stardust Dance*. New York: Harcourt, 2000.

Ferris, Jean. *Eight Seconds*. New York: Harcourt, 2000.

Garden, Nancy. *Holly's Secret*. New York: Farrar Straus & Giroux, 2000.

Hines, Sue. *Out of the Shadows*. New York: Avon Tempest, 2000.

Wittlinger, Ellen. *What's in a Name?* New York: Simon & Schuster, 2000.

2001

Cart, Michael, ed. *Love and Sex: Ten Stories of Truth*. New York: Simon & Schuster, 2001.

Hartnett, P.-P., ed. *The Gay Times Book of Short Stories: The Next Wave*. London: Gay Times Books, 2001.

Howe, James. *The Misfits*. New York: Simon & Schuster, 2001.

Killingsworth, Monte. *Equinox*. New York: Holt, 2001.

Reynolds, Marilyn. *Love Rules*. Buena Park, CA: Morning Glory Press, 2001.

Ryan, Sara. *Empress of the World*. New York: Viking, 2001.

Sanchez, Alex. *Rainbow Boys*. New York: Simon & Schuster, 2001.

Taylor, Kim. *Cissy Funk*. New York: HarperCollins, 2001.

Vande Velde, Vivian. *Alison, Who Went Away*. Boston: Houghton Mifflin, 2001.

Watts, Julia. *Finding H.F.* Los Angeles: Alyson Publications, 2001.

Withrow, Sarah. *Box Girl*. Toronto: Groundwood/Douglas & McIntyre, 2001.

Wittlinger, Ellen. *Razzle*. New York: Simon & Schuster, 2001.

Wolff, Virginia Euwer. *True Believer*. New York: Atheneum, 2001.

2002

Alphin, Elaine Marie. *Simon Says*. New York: Harcourt, 2002.

Chambers, Aidan. *Postcards from No Man's Land*. New York: Dutton, 2002.

Cohn, Rachel. *Gingerbread*. New York: Simon & Schuster, 2002.

Desai Hidier, Tanuja. *Born Confused*. New York: Scholastic Press, 2002.

Freymann-Weyr, Garret. *My Heartbeat*. New York: Houghton Mifflin, 2002.

Newbery, Linda. *The Shell House*. New York: Fickling/Random House, 2002.

Plum-Ucci, Carol. *What Happened to Lani Garver*. New York: Harcourt, 2002.

Shimko, Bonnie. *Letters in the Attic*. Chicago: Academy Chicago Press, 2002.

Shyer, Marlene Fanta. *Rainbow Kite*. Tarrytown, NY: Marshall Cavendish, 2002.

Wallens, Scott. *Exposed (Seven, Week 2)*. New York: Puffin, 2002.

Williams, Tamara. *Truth and Lies.* Toronto: James Lorimer & Company, 2002.
Wilson, Barbara. *A Clear Spring.* New York: Girls First/Feminist Press, 2002.

2003
Atkins, Catherine. *Alt Ed.* New York: Dutton: 2003.
Benduhn, Tea. *Gravel Queen.* New York: Simon & Schuster, 2003.
Brennan, Herbie. *Faerie Wars.* London: Bloomsbury Publishing, 2003.
Cart, Michael, ed. *Necessary Noise: Stories About Our Families As They Really Are.* New York: Cotler/HarperCollins, 2003.
Davis, Rebecca Fjelland. *Jake Riley: Irreparably Damaged.* New York: HarperTempest, 2003.
Doyle, Brian. *Boy O'Boy.* Toronto: Groundwood, 2003.
Frost, Helen. *Keesha's House.* New York: Farrar, Straus & Giroux, 2003.
Hartinger, Brent. *The Geography Club.* New York: HarperCollins, 2003.
Huser, Glen. *Stitches.* Toronto: Groundwood Books, 2003.
Johnson, Kathleen Jeffrie. *Target.* Brookfield, CT: Roaring Brook, 2003.
Levithan, David. *Boy Meets Boy.* New York: Knopf, 2003.
Matthews, Andrew. *The Flip Side.* New York: Delacorte, 2003.
Murray, Martine. *The Slightly True Story of Cedar B. Hartley.* New York: Levine/Scholastic, 2003.
Myracle, Lauren. *Kissing Kate.* New York: Dutton, 2003.
Oates, Joyce Carol. *Freaky Green Eyes.* New York: HarperTempest, 2003.
Peters, Julie Anne. *Keeping You a Secret.* Boston: Little, Brown, 2003.
Rapp, Adam. *33 Snowfish.* Cambridge, MA: Candlewick Press, 2003.
Ripslinger, Jon. *How I Fell in Love and Learned to Shoot Free Throws.* Brookfield, CT: Roaring Brook, 2003.
Sanchez, Alex. *Rainbow High.* New York: Simon & Schuster, 2003.
Taylor, William. *Pebble in a Pool.* Los Angeles: Alyson, 2003.
Wallace, Rich. *Losing Is Not an Option.* New York: Knopf, 2003.

2004
De Oliveira, Eddie. *Lucky.* New York: Scholastic/PUSH, 2004.
Earls, Nick. *48 Shades of Brown.* Boston: Graphia/Houghton, 2004.
Hite, Sid. *The King of Slippery Falls.* New York: Scholastic, 2004.
Jahn-Clough, Lisa. *Country Girl, City Girl.* Boston: Houghton, 2004.
Jinks, Catherine. *Pagan in Exile.* New York: Candlewick, 2004.
Johnson, Maureen. *The Bermudez Triangle.* New York: Razorbill/Penguin, 2004.
Kemp, Kristen. *The Dating Diaries.* New York: PUSH/Scholastic, 2004.
Levithan, David. *The Realm of Possibility.* New York: Knopf, 2004.
Lyon, George Ella. *Sonny's House of Spies.* New York: Jackson/Atheneum, 2004.
Martin, Ann M. *Here Today* New York: Scholastic, 2004.

Peters, Julie Anne. *Luna*. Boston: Little, Brown, 2004.

Sáenz, Benjamin Alire. *Sammy & Juliana in Hollywood*. El Paso, TX: Cinco Puntos Press, 2004.

Sanchez, Alex. *So Hard to Say*. New York: Simon & Schuster, 2004.

Sones, Sonya. *One of Those Hideous Books Where the Mother Dies*. New York: Simon & Schuster, 2004.

Wittlinger, Ellen. *Heart on My Sleeve*. New York: Simon & Schuster, 2001.

Wyeth, Sharon Dennis. *Orphea Proud*. New York: Delacorte, 2004.

Index

Compiled by Julia M. Derden and Kara M.K. Hagen

Numerals that appear in **bold** type refer to the annotation for the entry.

About the Authors

Michael Cart is a *Booklist* columnist and reviewer and the author or editor of twelve books, including the novel *My Father's Scar*, a gay coming-of-age story selected as an ALA Best Book for Young Adults. A nationally known expert in young adult literature, which he teaches at UCLA, he is the founding editor of the literary journal *Rush Hour* and a past president of both the Young Adult Library Services Association and NCTE's Assembly on Literature for Adolescents (ALAN). In 2000, he received the prestigious Grolier Award for distinguished service to young readers and literature. He lives in San Diego, California.

Christine A. Jenkins is an associate professor at the Graduate School of Library and Information Science, University of Illinois at Urbana-Champaign, where she teaches courses in youth services, young adult literature, literacy, and the history of children's literature and librarianship. Earlier in her career, she spent thirteen years as a school librarian in the Ann Arbor Public Schools. She received her Ph.D. from the University of Wisconsin-Madison in 1995; her dissertation was a historical study of the role of U.S. youth services librarians in defending young people's right to read during the early Cold War era. Her work has appeared in *Horn Book Magazine*, *School Library Journal*, *Libraries and Culture*, and *Library Quarterly*.